the Shadow Tiger

Billy McDonald

Wingman to Chennault

the shadow Tiger

Billy McDonald

Wingman to Chennault

WILLIAM C. McDONALD III
BARBARA L. EVENSON

Published in the United States by Shadow Tiger Press, Birmingham, Alabama.
First Edition
Hardback ISBN-13: 978-1-945333-03-3
Paperback ISBN-13 : 978-1-945333-02-6
Library of Congress PCN 2016940625

We have tried to portray events, locales and conversations from the letters, magazines, books, photographs and first-hand stories available to us. We have relied on personal accounts wherever possible. Some names and identifying details have been changed or left out to protect the privacy of individuals. However, we do not warrant that we always got it right, or that further information would not change some of our conclusions. We present much of our primary source material and stories told by or about individuals, so that readers can look further. We welcome corrections of any kind. Although the author and publisher have made every effort to ensure that the information in this book was correct at press time, the author and publisher do not assume and hereby disclaim any liability to any party for any loss, damage, or disruption caused by errors or omissions, whether such errors or omissions result from negligence, accident, or any other cause.

Research and writing by William C. McDonald III
Writing and editing by Barbara L. Evenson
Cover design, book design & production by Barbara L. Evenson
Graphics production by Adam Grigg, Collective Visions Design
Map conception and production, Christopher Bull

Cover photo of Himalayas by Gifford Bull, © 2016 Gifford Bull Family. Back cover photo with Hawk 75 by Frank Higgs. Photo of Selma Road, © 2016 George Cully. WWII Maps of China courtesy of the USMA, Department of History. Terrain maps derived from content courtesy of Google. Overlay U.S. and China map courtesy of MapFrappe.com. Terry & the Pirates comics used with Permission, © 2015 Tribune Content Agency, LLC. Citations from unpublished manuscripts, transcripts and letters used by permission of Amelia (Smith) Lucas, Sebie Smith Family; William C. McDonald Jr. letters and photos, © William C. McDonald Jr. Family; Frank Higgs photos used by permission of Jeannie Holder. Skip Adair photos used by permission of Stephanie (Adair) Vickery. Reprints and photos from *Wings Over Asia* and cnac.org used by permission of Peggy Maher and/or Tom Moore, © CNAC Association. Claire Chennault photos used courtesy of Nell Calloway, Chennault Museum. Photos of soldiers marching, Dragon's Gate used through Wiki Commons license. An industrial scene in Ensley, Alabama (February 1937), photographed by Arthur Rothstein for the United States Department of Agriculture's Farm Services Administration. U.S. government photos used under public domain; special thanks to the U.S. military for many photos of early aviators, airfields and airplanes.

Dedication

To my partners in all of life's adventures

My wife, Nancy
My children, Maggie, Lucy and Will

To the men Mac called his best friends during his adventures

Col. Sebie Smith, Montgomery, Alabama
CNAC Captain Frank Higgs, Columbus, Ohio
Lt. General Claire Lee Chennault, Waterproof, Louisiana

To organizations and people who remember Mac's life

Peggy Maher, president of China National Aviation Corporation
Association
106th Observation Squadron, Alabama Air National Guard
Bill Chivalette, curator at the Enlisted Heritage Research Institute
("Enlisted Heritage Hall"), Gunter Annex, Maxwell Air Force
Base, Alabama
Nell Calloway, The Chennault Museum, Monroe, Louisiana
Angie Chen, CNAC Association–China

Finally, to the Chinese people who graciously honor his service
to China during its time of need

Table of Contents

139 Moving the Flight Schools
145 Chennault's Joe
149 San Francisco in Kunming
150 Hugh Woods & Japanese Attack on CNAC Plane
152 Mysterious Flight to Burma Border
153 "30 Degrees Against That Mountain"
157 "We will probably move west again, on to Tibet"
158 News from Kunming
160 Christmas Holiday with the Colonel
161 Chennault Puts Mac in Charge
163 China Has Lost Its Air Force
166 CAF Memories

CNAC

171 Mac's Story So Far: Still Chennault's Wingman
173 "A Job with a Future"
174 Hong Kong – Chungking – Chengtu Route
179 The Mysterious Trip, June 16–July 10, 1940
184 Foxy Kent & the Chungking
185 Attacks on CNAC DC-2
187 Frank Higgs
189 It wasn't all flying and danger…sometimes
         there were Dachshunds in sweaters…
190 A Reverse Three-Point Landing: Three versions
195 Important People Flew with Mac
196 China to the Mountains
199 CNAC Loses a DC-3 But Gains a DC-2½

CNAC AT WAR

207 America and Britain Enter the Fight
209 Evacuation of Hong Kong: Dec. 8–10, 1941
216 A Brief Stop at Toungoo: Chennault
         & Flying Tigers, Guns Ready
217 Unhappiest Man in Alabama
219 Adventure Seemed To Seek Him Out
220 A Trip Home, With Submarine
220 Trip to India
222 Flying the Hump: Supply to China
223 Fire and Ice: Crashes
225 Navigation Tools: Maps

226 Reading Maps
227 Flight Plans and Air Traffic Control
         by CNAC Captain Gifford Bull
231 Trust in CNAC
232 Wartime Censorship, End of Detailed Letters
236 Terry & the Pirates
245 Mac is Operations Assistant & Chief Pilot
         Roster of Senior Pilots, mid-1943 CNAC report
246 CNAC Captain Pete Goutiere Meets Mac
248–253 The Crocodile Flight or Sandbar Surprise
         Forced Landing in the Manas River
            by Glenn H. Carroll
         Letter to Mac from Captain James Atlee
         Glenn Carroll's C-47 Flies Again by Mac
         Flying a Transport Off a 700-foot Sandbar
            by Fletcher Hanks, Saga of CNAC #53
257 Marrying the Princess
258 Perks of Dating a Pilot
259 1944 Wedding in Calcutta
261 Honeymoon in Cooch Behar
262 Chinese Citations
263 Accomplishments and Sacrifices
264 Fatal Crash of Frank Higgs
265 The 1946 Christmas Crashes
266 Christmas Crashes report
269 After China
271 Lt. Gen. Claire Lee Chennault

PHOTO ALBUM

280 CAF & CNAC
281 1944 Wedding in Calcutta, Mac and Peggy
282 Fun & Friends
288 Reunions
290 Mac's Kids
292 Mac's Kids Get Married
293 Mac's Grandkids
296 Mac's Great-Grandkids
298 Mac's Grandkids Get Married
302 2016 Trip to China
313 Remembering Mac

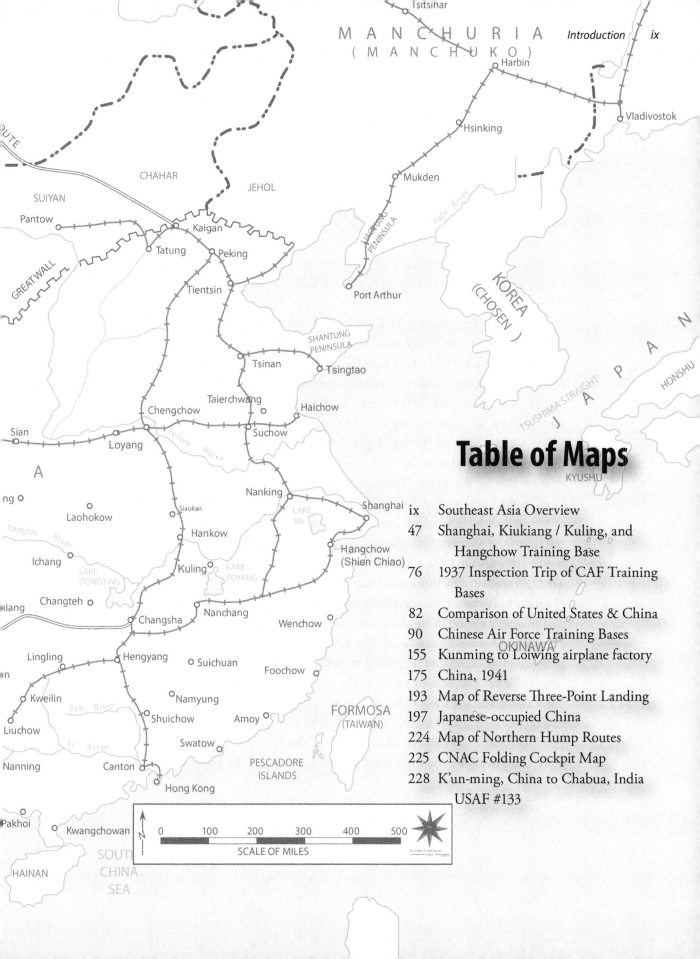

Table of Maps

MANCHURIA
(MANCHUKO)

CHAHAR   JEHOL

SUIYAN

Pantow
Tatung   Kaigan
                Peking
GREAT WALL   Tientsin

Sian   Chengchow   Taierchwang   Haichow
Loyang   Suchow

Laohokow   Siaokan   Nanking   Shanghai
Hankow   LAKE   Hangchow
Ichang   TAI   (Shien Chiao)
Kuling   LAKE
                POYANG
LAKE
DONGTING
Changteh   Changsha   Nanchang   Wenchow
Lingling   Hengyang   Suichuan   Foochow
Kweilin   Namyung
Liuchow   Shuichow   Amoy   FORMOSA
                Swatow   (TAIWAN)
Nanning   Canton   PESCADORE
                Hong Kong   ISLANDS

Pakhoi   Kwangchowan
                SOUTH
HAINAN   CHINA
                SEA

Tsitsihar
Harbin
Hsinking   Vladivostok
Mukden
LIAOTUNG
PENINSULA
Port Arthur
KOREA
(CHOSEN)
Yalu River
SHANTUNG
PENINSULA
Tsinan
Tsingtao

JAPAN
HONSHU
TSUSHIMA STRAIGHT
KYUSHU
OKINAWA

Yellow River
Yangtze River
Peh River
Si River

N
0   100   200   300   400   500
SCALE OF MILES

FOREWORD

THIS VOLUME FILLS A GREAT VOID, one that I hope will soon be alleviated with a new awareness of a very great man. A humble man overlooked until now, William C. McDonald Jr. is a man who contributed to world history, an unsung hero.

This is the story of his life written by his son, with a perspective that only a son could have. His rare insights make it hard to put the volume down. It is a must read.

The Shadow Tiger follows McDonald's life from his humble beginnings in Alabama to the faraway shores of a soon-to-be war-torn China. It traces not just his early life but when he was in the Army Air Corps and one of the three "Men on the Flying Trapeze." It delves deeply into the period when he was training Chinese pilots to fly before and during World War II. This volume captures him as a pilot flying the "Hump" while ferrying vital supplies in China for the famous "Flying Tigers," and as Colonel Claire Chennault's right-hand man and advisor.

As a 30-year Air Force Historian I have been privileged to research and learn about many remarkable individuals. But rarely have I researched one so overlooked by history but one so deserving of great accolades. I do understand how he slipped through the cracks though. McDonald is what every boy or girl wants to grow up to be, a hero who is also humble, whose life work needs no embellishment to stand out. Even his own children were not aware of most of his exploits because he rarely mentioned it.

The most exciting thing about this volume is that McDonald was continually a part of something special. The adventures he and his companions participated in all seemed to be critical moments in history. I remember the first time I read his first-hand account of the Japanese invading China; I couldn't put it down and felt I was there with him fending off the first assault. By the end of World War II this great man had saved thousands of lives.

McDonald was a pioneer who was one of the best at his craft or, for that matter, anything he tried his hand at. Even as a youth he became the first

Eagle Scout from Birmingham, Alabama. But he began to yearn toward aviation, to dream of becoming a pilot. As with most of his endeavors he far exceeded expectations to become one of the greatest pilots of all time.

But it helps to be in the right place at the right time. After McDonald became a pilot he left the service hoping to get an airline pilot job but nothing came from his efforts. He was driving to Auburn University to pick up his brother and decided to swing by Maxwell Field. There he ran into a friend who introduced him to Captain Claire Chennault. Chennault was in charge of a newly-formed aerial acrobatics demonstration team and McDonald was offered an opportunity to fly with them. He had to enlist again as a private with a promotion to sergeant in six months. Thus began his career as an enlisted pilot. He spent four years with the team, which drew crowds of between 25,000 and 100,000 people and over a million total visitors for their air shows. Their maneuvers were very exciting and considered impossible. The techniques they experimented with would help prepare them for World War II.

After realizing promotion to the officer ranks was not in his future, McDonald and fellow Trapezer Luke Williamson took an offer to train Chinese pilots and left for China in 1936. Chennault, believing his pilots had faced discrimination due to their association with him, stated, "…If I were to go to war and I were ordered to the front, I would choose these two men to accompany me into combat." It was one of the best things he could have said as their leader.

Reading McDonald's diary I gleaned insights into his many adventures teaching the Chinese Air Force to fly. At times they were humorous and at other times they were tragic. McDonald was the senior American instructor in the advanced flight section. His students did well and exhibited a trait favored by McDonald: they never quit. "They finish or they collapse," he wrote admiringly.

In 1937 on a dock in Shanghai, the Three Men on the Flying Trapeze were reunited as Claire Chennault arrived in China. In the coming years

Chennault would form the famous "Flying Tigers" which among their accomplishments brought the first defeats of World War II to Japan's air force.

As an aviation historian and museum professional I cannot but admire this great man and wonder why his story is not more visible to the reader. In our museum, McDonald has a full exhibit honoring his accomplishments. There I realize it was enough for him to have lived his adventures while rubbing shoulders with more famous people even though his exploits were as good, or better, than theirs.

The short synopsis above gives you, the reader, an insight to what is contained in this volume, which is the never-before-told story of an extraordinary man by a talented author who has captured the essence of the adventurous yet warm-hearted pilot. McDonald himself would simply shrug off all of the notoriety and would say he was an ordinary man caught up in extraordinary circumstances. But I see him as he really was and so will you, the reader. You will join him in his adventures as you read through this book. You will wish you had been lucky enough to be with him when he slipped the surly bonds of Earth and soared high above in flight, as I myself wished I too had been so lucky.

I am greatly honored to write the foreword for this book. McDonald was a great pilot whose life was filled with incredible adventures. I guarantee this book will keep you on the edge of your seat as much as it kept me on the edge of mine.

WILLIAM I. CHIVALETTE
Curator, Air Force Enlisted Heritage Research Institute

SGT. WILLIAM C. MCDONALD JR.
Permanent Exhibit

Air Force Enlisted Heritage Research Institute
Gunter Annex
Maxwell Air Force Base
Montgomery, Alabama

FROM THE CURATOR

We built the display in 1998 and through the kindness of Billy McDonald it contains McDonald's original WWII diary, pilot's books, flight logs, original photographs of Generalissimo Chiang Kai-Shek and Madame Chiang Kai-Shek, and much more. The artifacts contained in the display are so rare to aviation history that they are sought after by other institutions. Our visitors marvel at the treasures in the display and often comment on their rarity and the attractiveness of the display.

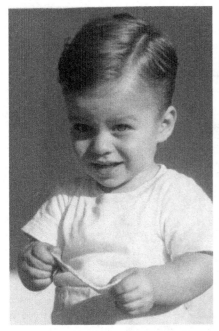

The Author as a young man

A FEW NOTES FOR THE READER
How I Found My Father Halfway Across the World

TOWARD THE END OF 2010, I was recovering from a heart attack and open heart surgery. During my recovery, my wonderful wife, Nancy, gave me a photograph of my father, William C. "Mac" McDonald, flying a P-12 airplane in 1934. Oddly, the plane was absolutely brand new, like a new car just rolling off the assembly line. Intrigued, I began a search to find the origin of the photograph. What I found was shocking.

While we had heard some stories, my sister Cameron and I had no idea that our warm-hearted and unpretentious father had been at the heart of one of the most incredible sagas of World War II.

In the Army, as one of three "Men on the Flying Trapeze," as an American instructor training Chinese pilots, as a "Hump Pilot" flying supply transports in China for Chinese troops and for the legendary "Flying Tigers," as Claire Lee Chennault's great friend and longtime wingman, my father witnessed and made history. Uncovering his story has been a six-year adventure of my own.

Beginning in the basement of Cameron's house, we found sixteen boxes of documents, some wet and many disintegrating. Some were lost, and others would have been lost within months. The history contained in those boxes is shown from my father's unique perspective and reveals some new information about this time.

Their loss would have been unknown, but a real loss nonetheless. I did not discover until then that he had started a book about his adventures. This experience fuels my continuing commitment to helping other families find and preserve the stories of these remarkable men.

As I looked through the boxes, my father's story and the stories of many others came to life in the letters, photographs and other documents. At the heart of his story is an adventure, a hero's journey from humble beginnings at the turn of the century in the steel town of Birmingham, Alabama, to an epic battle with powerful foes in a far-away and exotic land. Accompanied by brave companions in a quest to help a country from being overtaken for its resources and land, they directly saved thousands of lives amidst a war that threatened to engulf the world.

He and his companions participated in a unique and critical moment in history, the 1930s and 1940s in China as the Japanese attempted to take over that vast country by land, air and sea. Had the Japanese succeeded, it is impossible to overstate the difference this would have made to our modern world.

Remarkably enough, Mac came through those dangers relatively unscathed, and stayed in close touch with many of the companions who had shared in his adventures.

He enjoyed a long life with his wife and children, working in business until a stroke in 1977 cost the use of his right hand and his ability to speak. He died in 1984, a book about his adventures in China unfinished.

For the most part, the narrative follows Mac's letters to provide his first-hand and sometimes second-hand accounts of some of the war's most historic moments. His unique point of view provides a perspective on these events that general histories cannot.

My hope is that these pages honor his life and the lives of all of those who fought then and fight now to protect freedom.

BILLY MCDONALD III

ACKNOWLEDGEMENTS

AMONG THE MANY PEOPLE TO THANK, some have provided invaluable support, making this book possible.

Cameron McDonald Vowell, my sister, was smart enough to keep all of Dad's papers and nice enough to give them to me. Judge Scott Vowell, Cameron's husband, provided sound judgement on numerous questions brought up by the book. Peggy Maher, President of CNAC Association, was a wonderful source of information and encouragement during the writing of this book, and introduced me to Barbara Evenson.

Barbara Evenson is the editor/co-writer and so many other things associated with this book. Special thanks to her staff, especially her son Adam, who did so much for this book.

Angie Chen provided photos, fact checking and Chinese translation for this book, and an invaluable connection with China past and present. She arranged a remarkable trip for my family, as guests of several Chinese museums and groups who remember the Americans who flew for China in WWII. To express our appreciation for this remembrance, I commissioned reproductions of my father's Commanding Wing in sterling silver with gold plate to present to each of the museums. Angie's father, Mr. Chen Weiling (Willy Chen), was a CAF pursuit pilot and flew the Hump with CNAC while my father was Chief Pilot there. Since 2004, she has worked on the restoration and promotion of CNAC's contribution during WWII around China. In 2015, the Nanjing Anti-Japanese Aviation Memorial Hall (NAAM) honored her as its consultant. She is a great friend to me and to CNAC.

Chris Bull, son of CNAC pilot Gifford Bull, helped with photo permissions for his father's photography, and pitched in to help with maps, images and editing in the final version of this book. Will and Mary Bestor Grant translated my early manuscript into passable English that Barbara could work with. Retired Lt. Col. George Cully did such wonderful research and investigative work in Montgomery for this book. Tom Badham's article, *The Ghost Tiger*, inspired this book's name, though it translates better into Chinese as "Shadow Tiger." He also helped Barbara in editing drafts of this book. Tom has been a great friend since the 4th grade.

Michael Mixon at Hanging Around photo shop in Hoover worked hard to improve old pictures and introduced me to Dr. Ed Boyd. Ed Boyd has been a great advisor and supporter all along. His father-in-law was J.J. Harrington of the AVG. On December 17, 1941, my father flew Harrington and the ground crew of the 1st Squadron of the Flying Tigers from Toungoo to Kunming to start the Flying Tigers' fight against the Japanese.

Eugenie Buchan shared documents she found in the British Archives and provided candid advice, which I took. Nell Callaway, head of the Chennault Museum and Chennault's granddaughter, was encouraging and gave permission to use pictures of General Chennault. She has been a great friend to me.

Special thanks are due Amelia Smith Lucas, Sebie Smith's daughter, for agreeing to a mutual sharing arrangement where we each could use whatever our fathers shared. Sebie Smith's work was an invaluable resource for this book. Jeanie Holder, Frank Higgs' niece, became a great friend and shared a large quantity of pictures, stories and papers by and about Frank Higgs. She is a great friend to me and CNAC.

Captain Pete Goutiere was a great friend to Dad and flew 679 trips over the Hump for CNAC. The last five years he has been a great friend to me, and graciously wrote a story about his first meeting with Chief Pilot Billy McDonald.

My children, Maggie, Lucy and Will, have been steadfastly supportive for the past six years as the research and writing took over ordinary family life and conversation.

My wife Nancy, who supported me over many years in this endeavor, was also chief research assistant and photo editor for the book. She read endless drafts, encouraged me to pursue this difficult and time-consuming journey and was a patient and clever sounding board.

BILLY MCDONALD III

THIS WORK PROVIDED THE CHANCE to get to know the remarkable McDonald family, whose generous and warm natures were obviously inherited from Mac. They provide living insight into Mac's optimism, intelligence and charm.

None of this would have been possible without the introduction provided by Peggy Maher, who is a matchmaker by nature and design. Her longtime friendship has provided me with many of my favorite memories and many of my most useful skills.

While I was off flying planes in China from a desk in Alabama, my patient and brilliant staff held down the fort at our small press, taking care of everything beautifully. I am especially grateful to Mimi Currie-Lancsak and Leigh Songstad.

Adam Grigg, my son, took care of our home and business while working part-time and attending college full-time. He also proofed several versions of the manuscript and processed most of the scratched, dusty, ripped and torn photos and documents for the book. My mom, Bonnie Norrod, pitched in on layout and proofing. Having a talented and patient family makes all the difference at 4 AM under an impossible deadline.

All along our work has been supported by various beta readers and specialized editors. Scott Fish read the first draft and helped me understand the broader military context for China and Mac's story. Tom Badham came up with an evocative metaphor, the Ghost Tiger, to describe Mac's lifelong relationship with the famous Flying Tiger, Claire Chennault. He also read several versions of the manuscript, generously contributing his knowledge of aviation and Birmingham history. In addition, he wrote a beautiful pre-publication review which I cherish. Agreeing to put aside his own writing, Anton Kaiser generously and patiently improved the writing in this work by offering suggestions word by precise word.

Christopher Bull's varied talents were crucial to many areas of the book, including text and photo editing, as well as the concept for and creation of the detailed maps throughout the book. He too spent many hours reviewing the content and flow of the book, and his thoughtful and well-informed suggestions dramatically improved the book.

Finally, I want to thank Billy and Nancy McDonald for opening their home and hearts to me as we struggled together to find a way to tell the story of such a complicated and rich life in less than 1500 pages! Nancy patiently allowed the book to take over most of her home for a very long time, and was always ready to read, proof, discuss or provide moral support.

It has been a work of love for all of us, but Billy's incredible dedication in collecting and organizing such a massive amount of research amazes me still. In addition, his ability to place himself into a wide variety of situations and to sort the true heartbeat of the story from the details—which we have taken to calling "screen-playing it"—has consistently been the guiding star for this work. It is an honor to work with such a dedicated and creative author.

BARBARA L. EVENSON

INTRODUCTION

WHILE IT IS NEVER EASY TO REDUCE A MAN'S LIFE TO WORDS, in Mac's case, he lived in an extraordinary time, saw extraordinary events unfold, lived in an extraordinary place and maintained extraordinary friendships with people. It was never a question of having enough material—the author's archives began with 30,000 documents, 9,000 images, dozens of books and articles, and most importantly, dozens of letters that Mac wrote home to his family, detailing the ordinary and extraordinary elements of his life.

Mac lived during a time when aviation was changing rapidly, with new technology enabling ever more daring exploits by ever more daring pilots. Mac demonstrated this daring as one of two wingman for Major Claire Lee Chennault as part of the famous aerobatics team, Three Men on the Flying Trapeze, in the early 1930s.

Leaving the U.S. for China in 1936 to become an aviation instructor for the Chinese Air Force, Mac entered a new world. His wide-eyed observations help us understand what other young Americans in China saw, and why some of them, including Mac, were so devoted in their duties to that beleaguered and dangerous country. When the simmering conflict with Japan became outright war, some Americans stayed anyway.

This book shows and tells some of the stories of those who stayed in China to help the Chinese people in their struggle with Japan. It is impossible to know the effect of a single life, but Mac was present and participated in many historic events during these years. Mac was also the right-hand man—still the wingman—to Chennault in China. In many places and across many years, Mac and Chennault observed and sometimes made history together.

He was surprisingly aware of the importance of many of these events, documenting these in his letters home. Mac wrote home consistently despite the challenges of repeated relocations from one war zone to the next.

Some of Mac's letters home seem prophetic now, predicting many events years in advance. He was concerned by U.S. policy which left China without support as the undeclared war with Japan continued. He foresaw the havoc that Japan could impose if she were not stopped soon, and even predicted the attack on the United States at Pearl Harbor nearly four years in advance. Some of this prescience doubtless came from years of working and living with Chennault.

His respect and love for China and its people is evident throughout, and he is horrified at the atrocities committed by Japan upon the cities he and his pilots defended so hopelessly—Nanchang, Shanghai, Hankow, Nanking, Kunming, Chungking.

While many words have been written about Japan's actions, Mac's own words, written within a few days of witnessing events, add an immediacy that is both moving and horrifying. He, the other Americans and Chinese pilots saw the Japanese onslaught, fought bravely and retreated to defend the next target with too few planes, too few pilots and too little time for training against the might of Japan's military, decades in the making.

It is a special kind of bravery, to defend another's homeland, to long for its freedom as though it were your own country. This small handful of American advisers stayed to help China when even their own country threatened to disown them. Mac's bravery shows through the reassurance in the letters written from air fields bombed daily, from places of temporary retreat, after the deaths of comrades and while witnessing almost unimaginable savagery. His kindness shows as he takes the time to note the beauty in the hard lives of the people around him, and the natural beauty in his surroundings.

This is not the way that Mac would describe his own efforts. He dismissed praise and deflected credit, as did many of the men and women most deserving of it. But they were heroes nonetheless.

When Mac began flying for the Chinese National Aviation Corporation, it took an additional kind of bravery. These pilots flew over the highest mountains in the world often without maps, radio, beacons, and sometimes without enough oxygen or heat, in the worst and most unpredictable weather, and at night to avoid tempting Japanese attacks upon their unarmed transport planes. Their flight paths were littered with the aluminum of wrecked planes.

They carried heavier loads and took off in weather that grounded U.S. military planes, flying over Japanese-occupied territory. At times, they flew behind Japanese lines, including dangerous, low-altitude rice drops to starving troops.

What follows is not a complete history of the Golden Years of Aviation or the Second Sino-Chinese War. It is not an attempt to explain the complexities of geo-politics. It is instead the testimony of one man to both the best and worst in humanity, writing home to his family to try to explain why he did not come home, continued to work without a contract, stayed in cities although bombs were dropping around him. He described the beauty of the Chinese culture and its people, the admiration he felt for those he met, and the camaraderie among his companions.

Of many, one relationship stands out. Claire Lee Chennault was Mac's flying mentor, father figure, roommate and comrade in arms. He and Mac worked together for many years, developing a close friendship that continued until Chennault's death. Mac's perspective is unique, and adds a depth and humanness missing from discussions of his strategic brilliance, controversial ideas and notable outbursts.

The efforts of the American advisers are remembered and revered in China, and these men are considered heroes, with museums and literature devoted to their stories. Perhaps understandably, their stories are often overlooked in their own country.

But their efforts, and China's efforts, were critical to the interests of the United States and her allies. China's sacrifices kept a million Japanese troops engaged, when the Japanese planners expected a short war that would result in access to China's vast natural and human resources, materials and troops. Taking over China would have strengthened Japan's army immeasurably. It is hard to overstate the importance of that fact, and even a brief consideration of the consequences should China have capitulated is horrifying.

Instead, China overcame internal conflicts, difficult geography, scarce resources and international disinterest to successfully oppose the modern, well-equipped Japanese forces. Mac was a first-hand witness whose letters and photos, and those of his friends, provide a glimpse of the lives of the Americans who stayed to help China's people fight for its survival.

Mac's story includes some extraordinary experiences befitting a world-class flyer. But this is also the story of a boy from a small town in the deep American South who dreamed big, yet experienced things beyond his wildest dreams. It is the story of a hardworking young man who evolved from a mechanic into one of the world's best pilots. It is the story of a cheerful, outgoing man who maintained warm personal relationships with people who figure prominently in the history of the twentieth century and with others who didn't, a man who kept many of these people as lifelong friends.

William C. McDonald Jr. of Fairfield, Alabama, took a remarkable journey, and this book attempts to show part of that journey through the letters and photos passed down to his family, and letters and documents entrusted to him by friends and families who hoped he would use it to tell their shared stories. Some of these documents and photos have only recently come to light, and so we expect that even scholars may be surprised by some of the material here. But mostly, we hope that people enjoy the stories that Mac told, and that others told about him.

BARBARA L. EVENSON

For the sake of readability, we made minor grammatical, punctuation and typo changes in quotes from Mac's writing without inserting brackets or sics, which seem intrusive without being helpful to the majority of readers.

It is impossible to untangle history and know much with certainty—but it serves us well to ponder its lessons anyway. This story is complicated and involves many places, people, events and relationships. The more we learned, the more we saw how much more there was to explore. Our website at ShadowTiger.org will carry corrections, addendums, resources, stories, discussion areas and ongoing research. We welcome all of those, and the conversation.

We hope to publish other related material and welcome inquiries.

The steelmills at Ensley, Alabama, 1930s.

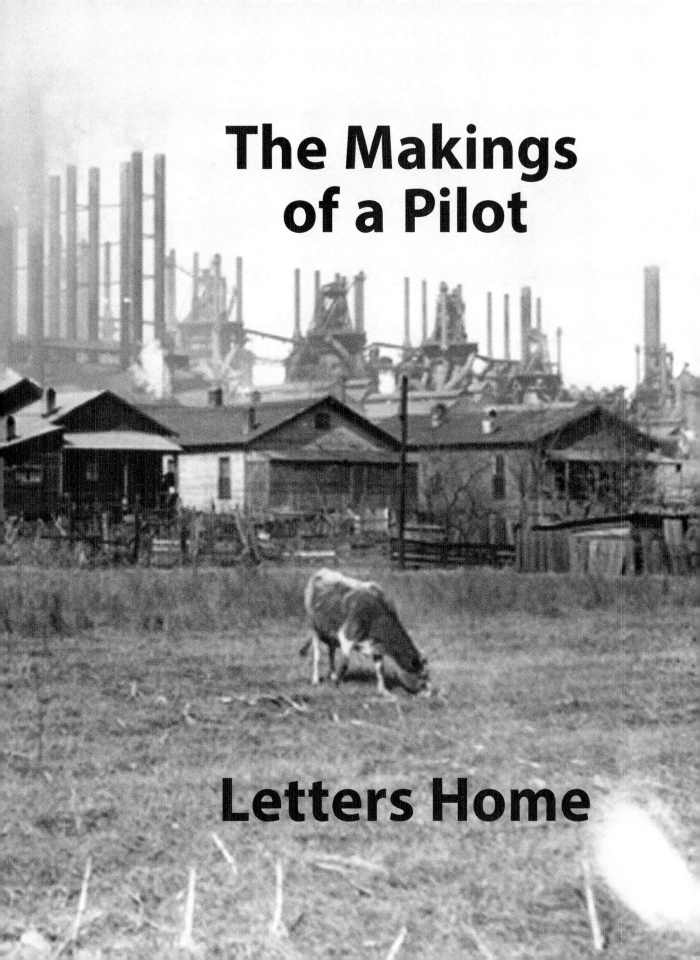

The Makings of a Pilot

Letters Home

ABOVE Baby Mac already flashing that smile.

OPPOSITE PAGE, FROM UPPER LEFT AND MOVING CLOCKWISE

Mac's parents Valerie and William McDonald Sr.

Standing portrait of sister Dorthea, "Dottie"

Formal portrait of sister Lucie

Siblings Mac (left), sister Dottie and brother Malcolm with beloved dog Punky

Standing, brother Malcolm

1906–1919
A Boy from Fairfield

William C. "Mac" McDonald Jr. was born May 24, 1906, in Pratt City, Alabama, and raised in Fairfield, near Birmingham. His mother, Valerie Henderson McDonald, was a school teacher and his father, William C. McDonald Sr., worked in the accounting office of a steel mill. The McDonald home was warm and loving, and throughout his life Mac was devoted to his family.

In 1906 in rural Alabama, a typical boy born into a modest family would follow his father into work at a steel mill or a coal mine, learn a trade or work the family farm. Graduating from high school would be an achievement, and college was unlikely.

But Mac was not a typical boy. His extraordinary journey took him from Fairfield across the world to China and the exotic Far East, where he was a key figure in one of the epic stories of history. His efforts earned a place among the heroes of history in that country, an effort still recognized today in museums across the world.

But to start with, he was just a hardworking kid from a small town with big dreams. He became the city's first Eagle Scout. He won a scholarship to Washington & Lee University for swimming, and then spent two years at Howard University on the football team.

Geography, Hard Work, Friends & Family

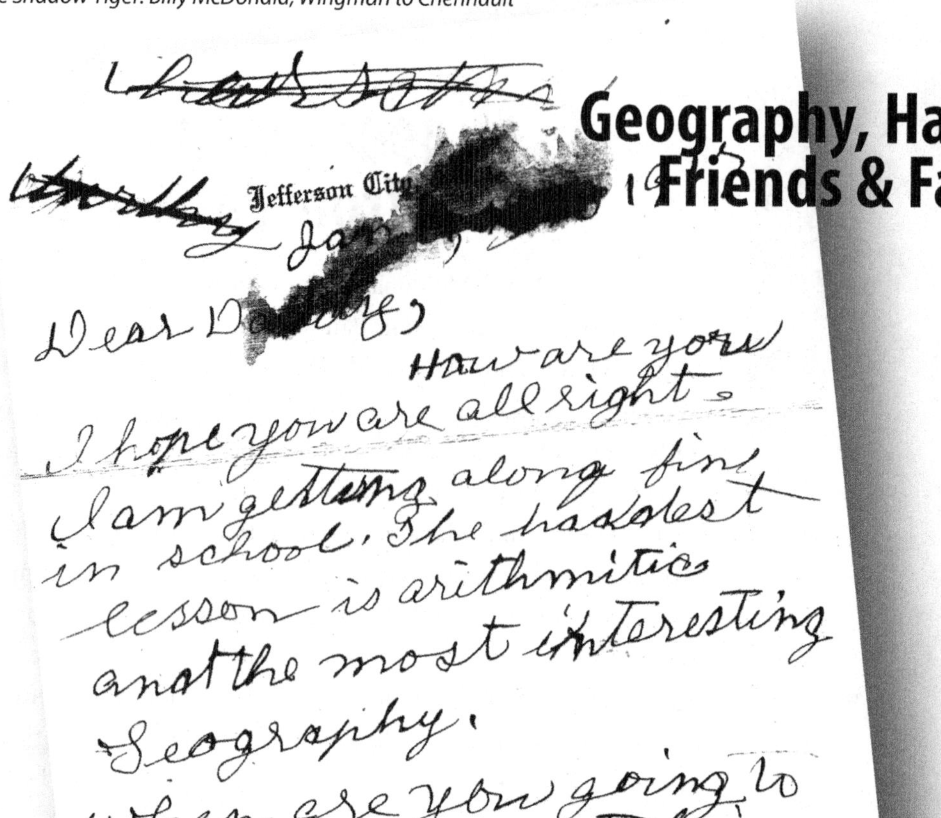

Jefferson City

Dear Daddy,

How are you
I hope you are all right.

I am getting along fine in school. The hardest lesson is arithmitics and the most interesting Geography.

when are you going to send me that watch and chain? answer this letter daddy tell Jiles Dunkin howdy for me.

your son
william

ABOVE Mac spent some time living with his maternal grandparents, the Hendersons, in Jefferson City, Tennessee. From there, he wrote this first of many letters home, assuring his father that he was working hard at his studies. He noted that geography was his favorite. He asked his father to say "howdy" to a friend.

This letter shows four of the basic anchors of Mac's life. He worked hard, he loved learning about new places and people, he always remembered his friends and he wrote home to his family!

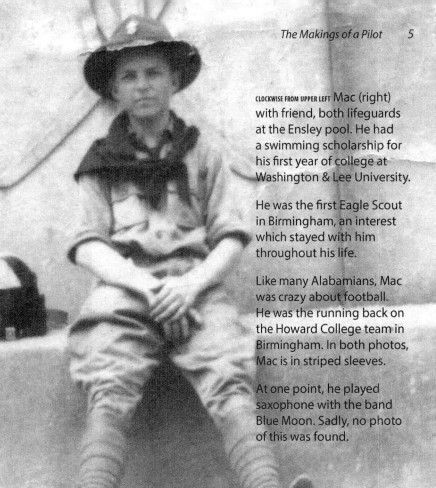

CLOCKWISE FROM UPPER LEFT Mac (right) with friend, both lifeguards at the Ensley pool. He had a swimming scholarship for his first year of college at Washington & Lee University.

He was the first Eagle Scout in Birmingham, an interest which stayed with him throughout his life.

Like many Alabamians, Mac was crazy about football. He was the running back on the Howard College team in Birmingham. In both photos, Mac is in striped sleeves.

At one point, he played saxophone with the band Blue Moon. Sadly, no photo of this was found.

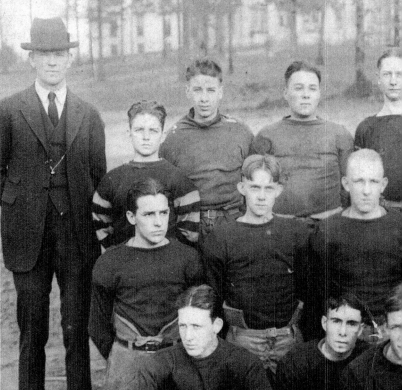

Major James (Jimmy) Armand Meissner

July 20, 1886 – January 16, 1936

- World War I ace
- Father of Alabama's National Guard
- Mac's next-door neighbor
- Took Mac on his first airplane ride at age 14
- Born in Nova Scotia; grew up in Brooklyn
- Shot down by German pilot Eric Just, Mac's next-door neighbor on a mission in China
- Twice flew home from battle minus the canvas on his plane's wings, with ace Eddie Rickenbacker taking out tailing enemy ships

From famous WWI ace Eddie Rickenbacker's memoirs, *Fighting the Flying Circus*: ....at the same instant came the sound of that sinister crackling that indicated to me that the strain had again been too much for the strength of the Nieuport's wings. The whole surface of the canvas on the right wing was torn off with the first wrench! It was the same familiar old accident that had so nearly claimed Jimmy Meissner a fortnight previously...[H]ere we were again at least four miles north of No Man's Land! Would he disintegrate here or would he be able to make some sort of landing in the forest-covered mountains below? It was a pitiable choice...

"The boy who can pilot a machine without any fabric on it, as that chap is doing, is certainly something of an artist," I again said to myself as I put on the sauce and hastened to overtake my wobbly companion, who was staggering towards our lines much like a drunken man. But at any rate he was getting there. I came up to within twenty feet of him and looked curiously into the pilot's seat.

There was Jimmy Meissner again, turning a cheery grin towards me and taking his ease while he waved a hand to me! Jimmy Meissner indeed! No wonder he could fly a machine without canvas. With the practise he was getting he would soon be flying without wings. This was the second time he had gone through with practically this same experience, and I had saved him from attack on both occasions. I stayed close beside Jimmy all the way in. When he finally settled down on our field for his final little crash he came wobbling over to me from the wreck as blithe and merry as ever.

"Thanks, old boy, for shooting down those Boches on my tail," said Jimmy, trying to be serious. "I'm beginning to like coming home without any wings on my machine."

1920–1928
Mac Dreams of Flying

As a boy, Mac spent a lot of time next door at the home of Birmingham's only World War I ace, Jimmie Meissner, listening to Meissner's tales of flying and combat. Like many boys he was thrilled by the daring and danger the ace described, and longed to fly. Unlike many boys of that era, Mac got the chance to fulfill his dreams.

Meissner died in 1936 after a bout of flu. His adopted city, Birmingham, Alabama, held a memorial service which included a flyover by planes from the Alabama National Guard unit Meissner had founded. His World War I wingman, Eddie Rickenbacker, was an honorary pall-bearer.

Also unusual for parents in 1920, his parents were willing to indulge Mac's passion for flying and arranged for a very special birthday present, his first airplane ride.

In a speech given much later in his life, Mac told a vivid story of this first experience, one that would set the course of his life:

> I hitched a ride to an airstrip in West End, just outside Birmingham, to meet Meissner.
>
> "You are right on time," Meissner said as I walked in.
>
> He explained the various parts of the plane, got me into my parachute and buckled me into the front seat. The plane was a two-seat biplane with an open cockpit.
>
> "Now here are the rules," and he quickly went over the instruments and explained what I could touch and should not touch. He also went over the emergency procedures and gave me a crash course on how to use my parachute. The thought of needing the parachute was more exciting than scary. I was ready.
>
> The one-man ground crew helped start the engine and the World War I ace and this would-be pilot were on our way.

OPPOSITE, UPPER RIGHT Official service portrait of Jimmy Meissner.

OPPOSITE, LOWER LEFT Meissner standing with plane that twice had the fabric of its upper wing ripped while in combat. Meissner managed to get it home each time, protected by WWII ace Eddie Rickenbacker.

For Mac, it was his dream coming true. But not even in his wildest dreams could the young man have imagined that this ride would be just the first of thousands of hours flying, or that his feats of daring in the face of great danger would rival those of the flying aces of World War I.

1928 – Out of the Blue
from Mac's unpublished manuscript

Six years after that first airplane ride and 20 years old, Mac joined the storied 106th Observation Squadron of the Alabama National Guard based at Roberts Field in Birmingham.

His earlier dream of being a pilot put aside, but still eager to work with airplanes, Mac worked as a airplane mechanic apprentice. Then out of the blue...

The year was 1928.

It was a warm June afternoon and I was standing in the shade of one of the hangers at Roberts Field, outside, Birmingham, Alabama. Little did I know that on this cloudless spring afternoon the most vital decision in my young life was about to be made.

Roberts Field, home of the 106th Observation Squadron, Alabama National Guard, was little more than a glorified skid strip. It was bounded on the East by a creek and a steel mill and on the North and South by wooded hills and residential areas.

In the distance I heard the rumble of an aircraft engine. I shaded my eyes and as the roar drew nearer I saw a tiny aircraft heading in the direction of the field from the South. The plane seemed to scrape the tree tops as it zeroed in on the landing strip.

The pilot drove straight at the field, leveled off a few feet from the ground, pulled up into a graceful loop and started down again. The pilot fishtailed and sideslipped into a perfect landing and taxied up to the flight line. The plane, a Curtiss Hawk biplane, was a beautiful thing to behold.

Meanwhile, the squadron personnel, from the commanding officer to the lowest yardbird private, had tumbled out onto the flight line chattering, waving and raising one helluva racket.

The plane's pilot waved to the surrounding crowd, drew off his goggles and helmet and jumped gracefully from the cockpit to the lower wing and to the ground.

Commanding Officer Col. Sumpter Smith, smiling and waving graciously, strode to the pilot, shook his hand, patted him on the back and turned toward the crowd.

"Gentlemen," he said, "I would like you to know Captain Melvin Asp, U.S. Army Air Corps."

That was when I made my decision—a decision that was to propel me into a flying career, expose me to the adventures in the sky, meeting the greats and the near-greats the world over.

I would be less than honest if I didn't admit my heart was pounding, my legs weak and I was happily fascinated by the sights and sounds occurring only minutes before. I knew from that minute on I wanted to be a military pilot and I swore on the faith of my Scots forebearers that I would be a good one.

When Col. Smith introduced me to Capt. Asp, I asked what he would suggest I do to get into the Air Corps. He said the best route would be a letter to Senator Hugo L. Black, junior Senator from Alabama.

I followed his advice and in May 1930 I was appointed a Flying Cadet at the U.S. Army Air Corps Flying Cadet School, Brooks Field, Texas.

It was an awesome feeling. William C. McDonald, Jr., a scrawny kid from Fairfield, Alabama, hard by the smoking steel mills, whose lone claim to fame was an Eagle Scout's Badge, was going to be one of Uncle Sam's "Fly Boys."

Mac at Brooks Field

1930 – THE CHANCE OF A LIFETIME
Learning to Fly
Brooks Field, San Antonio, Texas

Mac enlisted on June 25, 1930, and on July 1 he reported to Brooks Field in San Antonio, Texas, to be sworn into the Army Air Corps.

Lieutenant Mickle, the flight instructor for the group, was reputedly very good. But during introductions that day, he explained to the cadets that odds were good that 25% of the 110 new cadets arriving would not be there for graduation, having "washed out" of school.

During primary training, the group used an antiquated PT-3 and the new Fleet Primary Trainers. Mac was holding his own with the rest of the class when disaster struck. Hospitalized with a severe sinus infection, he lost a week of instruction and was the last to fly solo. Mickle informed Mac that he had fallen too far behind and would be "washed out" the next day.

Mac was sent to Lieutenant Pearcy for the first of two "wash out" check rides. During the flight, Pearcy yelled, "Forced landing!" Filled with adrenaline, Mac executed the difficult maneuver perfectly. After, Pearcy told Mac to pull off the runway because he wanted to have a smoke. Turning to the anxious and confused cadet, Pearcy uttered two small but important words, "You passed." Recovering quickly, Mac was elated. This second chance put him back with his class. His dreams were still within reach. After three months of primary training, Mac graduated.

Basic Training followed, with the same instructors. The cadets

ABOVE JN-4 of 106th Observation Squadron at Roberts Field. Note squadron insignia below pilot. This insignia is still in use today.

World War I Ace Jimmie Meissner had helped to found the unit, only the seventh unit in the U.S. Forty years later in 1966, Mac's son William C. McDonald III would join the same unit. It still exists today as the 106th Air Refueling Squadron.

BELOW Brooks Field was an airdrome, with planes taking off and landing in all directions, depending on the wind.

Pos... Telegraph

ALL AMERICA CABLES COMMERCIAL CABLES

WB121 8 GOVT

ST WASHINGTON DC 15 1115A

WILLIAM G MCDONALD JR 5148

1040 43 ST BELVIEW HEIGHTS BIRMINGHAM ALA

YOU WILL RECEIVE APPOINTMENT TO JULY FLYING CLASS

HUGO L BLACK.

TELEGRAM

Telephoned

AY 15 1930

Sender

Receiver

Flying time was so limited that the cadets supplemented with "bunk flying." After lunch, students would watch as one cadet got up on a bunk and practiced the instructions from class. In a letter home, Mac told his parents that he wished he had made better notes from the daily bunk flying. During one of these sessions, Mac learned how to do a chandelle, a sudden, steep climbing turn, executed to alter direction and gain altitude simultaneously.

were introduced to various flying formations and flew two types of aircraft, the very old and famous De Havilland biplane with a Liberty water-cooled engine, and the more modern Douglas O-38 biplane. Each cadet flew both types for experience. On November 1, 1930 at graduation from Basic Training, the group was down to seventy-five, with thirty-five "washed out."

In Advanced Training at Kelly Field, the cadets were assigned to the Pursuit, Attack, Observation or Bombardment section. Lucky again, Mac got his first choice, Pursuit. He learned one-on-one combat with an enemy plane, attacking formations of bombers, and supporting ground troops in combat. Formation flying and aerobatic maneuvers were stressed, including close formation, echelon formation, stagger formations and tactical orientation. Planes in these formations filled the sky over Kelly Field. Aerobatic flying training provided a basic introduction to aerial combat maneuvers.

Cadet Henry Myers became Mac's wingman. The two enjoyed competing in all phases of advanced training. This competition in part led to a spectacular accident that could again have cost Mac his dream.

As graduation neared, the cadets made their final cross-country flights. Myers was first to make his flight to Love Field in Dallas. With a favorable tailwind, Myers established a record time within the Pursuit group.

Mac started his cross-country flight on the same course, determined to beat Henry's record. He was careful with his "dead reckoning" navigation and spotted Love Field five minutes ahead of Myer's time. In his excitement, he made a crucial mistake. Approaching to the north with a strong southerly wind at his back, he began his landing without circling the field to fly into the wind, which slows the plane's speed. The plane was streaking along much too fast in the landing roll after touch-down.

He executed a good touch-down, but as he passed the operations office, Mac realized his mistake. Ahead, disaster loomed in the form of high-tension wires, telephone wires, towers and poles which ran the entire stretch of the field. Mac slammed on the brakes so hard that his aircraft nosed over and flipped onto its back with a sickening crunch. The plane was badly damaged, though luckily Mac was unhurt. He saw cars racing across the field.

The instructor in command was furious. For any pilot to land

At Brooks Field

ABOVE LEFT TO RIGHT Flying in arrow formation; Mac standing in front of Ford; Mac (second from right) dressed to the nines.

BELOW The planes of the 106th Observation Squadron, Douglas O-38s.

Wingman

The term originally referred to a plane flying beside and slightly behind the lead plane in formation.

In aerial combat, the presence of a wingman makes the flight both offensively and defensively more capable. Working together, their effectiveness is more than doubled. They can employ more dynamic tactics, cover vulnerabilities and increase firepower and situational awareness.

Taken less literally, throughout his life Mac was both lead and wingman in many situations in the air and on the ground.

downwind was unforgivable. Mac felt awful. He had lost the race to Myers and cracked up a plane. The instructor flew Mac back to Kelly.

He could have been washed out, but he was near graduation and normally one of the best pilots in his class. His instructor was merciful and allowed the young pilot to continue his training. Mac learned his lesson: never, ever land downwind!

On May 12, 1931, Mac passed his instrument rating check ride, a milestone for new pilots.

Several days later, the unit received exciting news. The Air Corps would be involved in operating maneuvers across the eastern part of the United States. With every type of available aircraft included, they were to make simulated attacks on various cities. This great air armada included 672 aircraft and involved Regular Army, National Guard units and instructors, cadets and airplanes from the Advanced Flying School at Kelly Field.

In an article about the 1931 maneuvers, which took place from May 20 through May 30, author Dr. Maurer Maurer gave the schedule:

> The armada put on its show at Chicago on Thursday, performed for New York on Saturday, moved to airfields in New England on Sunday, performed at Boston on Monday, returned to New York on Tuesday, flew over Atlantic City and returned to New York on Wednesday, took a day for maintenance, passed over Philadelphia and Baltimore on the way south on Friday, and completed the tour with a grand display over Washington on Saturday, 30 May. The show at the principal cities consisted of two parts, a combat demonstration by thirty-nine planes (Keystone bombers, Curtiss A-3s, and Boeing P-12s) and an aerial review with the division in formation. In addition, the Air Corps scheduled bombing raids on New York on Friday night, the 22nd, and on Boston on Sunday night, the 24th.

Shortly after these maneuvers, Mac took his final stage check ride with First Lieutenant Claire Lee Chennault. The flight went extremely well and the two men hit it off almost immediately.

Neither of them could have seen then that they would become the best of friends, comrades in arms, experience countless adventures together, both on and off the ground, travel to a far-away land and fight in war to save a country. Their friendship would see both of them survive war, peace and illness, lasting until the end of their lives.

But for now, graduation had finally arrived. Mac had reached his dream and was now a pilot. He re-enlisted on June 30, 1931, for another year.

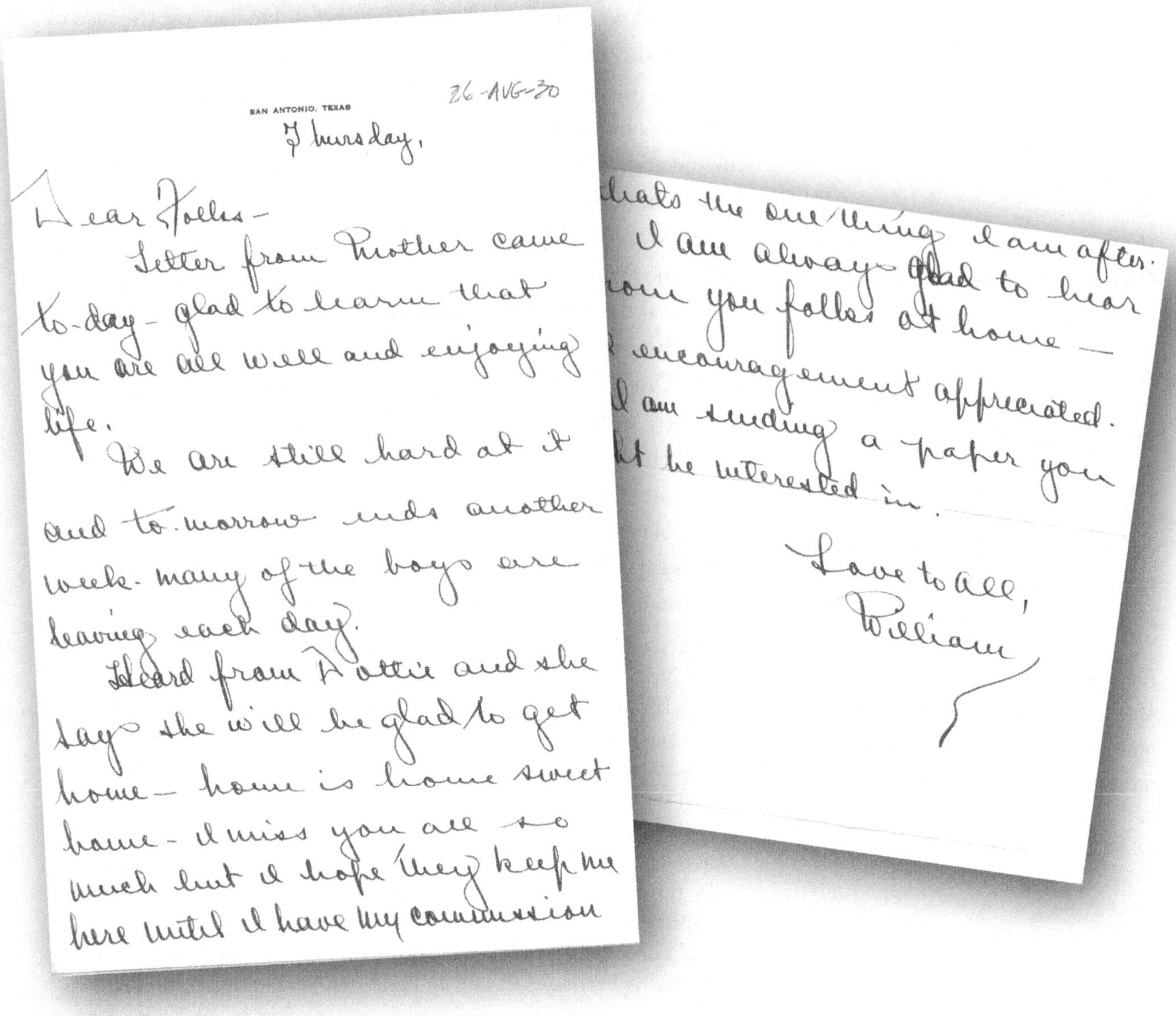

SAN ANTONIO, TEXAS

36-AUG-30

Thursday,

Dear Folks —

Letter from Mother came to-day — glad to learn that you are all well and enjoying life.

We are still hard at it and to-morrow ends another week. Many of the boys are leaving each day.

Heard from Dottie and she says she will be glad to get home — home is home sweet home — I miss you all so much but I hope they keep me here until I have my commission

— thats the one thing I am after. I am always glad to hear from you folks at home — encouragement appreciated. I am sending a paper you might be interested in.

Love to all,
William

Letters Home From Flight School

Mac started writing home in flight school, but if he wrote regularly, the letters have disappeared. He wrote occasionally, particularly when he was on a trip somewhere, but he didn't seem to have a schedule as he would later.

The letters he did write were enthusiastic, cheerful and positive. He mentioned friends, flying and that "home is home sweet home."

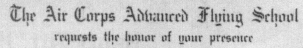

ABOVE Air Corps Advanced Flying School graduating class, June 1931, Kelly Field.

BELOW Mac passed the Instrument Flying portion of training.

1st Lt. James H. Doolittle made the first blind (instrument-only) take-off, flight and landing on September 29, 1929. Mac was among the first to be trained in this. According to a history of aviation in the U.S. Air Corps, written by author Mauer Maurer, instrument flying would not become a priority until 1934, and only then due to a scandal involving contracts for airmail delivery.

Lieutenant Colonel Henry Tift "Hank" Myers

Henry Tift "Hank" Meyers
September 16, 1907 – December 8, 1968

- First pilot of Air Force One
  Served from 1944–48
  Flew Franklin D. Roosevelt and Harry S. Truman
- Mac's Flight School Wingman
- First American to fly non-stop to Paris following Charles Lindbergh
- Set air-speed record that lasted for ten years, until it was broken by Howard Hughes

BOTH PHOTOS BELOW Hank Myers (left) and Mac (right), at Brooks Field.

SPECIAL ORDERS)
NO.   162)

WAR DEPARTMENT,
Washington, July 13, 1931.

E X T R A C T

X   X

30. By direction of the President, each of the followi
second lieutenants, Air Corps Reserve, is relieved from further as
and duty at Dodd Field, Fort Sam Houston, Texas, and will proceed
station specified after his name and report to the commanding offi
duty. Each officer if not sooner relieved will be relieved from d
time to enable him to arrive at his home, as indicated after his n
June 30, 1932, on which date he will revert to inactive status;

*

William Clifford McDonald, Jr., Birmingham, Alabama, Selfridge Field,
Mt. Clemens, Michigan.

Ronald Claire McLaughlin, Evanston, Illinois, Selfridge Field, Mt.
Clemens, Michigan.

Henry Tift Myers, Tifton, Georgia, Selfridge Field, Mt. Clemens,
Michigan.

Charles Harrison Pursley, Fort Myers, Florida, Selfridge Field, Mt.
Clemens, Michigan.

Herbert George Robinson, Norfolk, Virginia, Selfridge Field, Mt.
Clemens, Michigan.

Charles Wesley Schott, Providence, Rhode Island, Selfridge Field, Mt.
Clemens, Michigan.

Joe Malcolm Sutherland, Anderson, South Carolina, Selfridge Field, Mt.
Clemens, Michigan.

Claude Benjamin White, Norfolk, Virginia, Selfridge Field, Mt. Clemens,
Michigan.

*   *

The travel directed is necessary in the military service.
FD 1139 P4-0___, P_-0521, P4-1378, P4-0284, P4-0700, P4-0730 A 084-2.
(A.G. 210.313, A.C. Res.) (8-9-31.)

X   X   X

By order of The Secretary of WAR:

DOUGLAS MacARTHUR,
General,
Chief of Staff.

OFFICIAL:

C. H. BRIDGES,
Major General,
The Adjutant General.

A True Extract ___

Among others, William C. McDonald Jr. and Henry Tift Myers went to Selfridge Field in Michigan.

— AIR —
— MAIL —

Mentor Tour
1.

Mrs. Valeria McDonald,
c/o The Travel Guild,
33. Avenue de l'opéra,
Paris, France.

FIRST PURSUIT GROUP
SELFRIDGE FIELD
MT. CLEMENS, MICH.

July 31, 1931

My Dearest Mother —
I so sorry I have not been a good boy and dropped you a line. I have been stationed here in Mt. Clemens, Mich. and I like it very much. Things as a whole are very nice and we are expecting things to get better as we go along. I didnt go by home on the way up here — but I did go by Edmund Okla. to see Aunt Virginia. She looks so well and was so nice to me — I didnt see her long. I brought Wm Graham as far as Detroit with me — he is very young yet — needs a little real life —

A letter from you came the other day — it was sent on up from Kelly Field — I am so happy that you are having a good time. I think of you lots — because your boy loves you.

As soon as you get home I am going to get about ten days leave and come home.

Be a sweet Mother and have the time of your life and write to me.

Love,
William

1931 – THE CHANCE OF A LIFETIME
Critical Lessons
July 1931 – June 1932
Selfridge Field, 25 miles north of Detroit, Michigan

LEFT Newest member of the 94th Pursuit Squadron

For Mac, it was especially meaningful to go to the 94th Squadron of the First Pursuit group, the same unit that Jimmie Meissner flew for in World War I. Mac was proud to be assigned as Second Lieutenant to this storied group of fighters. Mac is front row, center.

On July 13, 1931, Mac, Myers and others were ordered to Selfridge Field in Mt. Clemons, Michigan, for their first assignment as pursuit pilots with the 94th Pursuit Squadron.

Due to the Depression, budget constraints usually limited flying to ten hours per month, and as low as four hours a month. Luckily, Mac was asked to participate in several other projects which gave him more hours flying under a variety of conditions and critical experience flying different aircraft, including those with multiple engines.

High-Altitude Formation Training was dangerous, as pilots would attempt to exceed the suggested ceiling on the Boeing P-12 C, the hottest new fighter plane at the time.

On one of Mac's flights, he climbed past 29,000 feet, the ceiling for this aircraft, in an attempt to get to 30,000 feet. After failing to ease through the last 100 feet, he dove hard for 2,000 feet to gain as much speed as possible for another try. It wasn't quite enough.

The group was testing out a new oxygen delivery system and suits

Fliers of Ninety-Fourth Pursuit Squadron

RIGHT Members of the 94th Pursuit Squadron from Selfridge Field, Mt. Clemens, Michigan. LEFT TO RIGHT, FRONT ROW Lieutenants R.C. McLaughlin, J.S. Anderson, W.C. McDonald, J.V. Crabb and C.R. Feldman. BACK ROW Lieutenants L.R. Black, R.L. Sansbury, Harry A. Johnson, commander, Jess Auton and H.O. Coleman.

—Post-Gazette Photo.

Members of the Ninety-fourth Pursuit Squadron from Selfridge Field, Mt. Clemens, Mich., who flew here in 16 Boeing pursuit planes. They are, left to right, front row: Lieutenants R. C. McLaughlin, J. S. Anderson, W. C. McDonald, J. V. Crabb and C. R. Feldman; back row, Lieutenants L. R. Black, R. L. Sansbury, Harry A. Johnson, commander, Jess Auton and H. O. Coleman.

High Altitude Formation Flying

December 4, 1931, *Air Corps News*

The first cross-country flight at an altitude of 20,000 feet, in which all the pilots used liquid oxygen, was completed by the 94th Pursuit Squadron on November 3rd, when twelve planes, under the command of Lieut. Harry A. Johnson, flew from Selfridge Field to Washington, D.C., in two hours and five minutes. At Selfridge Field two days prior to the flight, tests were run on gas consumption above 20,000 feet, and it was discovered that an economical consumption could be obtained at a fairly high RPM.

A short distance out of Washington, members of the flight noticed the plane piloted by Lieut. Hersam started cavorting crazily about the sky and then diving for the earth. Down he plunged out of sight of the remainder of the flight who, wondering, kept on towards Washington. They were delighted, indeed, to have him join the flight just before they landed.

It was learned that Lieut. Hersam had accidentally detached the tube leading from his oxygen supply to his face mask while reaching for his map. He was soon unconscious, and his plane, out of control, dove towards the earth until at 7,000 feet the pilot recovered and righted his ship. He joined the flight over Washington, and the 12 planes landed as one unit at Bolling Field, Anacostia, D.C., the first one touching the ground at 3:50 PM.

Liquid oxygen was used on this trip, and it is a marked improvement over the gas oxygen carried in cylinders. The regulation of the amount necessary for the pilot is entirely automatic and cuts the number of gauges and instruments necessary to keep on a flight of that type. Face masks in which a tube carried the oxygen to the nostrils, were used, and these proved superior to those which required the tube to be held in the mouth…

Most of the pilots encountered

trouble through the fogging of the goggles, one pilot losing his goggles 15 minutes after taking off and flying the entire distance without them. The maximum temperature encountered was 20 degrees below zero centigrade, which seems to be the dead line on temperature where goggles either will or will not fog. At a temperature below that, all B-6 goggles will fog until it is impossible to see through them.

The flying suits (B-7) were apparently warm enough for the first hour. After that, all pilots began to chill and during the last hour hoped that Washington would show up soon. The opinion of the members of the flight…was that the temperature of Washington was almost tropical.

It can be seen from this flight that, should Washington be endangered by an attack, a squadron could take off from Selfridge Field, arrive at Washington, drop the auxiliary tanks, and have sufficient gasoline…to go into combat at ceiling just two hours after leaving Selfridge Field.

OPPOSITE PAGE Mac (left) dressed for high altitudes. In Mac's High-Altitude Formation Training, pilots attempted to exceed the suggested ceiling on the Boeing P-12 C, the hottest new fighter plane at the time and the plane most suited to aerial acrobatics.

Mac's training under Ballard, particularly in navigation, would serve Mac well later in his career. A bad navigator can take the plane off-course, with the danger of running out of gas in the air and forcing an emergency landing.

Captain Ballard and Mac flew a Tri-Motor Ford transport plane to St. Paul to supply other planes with skis for a training exercise. A difficult plane to fly, this specific experience with the Ford would later put him at the scene of one of the twentieth century's pivotal moments.

to help pilots bear the cold at high altitudes. Above a certain altitude, roughly between 13,000 and 15,000 feet, pilots would become less alert or even pass out from lack of oxygen or being chilled.

Later that month, Mac piloted one of twelve planes flown in formation from Selfridge to Washington, D.C. in a high altitude, long-range mission designed to test equipment and pilots.

Selfridge provided many opportunities to hone his flying skills, but equally important to his career, to practice his landing skills.

Ski Testing was headed by Captain A. B. Ballard and involved a number of mechanics and six pilots. Pilots tested Ford Tri-motor planes equipped with flat, corrugated and amphibious skis for different landing conditions. The pilots practiced in a Douglas O-38, a two-seat observation aircraft, fitted with large flat skis. Everyone enjoyed flying this plane because it was twice the size of a P-12 and more stable when landing on snow or ice.

Mac loved landing on the frozen lake at Selfridge Field. Once the plane had slowed to 40 mph in the landing roll after touch-down, Mac would kick full rudder for a hard turn, causing the plane to spin on the lake like a top. This technique could be highly dangerous if a pilot did not know the exact air and ice conditions, which seemed to add to the fun for Mac.

In June of 1932, after fourteen months at Selfridge Field, Mac had completed his two years of active duty, graduated and was released from the Army along with hundreds of other new pilots. Against the odds he was now qualified as a pilot, but he still needed a job. He went home to Birmingham and spent over four months searching for work with no luck, as did the other newly-minted pilots.

In 1932, as the Depression deepened, jobs were not guaranteed. But he was a good pilot and fate intervened yet again, this time through Luke Williamson, who was destined to provide Mac with yet another unbelievable opportunity.

1932–1936 ANOTHER CHANCE OF A LIFETIME
Men on the Flying Trapeze
Maxwell Field, Montgomery, Alabama

Lᴇꜰᴛ Mac after re-enlisting as a private in the U.S. Army Air Corps, December 1932, to join Chennault's aerial acrobatics team

The United States government felt that America should take to the air. In 1927, the U.S. military embarked on a five-year plan to beef up its air power. The Department of Commerce did its best to encourage the development of civil airlines. Even the U.S. Post Office used its contracts for airmail to steer and develop commercial airlines.

But the Depression kept the military budget small, and the relatively new idea of air power competed for officers and funding with the traditional armed forces. Some believed that no country had ever been defeated without being occupied by the enemy's army; this led to the conclusion that air power could not be a dominating factor in war. Others disagreed, among them Claire Lee Chennault.

In December, 1932, Mac was on his way to Auburn University to pick up his brother Malcolm for the holiday break. He decided to swing by Montgomery, Alabama, to see friends at Maxwell Field, home of the Air Corps Tactical School (ACTS). Mac ran into Luke Williamson, a pilot who had been in the class ahead of him at Brooks Field.

Williamson took Mac to see Chennault, who told Mac about his newly-formed Army aerial acrobatics team. He offered Mac the chance to fly with this team as its fourth member and a rare chance to re-enlist, though as a buck private. Chennault promised a promotion to sergeant in six months, starting pay of $17.50 per month and a 50 percent bonus for flying ten or more hours per month.

Any job was a good job in those days, and the chance to fly with Chennault was too good an offer to turn down. Mac jumped at the opportunity and signed enlistment papers on December 20.

After a brief trip home for the holidays, Mac returned to Maxwell Field and reported to Chennault. Mac was assigned to a bunk in the barracks of Headquarters Company and began his career in the U.S. Army Air Corps as an enlisted pilot.

Maxwell was a pilot's heaven, with all four types of military planes—pursuit planes, attack planes, observation planes and a bomber—available due to the presence of the Air Corps Tactical School. In his first month at Maxwell, he logged over 100 hours, piloting all four types of aircraft.

Mac began to train immediately as the fourth man on the demonstration team, joining Chennault, John H. "Luke" Williamson and Haywood "Possum" Hansell. He had a lot of work to do.

Chennault put together a demonstration team to convince his fellow officers and the general public—anyone who would watch and listen—that pursuit planes were an essential part of strategy for war in the Aviation Age.

The original 4-man Army aerial acrobatics team, the Men on the Flying Trapeze
ABOVE, LEFT TO RIGHT William C. "Billy" McDonald, alternate, Haywood S. "Possum" Hansell, left wing man; Claire Lee Chennault and John H. "Luke" Williamson, right wing man.

BELOW The team at Maxwell Field ca 1933 in front of their Boeing P-12s.

Origins of the Army Demonstration Team

Colonel John Curry, Commanding Officer of Maxwell and the Army Air Corps Tactical School (ACTS), had gone to Auburn for the dedication of their airport on April 4, 1932. The Navy's formation team put on a spectacular show. In contrast, six Army planes from Maxwell flew over in competent but unimpressive formation. Martha Byrd in *Chennault: Giving Wings to the Tiger* gives Chennault credit for convincing Col. Curry that a demonstration team would serve several needs for ACTS. Colonel Curry authorized Captain Claire Lee Chennault to organize and train a three-pilot demonstration Army team that would compete with the Navy.

Claire Lee Chennault was originally from Louisiana, and had graduated from Louisiana State University and its Normal School, becoming a high school teacher. A good teacher no matter the subject, he was also a student of fighter pilots and warfare, and had been flying since World War I. In 1922, he graduated from pursuit pilot training. He was Chief of the Pursuit Section at the ACTS in the 1930s, and a great pilot.

Chennault decided on a simple but tough test to determine if a pilot was good enough to be a wingman. To make the team, a pilot had to stay with Chennault's plane during 30 minutes of aggressive acrobatic flying. Many tried, but only three men made the cut. Chennault selected Sergeant John H. "Luke" Williamson as his number one wingman and Lieutenant Hayward S. Hansell as his number two. Mac joined several months later as the alternate until Hansell left the team in May, 1933.

The team served as a lab for testing maneuvers and tactics which would become part of the training program for the Chinese Air Force and for the famed Flying Tigers.

Chennault also hoped to educate his fellow officers on the importance of pursuit planes. The military had switched its focus to bombers, and pursuit planes were not popular among the officers at ACTS or elsewhere. Chennault also did not believe the standard military book adequately prepared pilots for the new realities of air warfare, another belief which did not endear him to his fellow military officers. But the men he commanded were often fiercely devoted to him, and none more so than Mac.

Hansell (on right) resigned from the team in May, 1933, to train as a bomber pilot. He flew bombing raids over Germany and rose to the rank of general. He and Mac remained friends.

"Three Men on a Flying Trapeze," Billy MacDonald, Claire L. Chennault, Luke Williamson, with an unidentified pilot, stand before their Boeing P-12 at an early Carnival

Luckily, Mac would be flying the Boeing P-12, the plane he had flown as a pilot at high altitudes at Selfridge. He also loved the work and was thrilled that he could fly more than ten hours a month, the allotment at Selfridge Field.

At Maxwell, Mac gained invaluable flying skills and became fast friends with Chennault, the man with whom he would spend most of the next two decades.

After several months of intense training and practice, Mac was ready. At demonstrations across the country, Mac now performed a solo show in the fourth P-12, executing a show of aerobatics developed by Chennault. He also served as the announcer during the three-man demonstration flights at the National Air Races.

After the Cleveland National Air Races in May of 1933, Hansell left the demonstration team. Mac took his place in the main three-man acrobatic team.

LEFT Three Men on the Flying Trapeze (place and date unknown).

ANOTHER CHAPTER IN THE NEVER-ENDING CHANCE OF A LIFETIME
Training & Thrills with Chennault

Chennault believed that standard military training did not address modern warfare. Consequently, Mac's training was not standard Army fare. Even Chennault's wife Nell helped with her husband's unconventional approach to training. Selma Road ran in front of the Chennault home and continued straight for several miles.

Under Chennault's guidance, Mac practiced incessantly, learning to execute a variety of maneuvers without veering toward the left or right of Selma Road. Nell observed and made notes on his performance as he developed his skills. It was she who determined he was ready for the next step in his training.

In later correspondence, Mac credited Nell Chennault as an important contributor to the training he received. Chennault kept his promise and promoted Mac to sergeant after six months. In addition to the unique training he received as a member of Chennault's demonstration team, Mac was able to participate in several other activities which gave him enhanced skills and valuable experience in different kinds of flying. During the Air Mail Scandal, he flew mail. He got his transport pilot rating during a record-setting trip to South America. He also flew passengers. During one flight, he joined the Caterpillar Club, jumping from a plane whose engine had quit and was on its way to crashing.

BELOW LEFT Old Selma Road (left). Photo by George Culley.

BELOW RIGHT Chennault's home in Montgomery, Alabama, was big enough for his eight children, but in rough shape. Photo by Alex Bush. (Stone-Young-Baggett House, Old Selma Road. Historic American Buildings Survey, Library of Congress, Prints & Photographs Division)

Flying Trapezers Ready For Miami

12/8/35

After two mornings of intensive practice, Maj. Claire Chennault will lead his celebrated Flying Trapezers, army stunting team, to Miami Tuesday morning for the air maneuvers in progress there, it was learned last night.

Col. Fisher, post commandant, will fly down Tuesday with Capt. Storrie. There will also be a transport plane, carrying mechanics. Probably other ships will make the trip.

Lieut. H. S. Hansell, Jr., orignal member of the Flying Trapezers, already is in Miami, with G. H. Q. maneuvers now in progress.

The team led by Maj. Chennault, with Sergts. William C. McDonald, Jr., and Luke Williamson flying planes on his wings, will go into the air over Maxwell Field at 9 a.m. today for practice of their repertoire of aerial acrobatics. The practice will be repeated Monday at the same time.

Time for the take-off Tuesday morning has not been fixed definitely.

Flying Trapezers Invading Newsreel

Newsreel photographers representing five major companies will be at Maxwell Field this morning to make moving pictures of the Tactical School's famous "Flying Trapezers" in action.

Permission to make the pictures was given by the commandant, Col. John F. Curry, to Fox Movietone, Pathe, Universal, Hearst Metrotone, and Paramount News.

Operators for these companies will arrive at the post about 9 a.m. today and set the equipment and cameras to make sound pictures. Cameras probably will be taken aloft in planes furnished by the school to get first-hand views of the noted stunt team in action.

Making of the pictures which will be shown from one end of the country to the other, follows close upon the Maxwell Field pursuit team's triumph at the Cleveland air races early this year and at other air exhibitions. Civilian and army fliers have acclaimed the Trapezers, led by Capt. Claire L. Chennault, as one of the greatest teams in the nation.

Capt. Chennault is operations officer at Maxwell Field. Lieut. Haywood H. Hansell, Tactical School student, is one of the wing men, and Sergt. John Williamson, enlisted pilot, is the other wing man. Sergt. McDonald, enlisted pilot, is alternate wing man.

The Trapezers use tiny pursuit planes, capable of a speed of about 185 miles per hour, and they perform an amazing series of loops, rolls, spins, wingovers, barrel-rolls and other stunts.

As the National Air Races opened at Cleveland Airport yesterday. TOP—Part of the 25,000 spectators in the grandstand when the band opened the races with the national anthem.

LOWER LEFT—The army's stunt flyers, "three men on a flying trapeze." They are, left to right, Lieut. W. C. McDonald, Maj. C. L. Chennault, and Lieut. J. H. Williamson.

ABOVE, LEFT TO RIGHT As the National Air Races opened at Cleveland Airport: Lieut. W.C. McDonald, Maj. C.L. Chennault, and Lieut. J.H. Williamson.

Mac and Williamson were enlisted men with the rank of sergeants, but they arrived at shows with the lieutenant's bars they earned in the Reserves. Later in life, Mac explained that they were ordered to change their insignia because the Army did not want the public or press to know that an enlisted man was flying rather than a commissioned officer. The press reported Mac and Williamson as Lieutenants. However, the Army also did not want to pay them as officers due to Depression budget restraints. This situation greatly concerned Chennault as he believed the men had more than earned the right to become regular commissioned officers.

Breaking the Rules

Mac, from undated speech card

When we were flying in close formation, the distance between the planes was approximately two feet. The distance between the cockpits was about fifteen or twenty feet. Although we did not have radios in those days we could read lips and because we flew together so much we could anticipate anything that the General was going to do.

Every single maneuver that we performed was the original idea of the General. From the spectator's view point the three turn spin was the most spectacular and most thrilling; and of course the Boeing P-12C that we were flying was not supposed to be put into spins. Therefore, when we did this maneuver, the military pilots also got a thrill out of it. Yet together it was the easiest and simplest maneuver that we did. The most difficult was rolling the entire formation in close formation, and I also think it was the most dangerous.

Luke Williamson and I invented a maneuver and we begged the General for over a year to try it. We were young and forgot the safety rule that the General adopted. We never did any maneuver under a thousand feet. This meant in case of a collision we would have a chance to jump. We wanted to try a landing out of an inverted approach. Finally the General agreed and one Sunday afternoon, coming in to Maxwell Field from an air show in Atlanta, we thought that there would be no one at the field and we could get away with this maneuver unobserved.

Unfortunately it did not work out that way. We approached the field from the east, dove down to a low altitude, roared across the field and then pulled up into a loop and approached the field upside down in formation. We cut the power and glided on down to approximately 100 feet, crossed the fence and at a signal from the General rolled over right side up and landed. It was a real thrill and we were as cocky as three pilots could be. We taxied to the flying line and got out and were laughing about the approach and landing, when suddenly we realized someone was galloping across the field to us on a horse! The jubilee ceased at once.

It was Col. John F. Curry, the Commanding Officer. He gave us a dressing down on the spot, and we were all standing at attention. He promptly grounded the three of us. No more flying. And then as he walked away he said under his breath, "That was the most spectacular landing that I have ever seen in my life." Of course, the next day we were placed back on flying status.

12

FAMOUS AIRMEN TO APPEAR TODAY

Noted Army Trio to Perform at Aviation Show Here This Afternoon

20 PLANES AT AIRPORT

Large Crowd is Expected to Be on Hand to Witness Demonstrations

The army air corps demonstration team, commonly known as "The Men on the Flying Trapeze", will, with others of the pursuit and bombardment flights, put on an exhibition of flying at the municipal airport this afternoon at 4 o'clock the like of which Charleston has not seen before.

"The Men on the Flying Trapeze", led by Major Claire L. Chennault, and with Lieutenants John H. Williamson and William C. McDonald on the wings, is probably the most famous team of acrobatic fliers in the country. They were hailed as the outstanding team in both the National air races in Cleveland and the All-American air races in Miami.

They said that they were instructed to come here in connection with the Azalea festival on a training flight, rather than for demonstration purposes, but the program they have outlined for themselves shows that what they consider a training flight is practically a demonstration. They will go through the following maneuvers: Squirrel cage, slow roll to left in column, snap roll to right in column, two turn tail-spin in column, Immelmann turn figure 8's in V formation, half roll figures of "8", lufberry circle, assimilated bombing attacks on ground targets, and a power dive.

Tailspin in Column

Their two-turn tailspin in column should be especially interesting since they are said to be the only team able to put on the stunt.

All three of "The Men on the Flying Trapeze" are Southerners. Lieutenant Williamson is a native of this state, Major Chennault is from Louisianna and Lieutenant McDonald is from Birmingham.

The detail of planes is from the Air Corps Tactical school, Maxwell Field, Montgommery, Ala. Lieutenant Colonel William O. Ryan, commanding the flight, is president of the air corps board and a pilot with considerable experience with the Italian air forces during the World war. Besides the commander of the flight and the "Men on the Flying Trapeze," the pursuit detail is composed of Major Emil C. Kiel and Major L. A. Smith, instructor in attack aviation at the tactical school in Montgommery and also a pilot of much war experience.

The pursuit flight will be a single seater Boeing P—12C planes with engines of 425 horsepower, capable of 307 miles an hour as a maximum.

During the four years from 1932 to 1936, the team performed at numerous air shows in Birmingham, Atlanta, Cleveland, Miami and many other cities. The press estimated that over a million people attended the combined shows. One press clipping estimated that a crowd of 25,000 would come to see the Trapezers in their daring show.

Unlike other flying teams, the pilots were using innovative military maneuvers in their shows. The men developed new and unique combat strategies while performing for crowds. Four years of practice and development gave the three men outstanding experience in a new kind of aerial flying and warfare.

They also got to know the exact strengths and weaknesses of the aircraft they flew, trying to use anything to their advantage. The capabilities of their planes were carefully cataloged and taken into account at every stage of planning.

But the perception of difficulty did not always match the actual difficulty. What seemed dangerous or crazy was actually a carefully-planned show. They were excellent pilots, practiced hard, studied everything they could find, and understood their planes' capabilities and weaknesses completely.

Another perk of the job. Girls wanted a picture after a show where the crowd was estimated as over 100,000.

U.S. Army Air Service & the Airmail Scandal

February 19–June 1, 1934

The Trapezers were also military men who could be called upon for any reason. When commercial airmail contracts were cancelled due to scandal, President Roosevelt ordered the Air Corps to take over the job. Mac reported to the commanding officer at Chandler Field in Atlanta to begin flying the mail.

Mac flew this duty for just two weeks, likely in the P-12s which were noted as one of the planes which became dangerously off-balance when loaded with mail.

The U.S. Army Air Service delivered the first airmail for three months in 1918, then turned it over to the Post Office. The Post Office operated it for nine years, until Congress decided that private contractors with airmail contracts would encourage commercial aviation nationwide.

Some of these contractors took advantage of the lucrative airmail subsidies by arranging to carry junk mail and heavy objects, and many carriers were barebones operations. Using the Air Mail Act of 1930, the postmaster general for the Hoover administration, Walter Folger Brown, set out to "use air mail contracts to stimulate the growth of a stable and efficient airline industry," according to John T. Correll's article, *The Airmail Fiasco* (Air Force Magazine, March, 2008). His policies favored larger airlines and those which would increase capacity to carry passengers. The smaller carriers weren't happy.

After a change of administration, in September 1933, Sen. Hugo L. Black (D-Alabama) launched a Senate investigation. Headlines in the election year of 1934 announced that the Republicans had presided over a scandal, a collusion to misuse public funds.

Members of President Franklin D. Roosevelt's administration proposed cancellation of all commercial airmail contracts and the Secretary of War George H. Dern agreed to have the Army Air Corps carry the mail. The Air Corps was given just ten days to prepare, with first routes begun February 19.

The Chief of the Air Corps, Maj. Gen. Benjamin D. Foulois, presided over the Army Air Corps Mail Operation. Among its many difficulties, the Army's planes were for the most part built to special purpose, unsuitable and often dangerous to use to carry mail; they also were not equipped with the night-flying and instrument navigation systems of the commercial carriers. Consequently, its pilots had not received adequate training in instrument navigation or night flying. According to Correll, most of the 250 pilots were lieutenants with little flying experience. Few had experience flying in bad weather. When a pilot can't see the horizon due to clouds, fog or darkness, for instance, they risk flying in a descending spiral into the ground. Due to human physiology, without external visual cues, the pilot experiences this as flying straight and level, leading to judgment errors that might result in a "graveyard spiral" and crash.

The results were tragic, with several deaths due to each of these causes. The scandal reached the White House, yet despite strong attempts to correct the many issues quickly, there were 66 crashes and 12 fatalities before the contracts with commercial flyers were back in place in June of 1934.

Candler Field, Ga.,
March 2, 1934.

Dear Dad,

Larry and I are no longer carrying the mail. The Zone Commander decided that it wasn't fair for us to fly mail if Congress wouldn't appropriate money comensurate with the work that we were doing. Of course we want more money but we were not squaking over it since this was a job and it had to be done and since we are more qualified for the work we felt a little bit peeved about it. However we are still in Atlanta. Most of my work consists of Office work anything to keep things moving. Larry is doing the same thing except we work differant hours.

Don't know how long this will last but I am sure we will be here another two weeks anyway.

Lots of bad weather lately and the boys having a bit of tough time but they are not taking any chances when the weather is to bad.

My regards to the rest of the family and I hope that it won't be long until I see you again.

Just,

Mac flew the mail for at least a couple of weeks.

ABSOLUTELY FIREPROOF   700 OUTSIDE ROOMS ALL WITH BATH   2/16/34   LEON JACOBS, President

JUNG HOTEL
NEW ORLEANS' MOST MODERN HOTEL
MODERATE RATES

EVERY ROOM WITH CEILING FAN, SERVIDOR, RUNNING ICE WATER
ROOF GARDEN, AUDITORIUM, TURKISH BATH, FREE PARKING SPACE
UNEXCELLED FRENCH CUISINE

NEW ORLEANS
Friday

Dear Dad,

The Chief of the Air Corps took his ax and cut our flying to 4 hours a month — Then came the Air Mail work so the 4 hour business was out.

We were informed 3 hours before we took off for New Orleans — Just shows

how rapid things are moving. We are here to help dedicate the new Airport, and will remain thru Sunday

I don't think that Maxwell Field will be used in carrying the mail — however you can't say, for sure.

Will try to get home soon — Love to all.

Wm

> The chief of the Air Corps took his ax and cut our flying to 4 hours a month — Then came the air mail work so the 4 hour business was out...I don't think that Maxwell Field will be used in carrying the mail - however you can't say, for sure.
>
> Mac, February 16, 1934

It was a common rumor that the team tied their wings together, as it was believed impossible to make the synchronized moves they made without this artificial attachment. Later in his life, Mac went ballistic whenever the rumor was repeated. He felt strongly that the comment was a great insult to the passion, work and intelligence that they and Chennault had poured into the seemingly impossible maneuvers. A stunt team from the Navy did tie themselves together with 35-foot ropes, which may have been the origin of this rumor.

Each of the men brought different qualities to the group, but as a whole, they were willing to take calculated risks, inclined to skirt authority and somewhat cavalier about danger; often they displayed all three traits at once. These traits would serve them well and carry into the next phase of their lives.

This picture shows Mac in the center, with one of two dogs who took the trip with the team. Their names were "Whiskey" and "Sour."

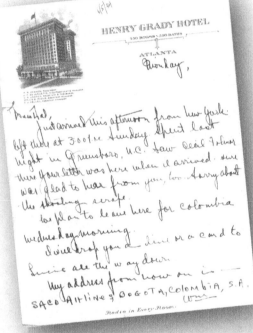

Ferrying Transports from New York to Bogotá

While flying the mail out of Atlanta, Mac met Dan Hughes, the Chief Pilot for Colombian Airlines, Servicio Aereo Colombiano, which was owned by Ernesto Samper Mendoza. He was a famous flyer and considered the "Lindbergh of Colombia." Hughes needed another pilot to ferry reconditioned Curtiss Kingbirds, recently purchased from Eastern Airlines, from New York to Bogotá.

This trip would give Mac his transport rating, the credentials to fly larger, multi-engine planes. Chennault approved and arranged a 90-day leave of absence for him.

The trip took sixteen days and was 4,200 miles long, and set a record for formation flying by transport planes. The trip served as good publicity for the new airline and also showcased commercial flying in South America. The South American press covered it widely, and Mac kept clippings showing him standing with large groups of people gathered to commemorate the trip.

Mac was offered a job but he turned it down and returned to Chennault's team.

Mac acquired experience that he would need in the future: his Transport Pilot Rating, Multi-Engine Rating, navigation over unfamiliar and rugged terrain and operating in foreign countries.

Curtiss Kingbird

'ALLU EL PRESIDENTE EN EL CONFLICTO DE

JUEVES 14 DE JUNIO DE 1934.

llegaron Ayer los Pilotos Colombiano

s acompañantes del aviador colombiano Samper

Muestra nuestra ilustración las personas que acompañan al señor Samper en su raid aéreo desde los Estados Unidos a Colombia. De pie en la línea posterior: los pilotos Wm. C. Mc Donald, Dan Hughes J., Floyd Addison, C. V. Patterson, E. F. Weast; y al frente: don Gamaliel Noriega, cónsul general de Colombia, Mrs Addison, J. Stanley B. Harvey, piloto.

En la tarde del domingo ingresaron al país tres aviones comerciales que hacen el raid Estados Unidos - Colombia para luego ser empleados en el servicio de pasajeros y expreso entre las ciudades de Medellín, Bogotá y Cúcuta, esta última en la frontera norte de Venezuela. Viene como je-

nesto Samper,, y en la madrugada de hoy los tres aviones salen del campo de Santa Ana para la próxima etapa de su largo vuelo desde la república del norte hacia Panamá. Saliendo de la capital de la república vecina los aviones aterrizarán por primera vez en territorio colombiano en

momentos después de la llegada de los bimotores de SACO. Los aviadores por aparecen

(M-779)   Crash 02 C1-4-15-35 12:55 P.M. Pilot Sgt McDonald

ABOVE Crash site, remaining bits of plane and curious locals

On April 15, 1935, Mac was flying a two-passenger Hell Diver Marine over Ashland, Kentucky when his motor began to miss badly, commonly caused by a bad batch of gas.

He bailed out at 500 feet, which is dangerously low, after setting the stick to try to avoid buildings. He was rattled when interviewed.

Mac was now a member of the famous "Caterpillar Club," which is composed of pilots who have been forced to abandon their aircraft in order to save their lives, using a parachute. Parachutes were made of silk, spun by silkworms (caterpillars).

It was his second forced landing but it would not be his last.

1935 - Hell Diver Bailout
From the Ashland Daily Independent - April 15, 1935
ARMY PLANE CRASHES ON BEECH ST; PILOT UNHURT
Sergeant McDonald Is Only 'Shaken Up'
As Plane Is Destroyed.

ASHLAND, KENTUCKY—A United States Army pursuit plane piloted by Sergeant William C. McDonald, Jr., 29, of Maxwell Field, Montgomery, Ala., crashed here at 1:55 o'clock this afternoon on Beech street and was destroyed by fire. McDonald bailed out in a parachute and escaped injury being only slightly shaken up when he landed at the intersection of Cumberland and Kentucky avenues in Grayson Roads.

Residents of Grayson Roads and Midland Heights heard the big ship droning overhead and heard the motor begin to sputter. Sensing that the pilot was in trouble, the residents watched the plane lose altitude and when it was only about 500 feet from the ground they saw the pilot bail out with his parachute. Bailing out at 500 feet is close by any measure.

The abandoned and pilotless plane glided, spun and finally crashed in the center of Beech Street just back of the Armco Addition, skidded

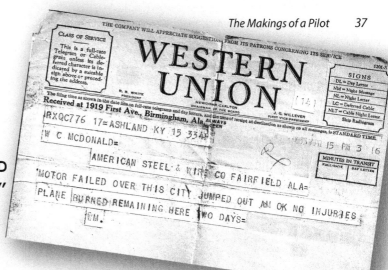

"MOTOR FAILED OVER THIS CITY JUMPED OUT AM OK NO INJURIES PLANE BURNED REMAINING HERE TWO DAYS"
WM.

across the street, turned turtle and burst in flames. Once the fire started, it burned furiously, setting fire to the pines and other small trees which dotted the south bank of Beech street. Firemen rushed to the scene and attempted to extinguish the blaze but in vain.

Sergeant McDonald came down pretty hard and he was unable to give a coherent account of events immediately preceding the crash. After alighting in the street he grasped a concrete mail post in order to keep from being blown about by the stiff wind blowing at the time.

Sergeant McDonald was picked up in an auto and taken to the spot where his ship crashed. There he was taken in tow by the police and driven around for a while in order to collect his wits.

He gave the following statement to an Independent reporter: "I don't really know exactly what happened," he began, "because I am pretty much upset, and unnerved. I dropped a passenger at the airport at Huntington, Va., and took on gas there. I was returning to my home airport, Maxwell Field, Montgomery, Ala., I arrived over this town."

Then he stopped to ask where he was. His memory failed him for a few minutes and then he continued: "I left Maxwell Field this morning at 7:30 o'clock and stopped at Knoxville, Tenn., on my way up. My passenger was Private B. F. Weatherford, of Huntington. I dropped him there and was returning to Maxwell field.

As I flew over this town my motor began to halt, then missed badly. I looked for a place to land all the while losing altitude fast. I didn't see any place to set her down and decided to bail out and now there's my ship in ashes." McDonald was deeply moved by the loss of his ship. "I have been flying five years," he said sorrowfully, and "this is the first time I have ever had to bail out."

McDonald's home is Birmingham. He was flying a Hell Diver Marine two passenger open ship number 8456-0261. Later, after he was taken to the Henry Clay Hotel, and after he had time to pull himself together McDonald said that after he found that a crash was inevitable and there was no place to bring his ship down in safety, he set his stick and turned her toward a clump of trees just at Beech street so she would miss the houses, then he jumped with his chute.

Another man might take a break after bailing out of a disabled plane.

Mac went right back to flying.

"A good landing is one you walk away from."

Mac

During the 1935 Cleveland Air Races, a spectator asked "The Men on the Flying Trapeze" for their autographs.

Roscoe Turner, a famous acrobatic pilot of the day, heard the request and exclaimed, "You folks had better get them in a hurry. The way these three fly, they won't be around long, and they won't die in bed either."

All American Air Races
Miami, January 1935

Although Chennault and his theories were unpopular with his peers at the time, his single-minded devotion to the value of pursuit planes and innovative combat maneuvers, and his creativity in intelligence gathering, would eventually be of great value in China and adopted by others.

Chennault's will to analyze and to teach meant that the maneuvers became a system which could be passed along to others. His skills in observation and documentation were also great strengths, along with his ability to persuade and his talent as a speaker.

The extent of Chennault's influence in Mac's life is hard to overstate, and from 1933 to the end of his life, Mac remained devoted to him.

YET ANOTHER CHANCE OF A LIFETIME
Destiny Knocks

In January 1935, the Army team won the Miami Air Race competition for demonstration teams. Afterwards, destiny knocked again in the person of William Pawley.

Bill Pawley was president of the Central Aviation Manufacturing Company (CAMCO), an American company which assembled and sold planes to the Chinese. He operated a factory in China and was well-connected with Chinese government officials. He invited the Trapezers onto his yacht to meet Chinese Air Force General Mow Pang-Tsu, who'd been impressed by the team's performance. The general invited the Trapezers to come to China and train Chinese pilots in advanced military flying using American techniques.

The three men declined the offer, planning to stay with the team and in the U.S. military, but by 1936, when Mow repeated his offer each of them had reason to reconsider.

Luke and Billy are as good friends as a man can hope to have, and I never seen finer pilots.

I threw official discretion to the winds and told the Advertiser for publication, "Williamson and McDonald are outstanding pilots in any airplane....If I were to go to war and I were ordered to the front, I would choose these two men to accompany me into combat, and that is the highest compliment a combat formation leader can pay."

This was no idle boast. Billy and I fought together in China for three long years against the heaviest odds….

Claire Lee Chennault, *Way of the Fighter*

No Future in the Army

Sargeants Williamson and McDonald were passed over for lieutenant, and in their late twenties, they could not expect another chance at promotion. Chennault took the decision as a personal slight.

Chennault was approaching twenty years of service, had severe hearing loss from years of open-cockpit flying and health issues from years of smoking.

However, the most important factor was the Army's changing priorities. Chennault spent his career advocating vigorously for the importance of pursuit planes and training, often putting him in conflict with his superiors. The Army's leadership followed the ideas of Italian General Giulio Douhet instead, believing that strategic bombing with the new generation of bombers would win wars. Pursuit flying lost favor and Chennault lost his teaching position at ACTS in 1936.

Despite continuing public acclaim, even requests for commercial endorsements, the Flying Trapezers were told their shows would be limited in the future.

Chennault advised Mac and Williamson to take General Mow's offer and indicated that he would likely join them.

Provoking the military establishment, Chennault boldly penned an open letter to the Montgomery Advertiser, alleging that his two wingmen had faced discrimination due to their association with him and his unpopular ideas. In the Montgomery Advertiser, Chennault was blunt:

"Williamson and McDonald are outstanding pilots in any type of airplane. If we were to go to war and I were ordered to the front, I would choose these two men to accompany me into combat, and that is the highest compliment a combat formation leader can pay."

None of them could know how those words would be tested and found true, but in a way they couldn't have foreseen. Chennault was sincere and prophetic in his praise—he would rely heavily on both men in the upcoming years of war.

Mac and Williamson bought out their remaining enlistment time and left for China on July 11, 1936.

Maj. Chennault, of Maxwell Field, leader of the "Men of the Flying Trapeze," in their daring maneuvers before the crowds at the Cleveland Air Races. Zooming down out of the sky at Maxwell Field, he perfected the maneuvers that brought national recognition to his ace team of fliers, the Major was met by Miss Mint, the Wrigley Representative, and for his opinion, he was paid a crisp new Wrigley dollar. "You will find that each"

Here I am. . .

in China

CANADIAN PACIFIC STEAMSHIP LINES — WORLD'S GREATEST TRAVEL SYSTEM

Sunday
JULY 19th 1936

R.M.S. _En Route_

Dear Folks:--

There are so many things to write about. I really don't know where to start.

We left Seattle on the Princess Kathleen - a small boat and went up to Victoria where we boarded the Empress of Russia. We left on time and have made close to 18 knots an hour, 440 miles a day. We have had fog for three days but it doesn't retard our

Page 1

our progress at all. Day before yesterday we saw land for the first time since departure. We passed within 25 miles of the Aleutian Islands - part of Alaska. The fog lifted just enough to get a fleeting glimpse of the snow capped mountains.

The sea has been exceptionally smooth. No one has been ill. Most of our mornings we spend playing numerous deck games - golf and tennis seem to be the most popular. The afternoons are spent without plot or plan. Mostly sleeping.

The food of course is excellent. We have appetites that would ruin us if we had to pay for it. I have gained seven pounds since I left B'ham - I am trying my best to keep from gaining - it doesn't do a lot of

Page 2

I think in the next month or two I will have some real news for you. If things work out as planned - we will be here at least 5 years.

I would love for everything to go along as we have planned - so money troubles will be over for awhile anyway.

This letter will be mailed from Yokohoma Japan. We are not even getting off the boat there. You know why.

Love to all,

Page 3

Dear Folks:--
There's so many things to write about. I really don't know where to start.

Mac's first letter home, dated "En Route"

I would love for everything to go along as we have planned—
if so money troubles will be over for a while anyway.

This letter will be mailed from Yokohoma, Japan. We are not even getting off the boat there. You know why.

Mac's first letter home, from page 3

BACK ROW, LEFT TO RIGHT Mary & Luke Williamson, Billie & Sterling Tatum, newlyweds Martha & John Holland. Front row: Sebie Smith, Billy McDonald, Rolfe Watson

INSET The *Empress of Russia*, July 11, 1936.

In his second letter to his parents, Mac stated, "We were all scared to death when we docked in Yokohama, Japan, on the way to China. We did not even think about getting off the boat."

According to Sebie Smith, a New York Times reporter offered to take them into Tokyo after questioning, Japanese officials provided the group with visas.

In Tokyo, they attended a big wedding at a hotel, where Mac was certain that they had all been photographed by the Japanese secret service, according to Smith.

CASTING OFF FOR CHINA
From Alabama, Take a Slow Boat to China

The U.S. government knew that Mac and friends were pilots traveling to China, but the Neutrality Act of 1936 legislated that Americans traveling on belligerents' ships traveled at their own risk. By taking the *Empress of Russia*, owned by the Canada Pacific Railroad, the group was still traveling under the protection of the U.S. government.

Mac sent his first letter and a photograph home to his parents, July 19, 1936, labeling it "en route." The photo shows an excited group of adventurers arm-in-arm.

Mac and Williamson were joined by others hand-picked by Chennault. He recommended men whose capabilities he knew and respected. Luke Williamson and Mac came from Maxwell Field, as did Sebie Smith, a mechanical genius, and Rolfe Watson, one of the best armorers in the U.S. military. Pilots Sterling Tatum and John Holland came from the Alabama National Guard.

METROPOLE HOTEL
SHANGHAI, CHINA.
Tuesday, 7/28/36

CABLE ADDRESS: "METHOTEL"
TELEPHONE: 12500

Dear Dad,
    Well here I am in china. It all seems like a dream. I don't think we had a single dull moment on our way over. The sea was calm and in every aspect the voyage was a success. We arrived at Kobe, Japan the morning after typhoon had struck there but it didn't touch us.

It is awfully hot here— sl... all the... very co... fans an...

> "Well here I am in China. It all seems like a dream. I don't think we had a single dull moment on our way over. The sea was calm and, in every aspect, the voyage was a success...It is awfully hot here, around one hundred degrees all the time, but we are very comfortable with fans and the like.
>
> Mac, second letter home, July 28, 1936. Metropole Hotel, Shanghai.

ABOVE Mac and Williamson, July 28, 1936, seventeen days after leaving the U.S.

1936 – THE ADVENTURE OF A LIFETIME
"Here I am in China"

Note to Reader: From here, most of the material has been taken from Mac's letters home. He wrote every week or every other week for most of his time in China.

At the time of their arrival, about forty Americans were involved with military aviation and commercial aviation activities in China.

Col. Roy Holbrook, an American and trusted advisor to the Chinese, met the group and guided them through two weeks of red-carpet treatment in Shanghai. Every aviation company in the world wanted to sell planes to China, and Mac's group attended dinners hosted by Holbrook, Pawley, officials of the China Central Trust Bank, and other representatives of American aviation interests. W. Langhorne Bond of the China National Aviation Corporation (CNAC) and Pawley were the most prominent in commercial aviation interests in China.

In addition to being wined and dined, the men were measured for uniforms, attended meetings, received inoculations and did a bit of sightseeing. After two weeks in Shanghai, the group took a comfortable trip to Kiukiang, the summer capital of China. Kiukiang was located at the base of Mt. Lushan, with the summer resort of Kuling perched on its peak. Mac thoroughly enjoyed the sightseeing tour of Kiukiang, as he had been anxious to see the interior of China.

Mac was enthusiastic about his new home, the people he met and the adventures ahead. He had no idea what was coming.

Shanghai, Kiukiang / Kuling, and Hangchow Training Base

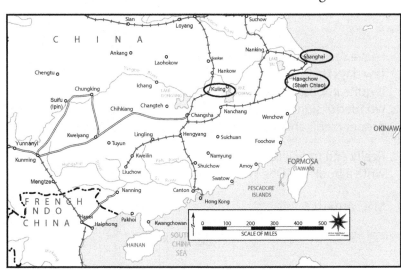

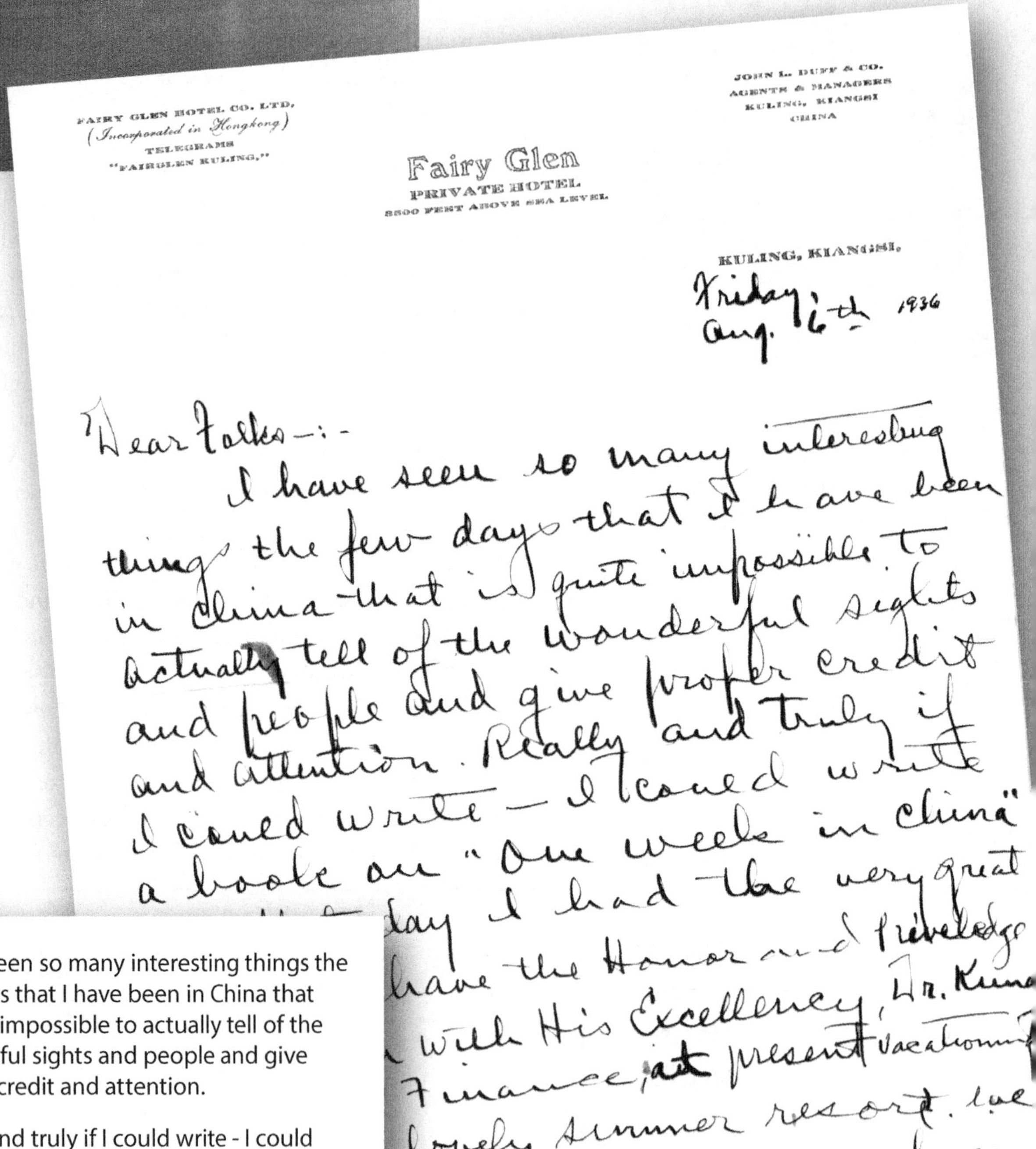

FAIRY GLEN HOTEL CO. LTD.
(*Incorporated in Hongkong*)
TELEGRAMS
"FAIRGLEN KULING."

JOHN L. DUFF & CO.
AGENTS & MANAGERS
KULING, KIANGSI
CHINA

Fairy Glen
PRIVATE HOTEL
3500 FEET ABOVE SEA LEVEL.

KULING, KIANGSI.

Friday
Aug. 6th 1936

Dear Folks —:—
I have seen so many interesting things the few days that I have been in China that is quite impossible to actually tell of the wonderful sights and people and give proper credit and attention. Really and truly if I could write — I could write a book on "One Week in China"

I have seen so many interesting things the few days that I have been in China that is quite impossible to actually tell of the wonderful sights and people and give proper credit and attention.

Really and truly if I could write - I could write a book on "One Week in China."

Mac, August 6, 1936

ABOVE, FRONT Mac in front kneeling, wearing a bow tie; STANDING, LEFT TO RIGHT Holland, Williamson, Tatum, Watson, unknown, unknown). Sightseeing in Kuling soon after arrival in China.

ABOVE LEFT The Williamsons & Sebie Smith with young scout (standing).

LEFT Mary & Luke Williamson (seated).

LOWER LEFT "Coming into Shanghai" and boat scene along the water.

A thousand or more interesting things seem to occur daily. I am not in a position to describe them, but will sure let you in on the sights when I see you.

I have met many lovely people, not only Chinese, but English and Russians. Shanghai is very cosmopolitan. Everyone seems to have gotten over their sea legs and are now accustomed to solid ground again. It took everyone about four days to adjust.

Unless a person is in a position to know, one would never suspect that anything ever happens in Shanghai or China. We are truly on the other side of the world. However, there is an abundance of activity. We are looking forward to our visit to Kuling; it will be history revealed.

Mac, August 2, 1936

FAIRY GLEN HOTEL CO. LTD.
(*Incorporated in Hongkong*)
TELEGRAMS
"FAIRGLEN KULING."

JOHN L. DUFF & CO.
AGENTS & MANAGERS
KULING, KIANGSI
CHINA

Fairy Glen
PRIVATE HOTEL
3500 FEET ABOVE SEA LEVEL.

KULING, KIANGSI,

character of the world. I will never forget it as long as I live.

The rest of the group will arrive here this afternoon and all of us will get the wonderful chance of meeting Her Excellency, Madame Chiang-Kai-Shek. I anticipate this interview with a great deal of enthusiasm.

As soon as I get back to Shanghai - I will get a typewriter and write a real letter.

A very interesting feature of our trip here was the different modes of transportation. By train, airplane, auto, Ricsha, and sedan chair. The latter four "coolies" carry you in a chair 3500 feet above sea level. It took 2:30 minutes for the "walk up".

A very interesting feature of our trip here was the different modes of transportation. By train, airplane, auto, richsha and sedan chair. The latter - four "coolies" carry you in a chair 3500 feet above sea level. It took 2 hours 30 minutes.

Mac, August 6, 1936

Madame Chiang

On August 6, 1936, Mac wrote home to his parents about his first of many meeting with two of China's most powerful leaders

> Yesterday, I had the very great fortune to have the Honor and Privilege of having tea with his Excellency, Dr. H.H. Kung, a financier and the Minister of Finance of China, at present vacationing here at this lovely summer resort. We talked of many things and my impression is that he is really one of the real characters of the world. I will never forget it as long as I live.
>
> The rest of the group will arrive here this afternoon and all of us will get the wonderful chance of meeting Her Excellency Madame Chiang Kai-Shek. I anticipate this interview with a great deal of enthusiasm…

Meeting with Dr. Kung and Madame Chiang Kai-Shek was indeed a great honor. Her husband, widely known by the Italian term *Generalissimo*, was leader of the *Kuomintang*, also known as the Nationalist party. Together they were the two highest-ranking officials in China. However, they held power in a country still run in part by warlords, in other places by the rising Communist party led by Mao Tse Tung, with still other provinces under the control of the Japanese.

Her wealthy and well-connected family held additional power. One of Madame Chiang's sisters had married Dr. Kung, Finance Minister, and the other was married to Sun Yat-sen, the revered founder of the *Kuomintang* and credited with beginning China's modernization. The three women were known in China as "The Three Sisters," and they held real political power which they would use consistently to support Chennault, Mac and the other American flyers in China. Their brother, T.V. Soong, was a businessman and held various positions of enormous influence.

The Chinese Commission on Aeronautical Affairs, headed by Madame Chiang, was the real power behind the aviation school. During the group's first meeting, Madame Chiang Kai-Shek assured the men that she and the rest of the Chinese government fully supported them, but

From Madame Chiang Kai-shek, the American advisors learned that they would have great power, but that they also had been given a nearly impossible job.

In just six months, they would need to create a cadre of Chinese pilots with the performance and skills levels necessary to fly the few combat-ready planes against the invading Japanese, believed to have 700 planes ready for the fight.

宋美

针就是兰

Madame Chiang was intelligent and had been educated in the United States. Her thorough knowledge of the political situation made her a potent political force and brilliant strategist. The entire group was won over by the persuasive and beautiful woman.

Other great men were also captivated by both her beauty and her intelligence, famously including Chennault and General Joseph Warren "Vinegar Joe" Stillwell, who agreed on little else.

that there was much to be done and very little time to prepare China's Air Force to fight the Japanese. After a tour of various countries' air forces and China's experience with training schools, she believed that the American model for training pilots was required to help China in its war with Japan.

Madame Chiang had reason to question the current system for educating flyers. Beginning in 1932, Mussolini sent forty military pilots and one hundred mechanics and support staff to provide training and sell planes to China's Air Force. However, students were generally from privileged families and all were passed, whether or not they knew how to fly.

The American schools, however, required that all students meet standards and "washed out" those who could not. Madame Chiang believed that the American model was necessary to train pilots who could defend China. She warmly welcomed the group and their skills to her country.

The Americans settled into the routine and began training pilots for the Chinese Air Force. American Jack May was already there. They would soon be joined by additional American instructors recommended by Chennault: Johnny Preston, Frank Higgs, C.B. "Skip" Adair, Jim Bledsoe, L.G. Hoston, Emil Scott, Harold Johnson, Billy Cherymisin, Harold Mull and Boatner Carney.

The Primary section, the first level, was taught by Robert S. "Bob" Angle. Higgs taught the Basic school, the second level. Mac was the senior American instructor, and Angle and Higgs reported to him. Most of Mac's student pilots in the Advanced flight section spoke at least some English so he found it relatively easy to conduct his lessons.

Hangchow flight line, trainers and cadets. Photography by Frank Higgs.

Central Aviation School
August 21, 1936 - Hangchow

Mac (right) with unknown Chinese officer.

After two weeks in Kiukiang and the momentous meetings there, the group returned to Shanghai to meet with William H. Donald, an Australian and Generalissimo's top foreign adviser. Donald too would prove to be a great supporter for the American advisors.

Donald came to China as a journalist and eventually became a trusted advisor to the Chiangs. He was dubbed by the Japanese as "the evil spirit of China."

By August 21, 1936, Mac and his group were in Hangchow. The Central Aviation School, expected to be their home base for some time, was about ten miles outside the city at Shien Chiao. Once at the school, the group immediately inspected the field and found that its equipment was "very much in advance of many fields at home." They joined American C.B. "Skip" Adair there, who had stayed from a previous group of advisors.

Chief officials and officers welcomed the group with a dinner party. Many of the Chinese spoke English. Mac claimed that despite that, "we are all going to try and speak Chinese."

The group seemed pleased with the setup and accommodations, and Smith and Mac became roommates, staying "in a building with 20 rooms and modernistic furniture."

BELOW Smith, Watson, Holland, Williamson, Donald, Tatum, Mac (far right), in Shanghai.

Mac bought a bicycle to explore the countryside and learn about its people. He lived two blocks from Hangchow Lake and could explore the numerous farms in the area as long as he did not walk on the crops. Mac learned a great deal about how people lived, and enjoyed most aspects of Chinese life, except for the noise he'd noted.

The boy was a long way from Fairfield, Alabama, but he seemed to be making himself at home.

The lake here at Hangchow is very large and affords a great deal of pleasure in that we are able to take boat rides. A 'coolie' will row you all over the lake for 30 cents 'MEX,' which means Chinese money. Don't know where they got the term 'MEX.' The last two nights have been exceptionally nice because of the full moon.

Mac, September 1, 1936

The lake here is very pretty and it is a lot of fun having a coolie row you around at night. It is so peaceful. Yet on the other hand, I think that China is probably the noisiest place outside of a structural mill in all the world. From early morning until late at night, one can hear bands, bugles, gongs, and soldiers singing all through the valley. Bands play at funerals and usually they are early in the morning. The gongs are banged upon at the different temples and when a gong is struck it means another evil spirit or devil is dead.

Mac, September 12, 1936

BELOW AND RIGHT As an Eagle Scout, Mac always noticed young scouts.

We plan to leave to-morrow for Hangchow. All of us will be stationed there for some time to come.

Mac, August 18, 1936

METROPOLE HOTEL
SHANGHAI, CHINA.
Aug. 18 1936

Dear Dad,
Back in Shanghai after a visit up the Yangse River to Kuling. Have been back about 4 days — we plan to leave to-morrow for Hangchow. All of us will be stationed there for sometime to come. The Central School of Aviation is located about 10 miles from Hangchow and we are all very happy at being

Mac's daily routine began at 6:15 AM to allow time for breakfast and the ten-mile car ride to the airfield. The American instructors gave four hours of classes and lectures in the morning. Lunch started with a ten-mile ride back to the hotel. After lunch, the men went back to continue instruction and observation of the students in the air from 3:00 PM until 6:30 PM Going home they rode the last ten miles, a total of forty miles commuting daily.

In early September, Smith was placed in command of the mechanical department, with the "unenviable task" of explaining, through interpreters, the principles of flight theory to the eager Chinese mechanics. Now and during his entire tenure, Smith would find that the lack of interpreters was a major issue in his work and teaching.

Watson, who was chief armorer, submitted a report on the school's armament section to the base commander, General Chih-Ju Chow. Watson reported finding everything in overall good condition, but also mentioned the need for more interpreters. He too would find that not having enough interpreters was a serious issue throughout his time in China.

Watson's biggest concern was the need for new coats of paint for bombs, in order to prevent rust. Much of the ammunition, bullets on belts fed through machine guns of that era, was close to corrosion, which would make it unusable.

In September, Mac and Smith got an apartment and a servant. This "man" cost just $7 a month and was on duty 24 hours a day.

A year ago last Monday Luke [Williamson] and I were at the National Air Races in Cleveland. This year they were held in Los Angeles. Sure wish we could have been there...Saw where old Roscoe Turner cracked up somewhere in New Mexico on his way out. And that the women flyers took all the honors. I guess next year the men will snap out of their sleep and start doing something. For the past two years, the races have been a failure in its real mission. That is the development of faster airplanes...

Mac, September 12, 1936

Graduation – October 12, 1936

In mid-October graduation ceremonies for the current class included a visit from the Generalissimo and Madame Chiang. The guards were doubled at the airfield for graduation, making it difficult to move around. Madame Chiang saw three of the advisers' wives, including Aimee May, and invited them to sit with her and Dr. Kung. Both the Generalissimo and Madame Chiang lived under tremendous strain at this time. Smith thought that the stress was beginning to show on the Generalissimo.

After graduation, the American advisers were invited to a large banquet in the evening. Mac's feelings sometimes wavered on the food in China. He enjoyed some dishes and found others questionable. But he seems to have tried them all. At this particular banquet, he thoroughly enjoyed the food served at the dinner, with the "bird's nest soup" being especially delicious. He even enjoyed the fat of bears' feet, which was a rare delicacy. The company held serious discussions at the dinner, and the tension was clearly rising.

At the same time, Mac was assigned to fly in the Generalissimo's squadron.

Today is the 4th birthday of the field. The occasion was properly celebrated. A parade at 6:30 AM very early this morning and speeches by high officials. Then, a morning box breakfast in the large area in front of the Main Buildings. After this a swimming meet was held in a very modern pool. The meet was excellently conducted.

Mac, September 1, 1936, on his new Swiss typewriter

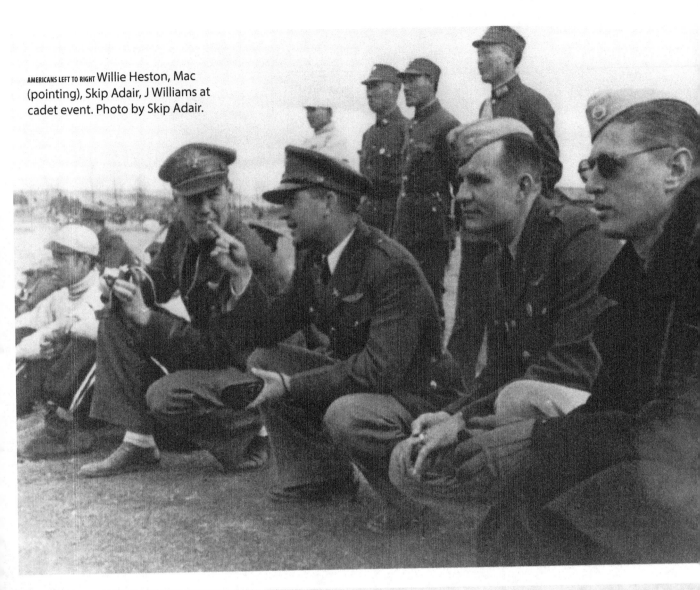

AMERICANS LEFT TO RIGHT Willie Heston, Mac (pointing), Skip Adair, J Williams at cadet event. Photo by Skip Adair.

Hangchow cadets in winter gear.

The boys displayed splendid technique in places and one thing that was noticeable was that they never quit. They finish or collapse. A remarkable trait so necessary in aviation. Mac, letter home, September 1, 1936

Despite his busy flying schedule, Mac enjoyed the people and experiences he encountered in his journeys.

Variety is the spice of life—so this time when I came to Nanking I decided to try this Chinese hotel [Foo Chong Hotel] and much to my surprise I found that there were quite a few foreigners, Italians, Germans, and Americans, that had already found the place. It is new in construction and very modern in every way. Even the food is a little above average.

Orders are changed so fast around these parts that it is almost impossible to know what one is supposed to do. I received orders from one source to report back to Hangchow for duty and just before I took off I was informed to stand by here. So again I say - I don't know how long I will be here and I don't know where I am going when I leave.

My mechanic and I were darned glad to get back to civilization once again. In the interior, Loyang and Sian, we had to eat Chinese food—take a bath once a week in a tin tub and until yet we have not been able to get our laundry done— now that we are here—Baths, food, picture show, radio, newspapers—latest editions and bright lights. All in all, we have been taking advantage of them. Because who can tell we may go right back from where we came.

I called Luke and Tatum and Cecil Folmar at Hangchow last night and talked to them. Sure was nice talking to some of the gang. They all seem to be getting along okay. I will try and get down there because I have a lot of mail...Even if I am ordered to stay with the Generalissimo's Squadron for a while longer, I will get a chance to go after my mail.

Mac, November 7, 1936, Nanking

LT. COL. REINBURG SELECTED
School Leadership

PREVIOUS TWO-PAGE SPREAD Sterling Tatum, an instructor with Mac at the Advanced School, is shown in the middle, bottom row. Mac most likely took this picture.

BELOW Training exercises in Hangchow.

OPPOSITE PAGE The Ford Tri-Motor (NC432H) shown at left was sold to China on March 14, 1932. The Young Marshall, Chang Hsiao-liang, bought a Ford Tri-Motor (NC406H) in September of 1931 and another in 1932. The China Aviation School bought NC8485 and NC8486 in April of 1936. Photos from online collection of San Diego Air & Space Museum.

Three days after the graduation banquet, all the high-ranking Chinese and foreign officers along with Madame Chiang and the Generalissimo attended a large meeting to plan for the future.

The group viewed the lack of leadership for the American advisers as a major problem, and Roy Holbrook offered a solution. Chennault had not yet retired from the U.S. Air Corps but Holbrook, along with Mac and Williamson, had continued to keep him updated on the situation in China, specifically the developments in war with Japan.

Orchestrated by Holbrook, retired Lt. Colonel George E.A. Reinburg, who had been the Berlin Embassy military attache, was placed in command for six months. Chennault would then arrive and take control. Mac was not certain if Reinburg knew the complete plan but the colonel was a friend of Chennault's and Mac believed that Reinburg was satisfied.

PS-Cecil Folmar is here at Hangchow on the same job as we are.
He is doing well and everyone is just one big happy family.

中 央 航 空 學 校

CENTRAL AVIATION SCHOOL

SHIEN CHIAO, HANGCHOW, CHINA.

Sat. November 14,1936.

CABLE ADDRESS:
"CENTRAVIA".

CODE USED:
BENTLEY'S SECOND

TELEPHONE: 3073
3074
3075

REF. NO.

Dear Dad,

Over here one looses track of the days and dates but I know
that to-day is the 14th because yesterday was FRIDAY the 13th but
no bad luck. In fact a little good luck.

Wednesday we returned again from Loyang to Nanking. To start
this better from the last letter -- Last Sunday the old Ford and
crew were sent back to Loyang with some very important Gov. Officials
that were to confer with the Generalissimo. One was the Foreign Minister of Affairs. We messed around up there until Wednesday and then
back to Nanking. Friday we were sent down here to have winter heating units installed on the Ford. It will take s[...]
get the installation and in the meantime I am v[...]
seeing and gathering all the local conversation[...]
to get back to friends again.

Luke and Tatum and their wives have gone [...]
week end - due to a birthday of Dr. Sun Yat Se[...]
Chinese Republic, they were able to go Thursday[...]
They will be back to-morrow night. Tatum is ha[...]
with his stomach and is going to get a thoroug[...]
Shanghai. Everyone else doing fine. The weathe[...]
right-anice fall season.

I still am assigned to the Generalissimo[...]
to be relieved within the next week or as soon[...]
to Nanking, then again I may be on the job all[...]
It is much nicer and pleasanter being here wi[...]
Also the type of work is more interesting and [...]

Have had a lot of fun complaining to th[...]
food that I have had to eat while I was away.[...]
cooks know more ways to ruin chicken than any[...]
chow in the interior is not as good as it is [...]
especially for the consumption of the foreign[...]
ed that in my letter last week.

Enjoyed all letters recieved last week[...]
and ran down here from Nanking before I wen[...]
after I wrote last Saturday. Letters are com[...]
makes life a lot more bearable with call thi[...]
folks.
Love to all and will write every Sat. [...]

PS. Cecil Folmar is here at Hangchow on the same job as we are. He is doing well and everyone is just one big happy family.

Last Sunday the old Ford and crew were sent back to Loyang with some very important Gov. officials that were to confer with the Generalissimo. One was the Foreign Minister of Affairs. We messed around up there until Wednesday and then back to Nanking. Friday were sent down here to have winter heating units installed on the Ford.

…

I am visiting around and seeing and gathering all the local conversation. So it is darn nice to get back to friends again.

I am still assigned to the Generalissimo's Squadron but expect to be relieved within the next week…I may be on the job all winter but I hope not. It is much nicer and pleasanter being here with the rest of the gang. Also the type of work is more interesting and far more comfortable.

Mac, November 14, 1936

1936 – Flying the Chief

In parallel, Mac came face-to-face with the greater political situation in China. On October 6, 1936, the Generalissimo traveled north to confer with his military commanders. Most of the American pilots were unaware of these plans, but since early October, Mac had been assigned to the Generalissimo's squadron. He was the only one with experience flying a Ford Tri-Motor. Although he did not name his passenger, Mac told his dad about flying to Loyang and then back to Nanking some time later. On October 29, 1936, Mac was very careful in describing his activities to his parents, stating he had flown government officials to an important meeting in Sian, Shensi, China.

On Wednesday, November 11, 1936, Mac returned again from Loyang to Nanking. On the previous Sunday, the "old Ford and crew" had been sent back to Loyang with several very important government officials, including the Minister of Foreign Affairs, to confer with the Generalissimo.

On Friday, November 13, 1936, they traveled to Hangchow in order to install winter heating units on the Ford. During the several days of installation, Mac spent his free time visiting and taking in the local conversation. According to Mac, "it was darn nice to get back around friends again." He was still assigned to the Generalissimo's Squadron, but expected to be relieved soon, possibly when he returned the Ford to Nanking.

BELOW Ford Tri-Motor flying over China. Photo from online collection of San Diego Air & Space Museum.

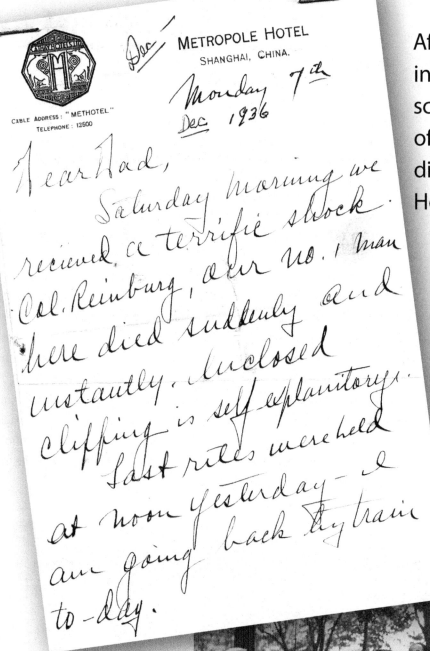

After just two months
in charge of the
school, in December
of 1936, Col. Reinburg
died suddenly.
Holbrook took over.

BELOW Believed to have been taken
at Col. Reinburg's funeral

Saturday morning we received a
terrific shock. Col. Reinburg, our
No. 1 man here died suddenly and
instantly.

Last rites were held at noon
yesterday. I am going back by
train today.

Mac, December 7, 1936

Waiting for Chennault

Unfortunately, after just two months at the school, Col. Reinburg had a heart attack and died quite suddenly. This loss again left the school without a leader.

Outside the church at Reinburg's funeral service in Shanghai, Madame Chiang approached Williamson and Mac and expressed her sympathy. She then asked the men about replacing Reinburg.

Williamson and Mac reiterated their recommendation for Chennault. Madame Chiang already knew about Chennault and Mac believed she simply wanted reassurance. The original 1935 delegation, headed by General Mow, had tried to hire all three members of the Flying Trapeze at that time. Madame Chiang was well-aware of Chennault's value and indicated that she would cable Chennault right away and told the men that they should do the same. In addition, she would also cable the Chinese Ambassador in Washington D.C. with instructions to do whatever was necessary to get Chennault to China.

Chennault had been engaged in an active dispute with high-ranking U.S. Army officials over the value of pursuit planes and pilots for much of his career.

Chennault believed that pursuit planes were critical to protect bombers during missions, and also to destroy enemy bombers before they arrived at their targets. Despite an ongoing, vocal and vigorous effort, with apparently little concern for his personal standing, he was losing the argument. Along with health issues including blood pressure, hearing loss and bronchitis, Chennault found himself without prospects in the U.S. military. He would retire as a Captain. He agreed to a three-month contract to evaluate the Chinese Air Force while still in the U.S. Chennault took retirement at twenty years and made plans to go to China.

He was forty-four, he had eight children to feed and China was willing to listen to his ideas.

In Roy Farrell's manuscript, he states that the job was originally offered to Mac. None of Mac's papers hint at this. At the time, he had very little management experience, and it seems unlikely that the Chinese would have offered this job to a low-ranking American. However, Mac had been the senior American instructor since his arrival, so it is possible. In any case, Mac made it clear in his letters home that he felt Chennault was the right man for the job.

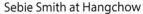

Sebie Smith at Hangchow

IN DECEMBER OF 1936 BEFORE CHENNAULTS ARRIVAL I HAD A N EXPERIENCE THAT BRINGS JIMMIE MESISSENER BACK INTO THE PICTURE.

BEFORE CHRISTMAS THE GENERALISSIMO FLEW TO SINFU IN NORTHWEST CHINA TO VISIT THE LOCAL GOVENOR AND OFFICIALS AND WHILE HE WAS THERE THE NOW INFAMOUS COUPE DE TAT TOOK PLACE AND THE GENERALISSIMO WAS CAPTURED BY THE YOUNG MARSHALL CHIANG SUEH LIANG. THIS CAUSED GREAT EXCITEMENT AND I WAS ASKED XX BY MADAME CHIANG TO LEAVE MY DUTIES OF TRAINING PILOTS AT THE SCHOOL IN HANGCHOW AND FLY A TRI MOTORED FORD TO SIAN WITH THE OVERALL EFFORT OF TRYING TO RECAPTURE THE GENERALISSIMO. THE FORD BELONGED TO THE GENERALISSIMOS TRANSPORT SQDN. THERE WERE ITALIAN PLANES WITH ITALIAN CREWS, GERMAN JUNKER TRANPORT WITH GERMAN CREWS, CHINESE AND AMERICAN FLYING THE AMERICAN FORDS.

THE REGULAR FORD PILOT WAS ON VACATION AND THAT IS THE REASON I WAS ASKED TO FILL IN. XXXXXXXX I JOINED THE SQDN AT NANKING AND WE ALL FLEW TO A CITY 60 MILES FROM SIANFU CALLED LOYANG. AT THIS FIELD THE ITALIANS HAD SET A TRAINING SCHOOL AND THE ACCOMODATIONS WERE UNUSUALLY GOOD FOR THIS PART OF INTERIOR CHINA. WHILE WE WERE WAITING FOR ORDERS THE CREWS LOAFED AROUND THE SLEEPING QUARTERS AND I SOON FOUND OUT THAT THERE WAS A LIBRARY AT THE SCHOOL SO I WENT TO THE LIBRARY AND THE ONLY ENGLISH BOOK THAT I COULD FIND WAS AN OLD AMAGAZINE CALLED AIR ACES. I TOOK THIS BACK TO MY ROOM AND WAS READING IT WHEN ALL OF A SUDDEN I REALIZED THAT I WAS READING A STORY ABOUT JIMMIE MEISSENER THE VERY MAN THAT HAD GOTTEN ME INTERESTED IN FLYING. THIS STORY WAS ABOUT THE FIRST WORLD WAR AND ABOUT A DOGFIGHT THAT TOOK PLACE BETWEEN THE 94TH HAT IN THE RING SQDN AND THE FAMOUS BARON VON RICHTOFEN AND HIS TERRIFIC RED SQDN. AS I READ MORE NATURALLY INTERESTED AS I HAD HEARD FROM JIMMIES OWN LIPS THE STORY OF THE FIGHT AND HOW HE HAD BEEN SHOT DOWN AND NARROWLY ESCAPED DEATH, MY SCALP SUDDENLY GOT TIGHT AS I READ THAT THE PILOT THAT SHOT JIMMIE DOWN WAS NAMED LT. ERIC JUST AND IN THE NEXT ROOM WAS A GERMAN PILOT BY THAT SAME NAME. I HAD KNOWN HIM ONLY A SHORT TIME BUT HE SEEMED FRIENDLY ENOUGH AND I TOOK THE MAGAZINE TO HIM AND TOLD HIM MY STORY AND SURE ENOUGH IT WAS THE SAME MAN. I THOUGHT THIS COINCIDENCE WAS THE MOST AMAZING THING THAT HAD EVER HAPPENED TO ME. SO HERE JIMMIE MEISSENER APPEARS AGAIN IN MY RAMBLINGS IN FLYING.

A FEW DAYS LATER THE GENERALISSIMO WAS RELEASED AND WITH EVERYONE HAPPY AGAIN WE FLEW BACK TO NANKING AND XXXXXXX WENT BACK TO HANGCHOW TO TAKE UP MY DUTIES AT THE SCHOOL.

One of Mac's speech cards, probably written in the 1970s.

Eric Just & Jimmy Meissner & Mac

Imagine you are waiting with a group of pilots somewhere deep in China to fly out the leader of a country after his kidnapping. Already, that would be extraordinary.

What are the odds that you'd pick up a book that tells a story about the pilot staying in the room next to yours, also a pilot in the Generalissimo's squadron? What are the odds that pilot, Eric Just, would be a famous German ace, the same one who, somewhere in Europe during World War I, shot down your hometown's only WWI flying ace?

Then what if that Birmingham ace was your next-door neighbor, Jimmy Meissner, who survived and also happened to be your first inspiration for becoming a pilot?

In notes for a speech that Mac is likely to have given in the 1960s or 1970s, he tells a story revealing much about the small world of aviation in the 1930s.

Some of the best flyers in the world came to China for the adventure, the money and the chance to fly. The coincidences and connections could be both unsettling and inspiring.

MAC AT A CRITICAL MOMENT IN HISTORY
An Historic Moment

On December 12, 1936, the tensions in the north came to a climax when Chang Hsueh-liang, known as the Young Marshal, Commander of the North Western Bandit Suppression Forces, kidnapped the Generalissimo. Marshal Chang and others believed the Nationalist and Communist factions within China needed to form a united front to successfully defend China against the Japanese aggression. The Generalissimo was not easily persuaded.

The kidnapping, negotiations and release of the Generalissimo were cloaked in secrecy. But Mac learned that Mr. Donald, who had tutored the Young Marshal as a boy, had flown to Sian. Eventually, the Generalissimo agreed that the Nationalist and the Communist forces would create a united front to fight the Japanese and his release was arranged.

In the middle of this tense situation, in a letter to his parents on Dec. 19, 1936, Mac worried that they were reading upsetting information in the papers concerning the situation in China.

Mac commented on a speech by Dr. Kung, Minister of Finance. Dr. Kung's speech was broadcast from Nanking, where it was relayed to Shanghai then on to San Francisco, with NBC eventually broadcasting it to the American public. He wondered if his parents had heard the speech, remarking on the excitement it had generated in China.

On December 19, Madame Chiang asked Mac and Sebie to travel to Sian with the Generalissimo's Transport Squadron. Mac flew one of two Tri-Motor Fords, while the second had a Chinese crew. A German crew flew a Junker Ju-52 and an Italian crew flew a Savoi-Machetti. On December 24, 1936, Mac wrote, "The Generalissimo has been released."

All four planes departed early the next morning, December 25, and landed at Loyang, 210 miles east of Sian.

In one version of events, after his release the Generalissimo and Chang flew back in the Boeing aircraft belonging to the Young Marshall, flown by Roy Leonard. In another, they flew back in the Generalissimo's Ford Tri-Motor, possibly the one Mac was flying, but he would never confirm or deny the story. We do know that the men flew back to Nanking on December 25, 1936.

Chiang's kidnapping, which resulted in an agreement to create a unified defense against the Japanese, is viewed by some as the single most significant event of the twentieth century. By altering China's future so completely, this event altered the world.

中央航空學校
CENTRAL AVIATION SCHOOL
SHIEN CHIAO, HANGCHOW, CHINA.

CABLE ADDRESS:
"CENTRAVIA"

April 30, 1937.   REF. NO.

CODE USED:
BENTLEY'S SECOND

Dear Dad,

To-morrow is the big day - Class 6b graduates to the tune of some 120 or more I am not sure of the exact count but I for one all ecited - that is the Cadets themselves and I for one glad when this is all over. I am keeping my fingers cro the field is very wet and muddy and it looks and feels might rain again to-night. There will be much sadness The field is all decorated up and everything is spick will be a pretty nice show if every little thing is ca perfection but who knows anything can happen.

Planes from other stations have been arriving the Generalissimo and the Madam will be here. Then of high officials from Nanking. All in all quite a crowd

Details of the exercises of course cannot be I can't write much about it. Several rehearsals have I am very well pleased with my bunch. Hope they perf morrow.

I don't know what will happen after this gr think that there are going to be a few changes. That out of the units. There are too many activities goi field. So I imagine some of us will have to go with won't be so bad if several of us are at one place b alone it makes things almost unbearable. But that's for so I guess one shouldn't complain.

I haven't heard from you in about two wee the sergice is all balled up again. When I do hear probably be two or three letters at once.

Hope Lucie is much better now and back o said you were taking her to the hospital for exam

No news from the Judge - I hope that no in this case.

Love toall - Tell Mother I will try and the Madam about her trip to the States.

Wm

MAY 1, 1937
GRADUATION FOR THE FIRST CLASS TRAINED ENTIRELY BY MAC & FRIENDS

To-morrow is the big day - Class 6b graduates to the tune of some 120 or more. I am not sure of the exact count, but they are all excited...and I for one will be glad when this is all over. I am keeping my fingers crossed because the field is very wet and muddy and it looks and feels as if it might rain again to-night. There will be much sadness if it does. The field is all decorated up and everything is spic and span. It will be a pretty nice show if every little thing is carried out to perfection, but who knows anything can happen.

Planes from other stations have been arriving all day. Also the Generalissimo and Madame will be here. Then of course all the high officials from Nanking. All in all quite a crowd.

Details of the exercises of course cannot be revealed. So, I can't write much about it. Several rehearsals have been held and I am very well pleased with my bunch. Hope they perform well tomorrow.

I don't know what will happen after this graduation but I think that there are going to be a few changes. That is spreading out of the units. There are too many activities going on at this field. So I imagine some of us will have to go with the units. It won't be so bad if several of us are in one place but if you are all alone it makes things almost unbearable. But that's what we are paid for so I guess one shouldn't complain.

Mac, April 30, 1937

Graduation is over. Our first class finished, but they were a sad outfit because it rained out the flying program. Many of the High Officials from Nanking were down for the exercises. To make the matter a complete success Generalissimo and Madame Chiang came down and will stay in Hangchow for a few more days.

Madame Chiang is as lovely as ever. Generalissimo hasn't fully recovered from his late mishaps. Last week, he had several teeth extracted in Shanghai and looks a little tired. It has been four months, and he has not recovered. Teeth being extracted would imply he was beaten up or worse when he was captured in December.

Mac, May 4, 1937

"AN UNHEALTHY INTEREST IN HARBORS AND AIRFIELDS"
Mac and Chennault in Japan

Just after graduation, Mac prepared for another mission unlike anything he'd done before. Mac was going to Japan, the sworn enemy of the country he lived in and worked for, to pick up Claire Chennault.

The Japanese knew that Americans were teaching Chinese pilots. Mac and Chennault weren't low-profile, given that they were members of the famous Flying Trapeze.

Would the Japanese recognize them? Would their American citizenship protect them?

Chennault retired from the military on April 10, 1937. He had a deal with the Chinese to make a three-month inspection trip across the vast country to evaluate the Chinese Air Force. He was on his way almost immediately.

On May 8, 1937, when Chennault left the United States for China on the USS *President Garfield,* he promptly started a diary titled "the Great Adventure." He expected to meet Mac in Japan. Chennault said nothing in his memoirs about planning for the trip, but he must have done a good deal of it [per CIA report in *Studies in Intelligence,* Vol. 54. No.2 (June 2010)].

Meanwhile, Madame Chiang ordered Mac to pick Chennault up in Japan. Mac needed a plausible cover story, a new identity, new passport and transportation.

Mac's answer came while having a drink in a bar in Shanghai, where Mac struck up a conversation with Dave Harvey, who happened to share the same college fraternity as Mac. Mac informed him about his problem.

Dave Harvey immediately devised a solution. He was taking forty-two entertainers to Japan in two weeks and Mac could go as the co-manager of the group. It was a large show, which included a singing act made up of three women from Manila who called themselves "The Dixie Girls," a group of Russian acrobats, and various other acts. They were scheduled to perform in a number of large Japanese cities.

They arrived a week before the *Garfield.* Although slightly apprehensive, Mac followed Harvey's instructions when they arrived in Japan. Harvey placed Mac at the front of the line. He walked forward and handed the Japanese officials a large stack of passports with his on the top. Mac never explained how he got a new passport with a different name and occupation in such a short period of time.

The entry into Japan went off without a hitch. The Japanese secret service never even looked at Mac.

The troupe's first stop was Osaka at the New Osaka Gekicho theatre. Mac stood backstage during rehearsal and nodded, pretending to be the manager. They were very pleased and slightly surprised that the plan had worked so well. If Harvey was not an intelligence agent, he certainly could have been one.

Visiting Japan with Chennault

Mac's speech card, undated

MADAME ORDERED ME TO GO TO JAPAN AND JOIN CHENNAULT WHEN HIS BOAT ARRIVED AND BRIEF HIM ON THE SITUATION. SINCE NEWS OF OUR WORK HAD SPREAD TO JAPAN WE WEREN'T EXACTLY WELCOME AND I HAD TO MAKE THE TRIP IN AN UNUSUAL FASHION. I HAD THE GOOD LUCK TO RUN INTO A FRATERNITY BROTHER WHO WAS TOURING THE EAST WITH A THEATRICAL TROUPE. HE IMMEDIATELY SIGNED ME AS MANAGER AND I ENTERED JAPAN WITH A DANCE TEAM OF INDIANS FROM CALCUTTA, RUSSIAN SINGERS, CHINESE JUGGLERS AND THREE RATHER DARK GIRLS FROM THE PHILLIPPINES BILLED AS THE DIXIE SISTERS. WHEN MY PASSPORT WAS PRESENTED WITH THEIRS IT WASN'T EVEN NOTICED.

I WAS AWFULLY GLAD TO GET BACK TO CHINA HOWEVER FOR THE CONFLICT WAS SHAPING UP AND IT WAS JUST A COUPLE OF MONTHS LATER WHILE WE WERE ON AN INSPECTION TRIP THAT WORD CAME OF THE BOMBING OF THE MARCO POLO BRIDGE ON JULY 7TH, 1937 WHICH BEGAN CHINA'S LONG STRUGGLE WITH JAPAN. WE WIRED THE GENERALISSIMO AND VOLUNTEERED TO SERVE WHEREVER HE WANTED US. WE WERE ASSIGNED TO NANCHANG WHERE WE RAN AN ADVANCED COMBAT

OPPOSITE PAGE. Like other times during their long association, this episode was inaccurately reported and Chennault and Mac were confused in the press. In a U.S. comic strip in 1943 entitled "Tiger in Tokyo," Chennault was depicted dressed as a dapper vaudeville tour manager.

The caption read, "Nips were caught napping a few years ago when they gave entry to an American Vaudeville Troupe and its Manager to tour Japan. The Innocent-seeming 'Manager' was one of the world's crack fliers then employed by China--who used this ruse to enter the enemy country and study its air force. His name? Brigadier General Claire Chennault of the Flying Tigers."

In addition to mixing up Mac and Chennault, the two did not go to Tokyo.

Mac mailed a letter to his sister Lucie from Japan that never arrived in the U.S. Later, he realized that mailing the letter was probably a careless thing to do.

Mac told the story of this trip in speeches after the war. He remembers going to Yokohama instead of Kobe. This is the story as he told it.

The day before the *USS President Garfield*'s arrival, Mac quietly slipped away and took a train to Yokohama, the first stop in Japan listed on the Dollar lines website for the *Garfield*.

He was cautious when he boarded the boat just after dark to meet Chennault in his stateroom. They were happy to see one other. They spent almost two full days driving by car to Kobe, the *Garfield's* last stop in Japan. During those two days they toured Kyoto, Osaka, and Kobe. They went through industrial districts, near construction sites, and to "areas where industry seemed to be expanding with the suspicious speed of a military enterprise." Mac took photos and Chennault made careful notes about everything they saw from a combat pilot's view point.

They then boarded the *Garfield*. Once the ship was underway "they tried to identify shipping routes and islands where new war industries were being established" as they traveled the inland sea. Mac updated Chennault on the current state of affairs in China so that he was prepared for his meeting with Madame Chiang.

A Window on the Development of Modern Intelligence

Claire Lee Chennault and the Problem of Intelligence in China

Bob Bergin

> " As an officer in the Army
> Air Corps, Claire
> Chennault came to
> realize the importance of
> intelligence in the early
> 1930s. "

Claire Chennault went to China in 1937 as a military adviser to Chiang Kai-shek as Japan's war on China expanded. During late 1940–41 he would organize and command the American Volunteer Group (AVG), popularly known as the "Flying Tigers," an air unit supported covertly by the United States before Japan's attack on Pearl Harbor. Chennault understood the value of intelligence and wrestling with the problems of acquiring it during most of his career. Most of what has been written about Chennault has focused on his leadership of the Flying Tigers, his relationship with the Republic of China, and his service during World War II. This article draws from his memoirs and other material to specifically address Chennault's approach to intelligence.

As an officer in the Army Air Corps, Claire Lee Chennault came to realize the importance of intelligence in the early 1930s, when he was the senior instructor in fighter tactics at the Air Corps Tactical School at Maxwell Field in Alabama. He had been trying to modernize fighter techniques and concluded that the "biggest problem of modern fighters was

intelligence. Without a continuous stream of accurate information keeping the fighters posted on exactly where the high-speed bombers were, attempts at interception were like hunting needles in a limitless haystack."[1]

Fighter planes had dominated the skies and military thinking during World War I, but that changed quickly when the war ended. In 1921, Billy Mitchell showed that airplanes could sink captured German battleships and "popularity shifted from the fighter boys… to the lumbering bombers, even then growing bigger and faster." Bomber advocates believed that the more powerful bombers would always get through and that the fighter planes sent against them would be ineffective. Advances in technology gave weight to their arguments. When the B-10 bomber appeared, it was heavily armed and capable of flying at 235 mph, faster than the P-26 "Peashooter," the standard fighter of the US Army Air Corps. Major air maneuvers during the early 1930s seemed to prove that "due to increased speeds and limitless space it is

All statements of fact, opinion, or analysis expressed in this article are those of the authors. Nothing in the article should be construed as asserting or implying US government endorsement of an article's factual statements and interpretations.

1

This report discusses Chennault's use of intelligence gathering by various methods and the use he made of the information. The report discusses the spying Chennault and Mac did while in Japan. [CIA report in *Studies in intelligence*, Vol. 54. No.2 (June 2010)]

SHE WILL ALWAYS BE THE PRINCESS TO ME
Chennault Meets His New Boss

On May 31, 1937, Williamson, Donald and Holbrook met Mac and Chennault at the dock in Shanghai. The the Flying Trapezers were reunited halfway around the world.

They had a "Walla Walla" that night, meaning they got a bit drunk. Chennault refrained, knowing he was to meet Soong Mei-ling, Madame Chiang Kai-shek, the next morning. Both Williamson and Mac had horrible hangovers the next day, while Chennault was sober. Mac accompanied Chennault, who first visited the American Embassy in full dress uniform to pay his respects.

Holbrook arranged Chennault's first meeting with Madame Chiang. An early adviser on aeronautical matters, Holbrook had become a trusted aide. When she entered the room, Holbrook stood up but Chennault remained seated, believing she was simply an attractive young member of the staff. Chennault was shocked when Holbrook introduced her as Her Excellency Madame Chiang Kai-shek.

They had a long, detailed meeting. Madame Chiang expressed concern about Chennault's rank as captain considering he would be dealing with admirals and generals. Chennault suggested he ask his cousin Jimmy Noe, a former governor of Louisiana, to appoint him as an honorary colonel in the state militia. Chiang responded by saying to Chennault, "Well, Colonel, that will do nicely." There is no evidence that Chennault took any action with his cousin or the state militia.

They agreed that Chennault would make a three-month inspection trip of all of China's air installations in order to develop a complete and honest report on the condition of the air force. Chennault, in his Louisiana drawl, said, "Well, I reckon you and I will get along just fine while I am fixing up your Air Force." Madame Chiang replied in her best Southern accent, "I reckon we will." With that exchange, the meeting was over.

Chennault was deeply impressed by the beautiful and intelligent 24-year-old, and they developed an almost instant friendship and trust. Madame Chiang loved her people, who desperately needed help, and Chennault was prepared to help. Chennault later wrote in his diary, "She will always be 'The Princess' to me." They would not always agree as Chennault argued for what he believed was necessary to defend China. However, they appear to have started with mutual respect. Mac stated, "All of us felt that way about The Princess."

When Mac saw Chennault, he congratulated him on the "promotion." In his final years with the Chinese Air Force, Mac would be referred to as Colonel by General Wu, a senior commander, and Colonel Shu, Chennault's translator. It is unknown if this title was an official rank or simply a sign of respect from these officers.

With instructions from Madame Chiang, plans were developed for the inspection trip and Chennault began assembling his team.

LEFT TO RIGHT: Sebie Smith, Colonel P.Y. Shu, Colonel Chennault, General Mow and Mac (with camera) getting ready to leave on inspection trip.

Chennault and his team were tasked with evaluating the readiness of the Chinese Air Force. During this trip, an incident at the Marco Polo Bridge on July 9, 1937, set off the Second Sino-Japanese War. The American advisors were thrust immediately into war.

1937 Inspection Trip of CAF Training Bases

ABOVE Chennault on the inspection trip, taken from the passenger seat of the other plane. Photo by Sebie Smith.

It felt good to be in the air again with Billy on my wing and a broad muddy river below that could easily have been the Mississippi instead of the Yangtze.

Chennanult, *Way of a Fighter*

The Inspection Trip

Two hard-used Douglas BT-2 biplanes were assigned to the group in Nanking. Their open cockpits and limited range added to the other perils of the journey, which included flying over poorly mapped territories, unfriendly tribal areas, the usual potential for weather-related problems, no instruments, no radio and visual navigation only.

Chennault piloted one plane while Mac flew the other. Mechanic Sebie Smith and Colonel P.Y. Shu were their passengers. During all of Chennault's time in China, Col. Shu would serve as his interpreter. Mac also took along ten rolls of film and a movie camera. As the inspection team took off in the two open cockpit planes, Chennault looked over and smiled at his old wingman. Chennault seemed truly happy to be a part of another adventure.

They stopped first for three days in Nanchang, on the southwestern side of Lake Poyang. The group took advantage of the mild weather to study the stars at night and brush up on their celestial navigation. Mac bought a hand-painted porcelain vase there, made from the special clay found on the lake's shores.

From Nanchang, they flew nearly five hours to Canton on July 1, 1937. Mac was very tired after. They reviewed Canton for four days.

Mac commented, "Spending the 4th not so glorious because we are in the British concession. Seems like the British still sulk over the Americans celebrating the 4th of July—funny people?!!"

They made a stop at Suichow to inspect a factory that assembled Martin B-10 bombers for the Chinese run by American Charlie Day.

During the next leg of the trip, the men were forced to pilot over one of China's wilder areas, as Mac explained in a July 11, 1937, letter.

> We flew over some territory that is still uncivilized. Certainly glad we did not have motor trouble in that region. The people there are somewhat like the American Indians, wearing similar clothes, nothing modern, depending on hunting and farming for a living. The government will not OK passports into this section. This is what they think of it. (Mac, July 11, 1937)

Then, after more than four hours flying in terrible weather in the open-cockpit planes, they arrived in Hankow. Smith spent most of his time there working on the aircraft.

Sunday, June 20, 1937, Shanghai

Colonel Chennault is here with us now and Thursday I am going on a 2500 mile inspection trip.…We are taking two planes, two-seaters and carrying Smith as our mechanic and an interpreter.

Mac, June 20, 1937

Sunday, July 11th
Loyang, Honan

Dear Dad,

On Monday last we left Canton in fairly murky weather but got thru to Hankow about 5:15 in the afternoon.

About 150 miles from Canton we flew over some territory that is still uncivilized. Certainly glad we did not have motor trouble in that region. The people there are somewhat like the American Indian wearing similar clothes. Nothing modern. Depend on hunting and farming for a living. The Gov. w not O.K. passports into this section — that's what they think about it. The "New Life Movement" is try to reach these people but it is slow work.

We have been doing a little sight seeing i this very ancient section. It is nothing to s something 2000 years old here. "Dragon Gate is located some 15 miles south and is a pass in the mts. In the rock walls there are many carved figures of Gods and Buddhas, some over 50 feet high will write more in detail about this. Should return to Nanking this coming week.

Love to all,
W —

Sunday, July 11, 1937, Loyang

We have been doing a little sightseeing in this very ancient section. It is nothing to see something 2000 years old here. "Dragon Gate" is located some 15 miles south and is a pass in the mountains. In the rock walls there are many carved figures of Gods and Buddhas, some over 50 feet high. Will write home in detail about this. Should return to Nanking this coming week.

Mac, July 11, 1937

Mac's Logbook from the Inspection Trip

June 26–July 14, 1937

26年

日期 Date	飛機式樣 Type of Plane	任務記號 Mission (Code No.)	任務概 A BRIEF STATEMENT	略 OF MISSION	飛行時間 FLYING TIME 任飛航員 As Pilot 點 Hrs.	分 Min.	任觀察員 As Observer 點 Hrs.	分 Min.	飛行次數 No. of Flights
7月									
補6月26	達机	長途	杭州 - 南昌	長途	3	00			/
1	"	"	南昌 - 廣東	"	4	45			/
5	"	"	廣東 - 韶州	"	1	05			/
5	"	"	韶州 - 漢口	"	4	10			/
7	"	"	漢口 - 洛陽	"	3	20			/
13	"	"	洛陽 - 西安	"	2	00			/
14	"	"	西安 - 洛陽	"	2	10			/
"	"	"	洛陽 - 孝感	"	3	00			/
									/

Loyang is near one of China's great wonders, the Dragon Gate or Lung-men Grottoes.

Chennault wanted to see them, despite the danger from hostile natives. Two Chinese colonels and Mac carried weapons for protection. Both colonels knew Mac from his previous visits in the area and treated him with great respect, which Chennault noticed.

About 1,400 caves carved from the limestone cliffs house about 100,000 statues, as well as 2500 stelae and 60 pagodas. Carvings range from 1 inch to 57 feel high. The grottoes are located on both the west and east sides of the Yi River.

One of many remarkable experiences for the Americans, it added to the respect and admiration they had for China and its people.

Gods and War

On the evening of July 7, 1937, they arrived in Loyang, Henan Province, where the main Italian aviation training base and airplane factory had been, to continue their inspections. They found time to visit the famed Lung-men Grottoes. Mac described the experience:

> We've been doing a little sightseeing in this very ancient section. It is nothing to see something 2000 years old. Dragon Gate is located some 15 miles south and is in a pass in the mountains. In the rocks there are many carved figures of gods and Buddhas, some over 50 feet high.

Later, they attended an opera staged at the base.

While the inspection team took in some of the timeless, beautiful treasures from China's long history, the ugly present was about to intrude.

Due to a lack of communication, news of the July 7 incident in northern China near the Marco Polo Bridge, believed by many to be the unofficial start of World War II, had not yet arrived. It would change everything.

龍門石

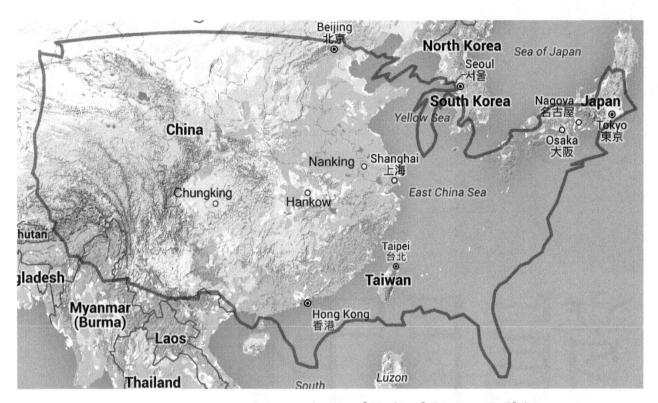

NOTE: The unfamiliar bulging at the northern U.S. border is due to the map projection method used, which emphasized the curve of the earth.

Comparison of United States & China

The outline of the U.S. in this figure does not cover all of China. Rather, this gives an idea of how close Japan and China are. It also labels many of the cities which figure prominently in the early story, as Mac and the Central Aviation School must respond to the invasion of Japanese planes.

The two countries are reasonably close in land mass. China has about 9,596,960 square kilometers of land, while the United States has about 9,161,966 square kilometers.

Population is entirely different. Estimated population for July 2014 was 1.3 billion for China and 319 million people for the United States.

China and Japan

The First Sino-Japanese War had ended in 1895 but Japan continued to expand its control over territory. The Japanese had overtaken Korea and Taiwan, and in 1931, Japan took the five northeastern Chinese provinces known as Manchuria. After several battles, a truce was negotiated that year, but in 1932, the Japanese invaded the Rehe Province and annexed it into its Manchurian holdings. Some consider this the start of the Second Sino-Japanese War.

Since the early 1800s, China also had foreign enclaves and troops in concession areas in key trading cities, called Treaty Cities, under several treaties intended to enforce trade policies favorable to Britain, France, the United States, Japan and others.

Under the rules of these treaties, Japan was able to expand its forces in China, outnumbering the European powers there. By 1937, it had troops there estimated from 7,000 to 15,000, most strategically stationed along railway lines in northern China. Internally, many Japanese were calling for an expulsion of Europeans from Asia, under the slogan "Asia for the Asians." Coupled with a belief in the superiority of the Japanese people, Japan felt called to embark on a campaign to "liberate" countries like China, where Western powers had significant influence.

Many historians consider the war's start as July 7, 1937, when outside the town of Wanping, the Imperial Japanese Army with approximately 5600 troops exchanged gunfire with approximately 100 troops from China's National Revolutionary Army, for reasons which are debated. The Japanese Army initially claimed that one of its soldiers was missing, and must have been taken by the Chinese. The situation escalated, with reinforcements for both armies arriving early the next morning. About 5 AM on July 8, the Japanese attacked the Marco Polo Bridge, with several skirmishes following. A ceasefire was brokered, then broken, with full-scale war between the two countries breaking out shortly after.

Japan was careful to refer to this invasion as the China "incident" because an official declaration of war would have triggered the latest U.S. Neutrality Act, passed by isolationists and pro-business interests in Congress. As long as war was not declared, U.S. companies could continue to trade with all sides in a conflict. In particular, Japan could buy scrap metal and other resources which they turned into war materials.

Despite President Franklin D. Roosevelt's desire to support China, the Neutrality Act of 1937 was especially difficult for the flyers in China. Americans aiding a belligerent could be court-martialed or even lose U.S. citizenship.

Mac and his group had come into this simmering cauldron to help build the Chinese Air Force. Now war with Japan was fully upon them. The American advisers to the Generalissimo and Madame Chiang Kai-Shek were caught in a war between two countries which would eventually become the China–Burma–India Theater of World War II.

Due to the Neutrality Act of 1937, the activities of Mac and his fellow advisers suddenly bordered on illegal, not just inadvisable, and they might face serious penalties if they didn't leave China immediately. Some of them chose to go home but several stayed despite the risks from Japanese bombs and the United States government.

War with Japan

July 16, 1937, Nanchang

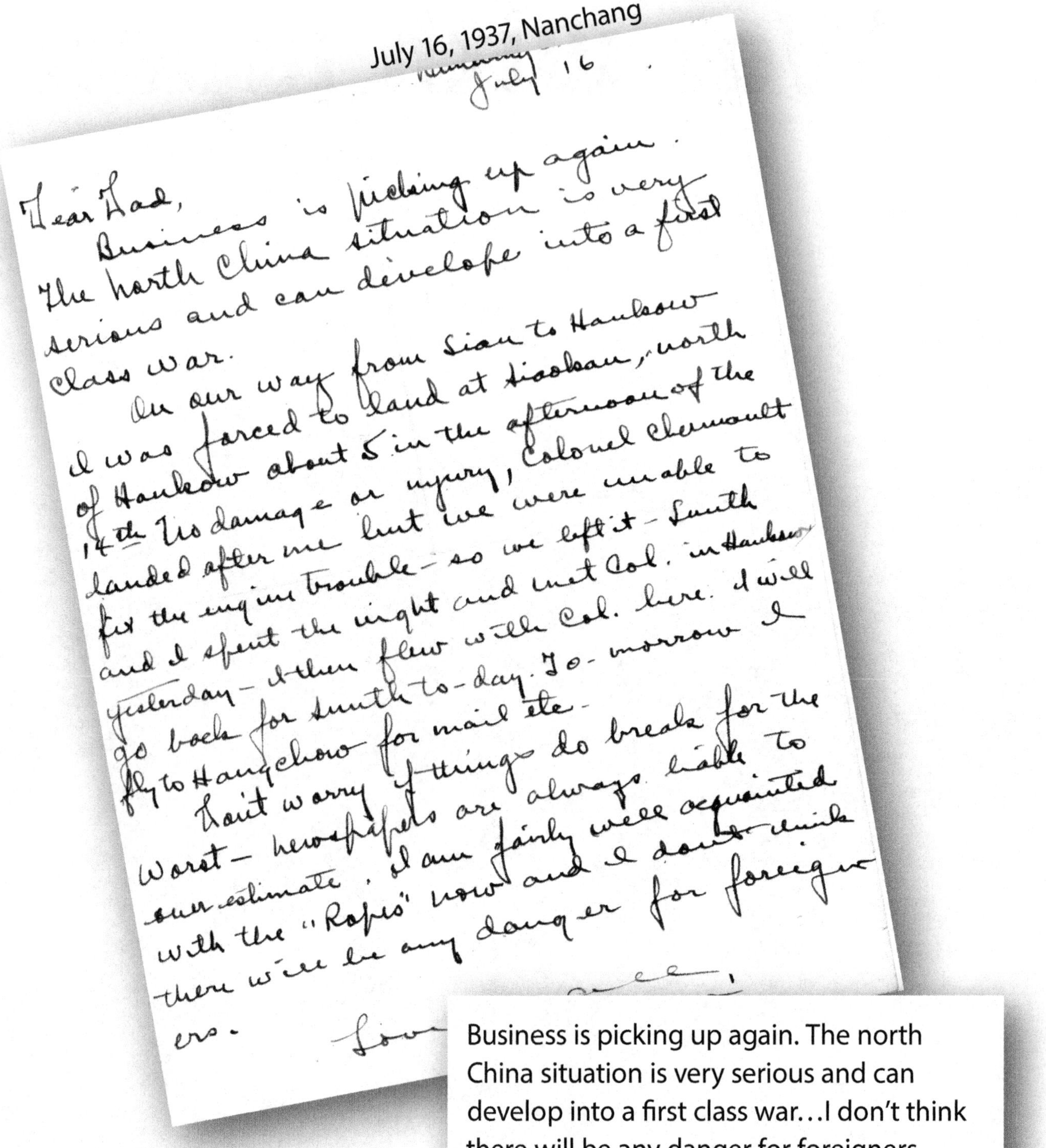

Dear Dad,
  Business is picking up again.
The North China situation is very
serious and can develope into a first
class war.
  On our way from Sian to Hankow
I was forced to land at Siaokan, north
of Hankow about 5 in the afternoon of the
14th No damage or injury, Colonel Chennault
landed after me but we were unable to
fix the engine trouble — so we left it — Smith
and I spent the night and met Col. in Hankow
yesterday — I then flew with Col. here. I will
go back for Smith to-day. To-morrow I
fly to Hangchow for mail etc.
  Don't worry if things do break for the
worst — newspapers are always liable to
over-estimate. I am fairly well acquainted
with the "Rofes" now and I don't think
there will be any danger for foreign
ers.
  Love

Business is picking up again. The north China situation is very serious and can develop into a first class war…I don't think there will be any danger for foreigners.

Mac, July 16, 1937

CHENNAULT, MAC & SMITH STAY
"...until it becomes dangerous"
July 11, 1937, Loyang, Henan

On the morning of July 11, base commander Colonel Wang informed the inspection team that he had received a 2 AM message that he must be prepared to mobilize in response to the conflict at the Marco Polo Bridge near Peking.

The Americans knew how badly the deck was stacked against the Chinese in the air. In spite of that, or perhaps because of it, they elected to stay anyway. The three men discussed it, and Chennault then sent word to the Chiangs offering their services in any capacity.

In *Way of a Fighter*, Chennault gave the following as his reasons:
1. I never run from a fight.
2. After all the years of classroom argument and theoretical debate over my theories of air warfare, I wanted a chance to give them an acid test in combat.
3. I was convinced that the Sino-Japanese war would be the prelude to a great Pacific war involving the United States. I felt that the more I could learn about the Japanese and the more damage I could inflict in the early phases of the conflict, the better I would be able to serve my country eventually.

A few days later, Mac told his family not to worry, as he would get out if it got "so dangerous." Mac's idea of "so dangerous" was notably different than most people's, as has been mentioned by many. He did get out, but only many years later, after staying through the Second Sino-Japanese War and World War II, and after thousands of hours flying through war, weather and wreckage.

Madame Chiang assigned Chennault as Senior Air Adviser and the Senior Tactical Instructor at Nanchang with General Mow, who commanded the elite of the Chinese Air Force combat units.

From Loyang, they flew to Sian to continue their inspections. On the next leg of their trip, Mac's plane lost oil pressure and Mac made a forced landing at Siaokan. Chennault and Colonel Shu flew on. Smith admitted later that he was quite nervous about spending the night in the wilds of China, but Mac and Smith eventually arrived in Hankow.

After retrieving their belongings from the Central Aviation School in Hangchow, they flew on to Nanchang to join General Mow and China's best combat pilots.

> We will not engage in any fighting but plan to stay on the job until it becomes so dangerous that we should have to leave. Definite plans have been made for departure if necessary.
>
> Mac, August 1, 1937

Aerial photo of Marco Polo Bridge. Beijing is opposite side of the river

Just one year ago to-day I landed in this country, eager to do what could be done in my line and to see what was what in the real Orient… Visiting most of the largest and most historic cities, meeting practically all of the ruling people of the different communities and of course the National rulers, many Americans, Germans, Italians, Danes, Russians, Chinese foreign educated, English, French and some nationalities I did not know…My year here has been packed with excitement of all kinds. Both National and International affairs have caused the blood to race through my veins…

Mac, July 27, 1937

Nanchang
July 27, 1937

TELEPHONE 400

CABLE ADDRESS "0400"

BURLINGTON HOTEL

Nanchang, _July 27_ _1937_

Dear Dad,

Just one yaer ago to-day I landed in this Country, Eager to do what could be done in my line and to see what was what in the real Orient. Now after one year I really think I am in a position to make almost any statement that I wish to make and back it up to the limit. Having traveled or rather flown over most of China under control of the Central Government and in doing so visiting most of the largest and most historic cities, meeting practically all of the ruling people of the differant communites, Germans, Italians, Danes, Russians, Chinese foreign educated, English, French and some of natioanlities that I did not know – therefore I think that I have apretty fair conception of of the above peoples ideas of China and naturally I have formed an honest and frank opinion of my own.

Now starnge as it may seem, though it is common knowledge in China among foreigners and most intelligent Chinese, the real rulers of China and the brains back of the Governement are "Three Ladies". These Ladies are all sisters. The number one of the trio is Madame Chiang Kai-shek, the next is Madame Kung, the wife of the present Minister of Finance, and last but by no means least is Madame Sun Yat Sen, the wife of Dr. Sun Yat Sen, the late Revolutionary leader and Martyr of China. So it is fairly easy to see at a glance that they are really in a positon to do the things that should be done and believe you me they are doing just that very thing. Ladies of real vision and love for their country and the people in it, they have planned and wprked to the hope of a real goal. And truthfully at this writing I think that they will egt there sooner or later.

My year here has been packed with excitement of all kinds. Both Natioanl and International affairs have caused the blood to race through my veins in a real rapid manner. Time and time again I have tried to write to you and tell you briefly of what was going on and how it was effecting me. I think that most of my efforts were wasted because I think that it is almost impossible for me to write exactly what I feel and see. Although at times I have tried real hard to do so. Most of the time I was always afraid that censoes would open the mail and misunderstand my attitude or intentions and get me in a little trouble with the government. Gradually this idea is fading from my mind. Now I think that I can write with more freedom. So in the future I will attempt to do so.

Now I guess the thing that you are mos interested in is the present difficulties in North China. In my last few leters I have tried briefly to cover the situation as best I could but under the circumstancs

Mac's Year in China

Mac had been in China about a year. He had come eager to work and learn about its land, culture and people. He'd accomplished that. He'd traveled widely across much of the country for a variety of reasons. He appreciated many different aspects of Chinese culture, its language, food, customs, art, architecture, agriculture, work. He had met and liked poor peasants and the leaders of the country. He'd made some friends that would last a lifetime. Not bad for a year, and a kid from Fairfield.

```
 I could.. .  ...   .ll what it was all about because I had          s
other than goss    nich at this time is more unreliable th          ther
time.

        I am at this writing almost positive that China and Japan will go
to War be  .se of this trouble in the North around Peiping. To the out-
side wor'  pictures are being painted first of one color and then another
until th  .verage newspaper reader doesn't know what it is really all
about. One thing I am sure and that most all,Americans an  Englsihmen,
are in favor of China and they are hoping that China will take the Japs
down more than just a couple of notches.

        The situation is indeed grave - The Generalissimo is doing every-
thing in his power to keep peace but on the otherhand it looks as if
the Japs are doing everything in their power to defeat his purpose. Of
this fact I think that in the long run they will be sorry. One thing
the envaders have overlooked - they think that they are th. only people
in the world, superior in knowledge, strength and wealt. Overconfidence
has caused defeat in more than one line of endeavor and it is to the
advantage of the opposition to have the enemy feeling that they are
overconfident.  I guess the answer will have to be put aside for a while
but as you read this maybe the answer will have reached you via news-
papers.

        It is really a lot of fun being really on the inside and knowing
all of the minor details. Many funny things creep up now and then and
one just can't help but get a good healthy laugh - and one good thing
they say as long as you laugh everything will come out all right inthe
long run.

        To-morrow I should get some mail bcause several more of the boys
are coming up here to do a little work. Kind of like old home week or
something.

        A brief idea of daily routine is as follows - Rise and sing at
the pleasant and quiet hour of 5:30 A.M. excluding Sundays - maybe???
arrive on the job at 6:00 - duty until 11:00 and back for tiffin at
12:00 - a short nap and back  n duty at 2:00 and stay in this capacity
until 5:00 - race home for a beer and a bath, shave and dinner at 8:00
write a few letters and then to bed and speaking of bed and plesant
dreams I think that I had better do that thing and crawl on top of the
sheets. Yes it is hot as the seven hinges of hades , but I am managing
to stand it o.K. - only a few spot  of prickly heat.
                                                        .pers -
```

The situation is indeed grave. The Generalissimo is doing everything in his power to keep peace but on the other hand it looks as if the Japs are doing everything in their power to defeat his purpose. Of this fact I think that in the long run they will be sorry. One thing the invaders have overlooked, they think that they are the only people in the world, superior in knowledge, strength, and wealth. Overconfidence has caused defeat in more than one line of endeavor and it is to the advantage of the opposition to have the enemy feeling that they are overconfident.

Mac, letter of July 27, 1937

Chinese Air Force Training Bases

PLACE	DATES	TRAINING BASE	CAF/FT BASE	FACTORY
HANGCHOW	1932-1937	Primary and Basic - Jouett 1932-1935, Reinburg 1936, Holbrook, Chennault 1937		CAMCO 1934-early 1938
LOYANG	1935-1937	Italian flight school, intermediate		Italian assembly plant
NANCHANG		Advanced	CAF base until Aug 1937	
NANKING	July-Dec, 1937		CAF defense Shanghai & Nanking	
HANKOW	Dec, 1937 - Oct, 1938	Regroups until March, 1938	CAF regroups 12/1937 - 10/1938	CAMCO early - late 1938
KUNMING	March, 1938 -	Advanced, Chennault 7/1938 - 1941, McDonald 4/1938 - 3/1940	Flying Tigers 1941-1942	
LIUCHOW	March, 1938 -	Primary and Basic		
MENGTZE		Basic		
YUNNANYI		Primary		
LOIWING	7/39 - ?/1942		Flying Tiger base: 1942	CAMCO late 1938 - 1942
HENGYANG				CAMCO, Greenlaw until late 1939
SUICHOW	1934? - 1940			C. H. Day - 1940

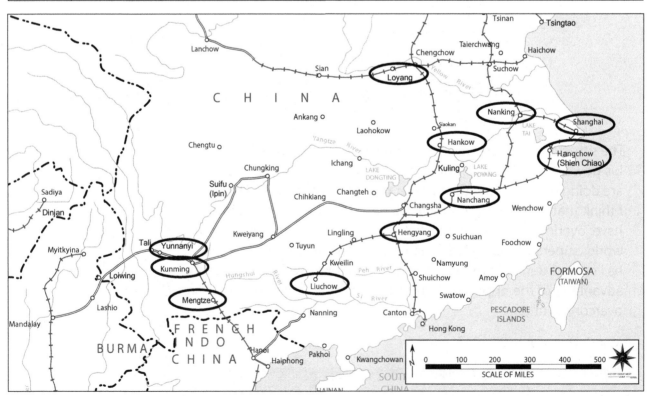

With the Chinese Air Force
Nanchang, late July into August 1937

Nanchang was the site of the Advanced Training program for the Chinese Air Force, under General P.T. Mow. Here were the pilots and equipment that would serve shortly in the defense of China. Now these were needed to prepare a country to defend itself against a foe equipped with modern strategy, equipment and training, years of planning, more and better planes and well-trained pilots.

Mac had learned dive-bombing in military training and as Chennault's protege, perfected and extended his flying and tactical skills with the Flying Trapeze team. Mac continued the evaluation of pilots for the Chinese Air Force. His records indicate that many pilots lacked adequate combat skills such as technique, approach, formation, dive, aim, maneuvers, targeting and planning. Only a handful were ready for the challenges of war,.

Many of these pilots had trained at the Italian school at Loyang, which had a policy of passing all surviving cadets regardless of competence. This school was an indirect result of U.S. policy, including the various Neutrality Acts passed by Congress, that prohibited sales of military aircraft to China. In contrast, the Italian government eagerly sought to sell Italian planes and offered to set up training schools and factories in China.

Training fields for aviation classes

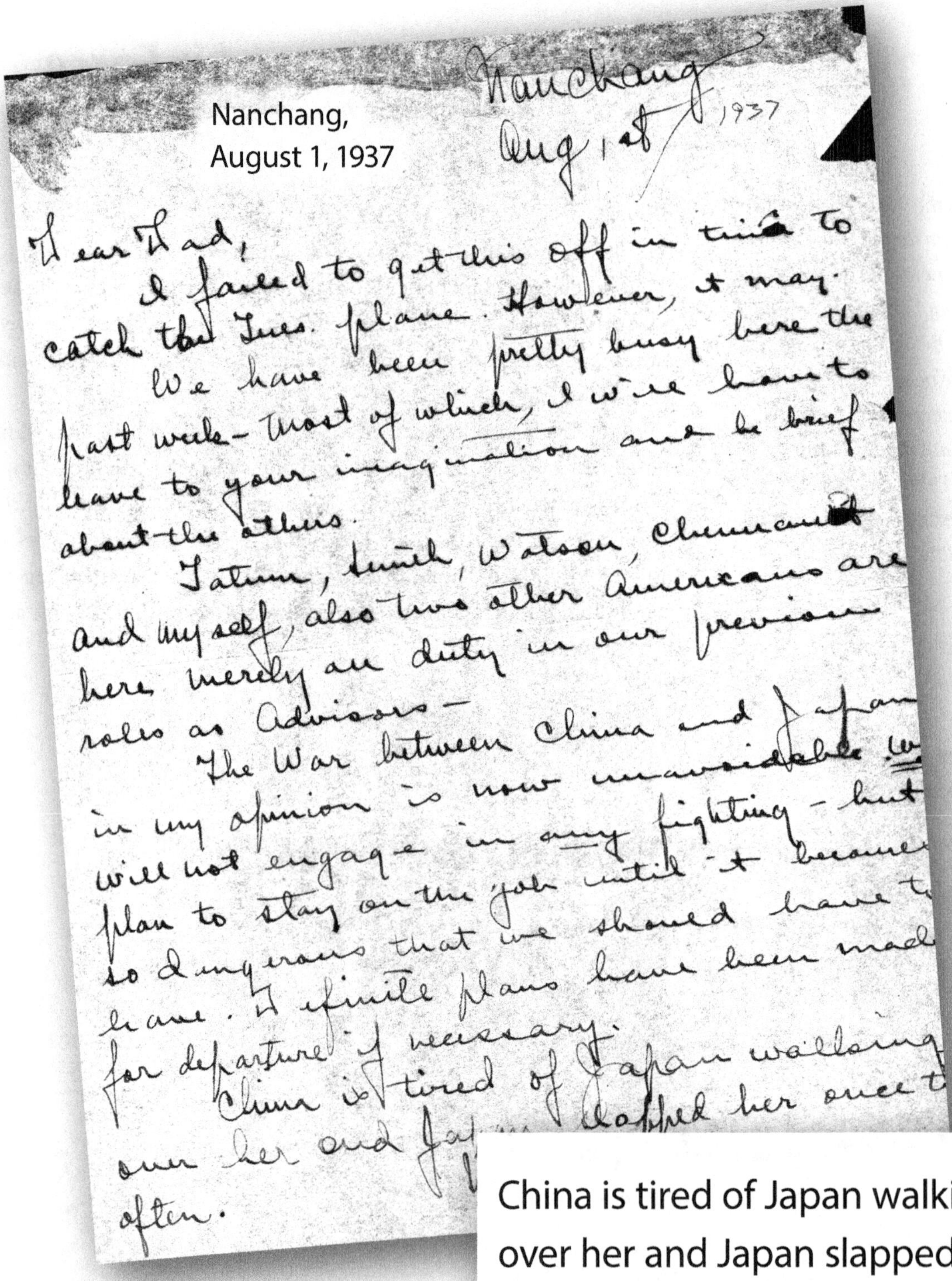

Nanchang,
August 1, 1937

*Nanchang
Aug 1st 1937*

Dear Dad,

I failed to get this off in time to catch the Tues. plane. However, it may.

We have been pretty busy here the past week – most of which, I will have to leave to your imagination and be brief about the others.

Tatum, Smith, Watson, Chennault and myself, also two other Americans are here merely on duty in our previous roles as Advisors –

The War between China and Japan in my opinion is now unavoidable. We will not engage in any fighting – but plan to stay on the job until it becomes so dangerous that we should have to leave. Definite plans have been made for departure if necessary.

China is tired of Japan walking over her and Japan slapped her once too often.

> China is tired of Japan walking over her and Japan slapped her once too often.
>
> Mac, August 1, 1937

Mobilizing for War
Nanchang & Nanking, August 1937

…the inspection trip had uncovered that of five hundred planes, only about ninety were fit for combat. The Chinese Air Force was not ready for war.

Nanchang was located in the interior of southern China, far from the events unfolding in the north. In response to the Marco Polo bridge incident and the possibility of war nearby, these pilots and planes needed to move to the north to counter the Japanese threat there. Shanghai airport and the training fields at Hangchow were too exposed to Japanese attack from carrier-based aircraft.

Nanking was farther inland and its airport would become the new base of operations. The base at Nanchang began closing in late July.

in *Ding Hao: America's Air War in China, 1937-1946,* Wanda Cornelius described an historic meeting on August 6, bringing together many of China's factions, including warlords and political parties. Chennault and W.H. Donald were the only two foreigners attending. These parties struggled with one another internally, but now agreed to set aside their differences and unite against their common enemy, the Japanese. Mac waited outside the meeting for Chennault.

By August 7 the majority of mechanics were gone from the base at Nanchang.

Events escalated rapidly when a Japanese officer, Lieutenant Oyama, and his driver were killed on August 9 in Shanghai leading to the outbreak of war there.

On August 10, Chennault and General Mow met with the Chiangs and reported that the inspection trip had uncovered that of five hundred planes, only ninety-one were fit for combat. The Chinese Air Force was not ready for war.

The Generalissimo was understandably outraged and threatened Mow with execution. Madame Chiang encouraged Chennault to be truthful and direct. Chennault bluntly described the dire situation, maintaining constant eye contact with the Generalissimo as he spoke. From that conversation, the Generalissimo determined that Chennault was the right man to serve as his Air Advisor. Mac would remain Chennault's wingman in this endeavor.

By August 12, the Nanchang base was closed. Mac, Watson, Smith, Folmar and Chennault went to Nanking.

They would all fight together for many long years.

Nanchang, Kiangsi,
August 6, 1937.

Dear Dad,

Seems only yesterday that I wrote you last - that is an example of how fast the time is flying.

Up early every morning includinh Sunday and back to the Hotel for food and sleep and that about covers the activity. Several of us have been playing a little cribbage after dinner until we get sleepy.

Tatum is now the most nervous of men - he is to become a father in a very few days and is expecting a telegram from Shanghai almost any day now. He will of course fly down for the event.

Mrs. Tatum is staying at the Metroploe Hotel until she must go to the Hospital. She has for company my dog the Baron and their dog, Barons Brother and in a letter to Tatum here the other day she said that the two dogs were having the time of their lives their at the Hotel. She says that I have lost my dog - that she is positive that the Baron will not leave her for me. Funny how one can grow so attached to dogs they are really a lot of company. I wish I had the Baron up here but I don't think he would like it.

Right at this moment things in the North have quieted down and just minor skirmishes here and there. One thing this trouble has brought out and that is the complete unification of all China. Just last week three Provinces joined hands with the Central Government. All three have been opposed in the past and all three have large armies and are quite wealthy. The provinces of Schechuan, Kwangsi and Yunnan are the new jioners. So it looks like so me serious business is ahead. Because one of the main reasons why these provinces have held out on the Central Government is because they wouldn't fight the Japanese. Now draw your own conclusions why they have come across.

It has been hot as the very hinges of hades the last several weeks. Showers have invaded our fair city for the past two nights and we were able to sleep a little better than usual. Even with an electric fan going all night - onesleeps very restless. *most are of us are — weather*

too hot ... *from upset stomachs —*

Sure ...

you foll ...

Some ...

P.S.
there must ...
her addre ...

Tatum is now the most nervous of men—he is to become a father in a very few days and is expecting a telegram from Shanghai almost any day now. He will of course fly down for the event.

Right at this moment things in the North have quieted down and just minor skirmishes here and there. One thing this trouble has brought out and that is the complete unification of all China. Just last week [the provinces of Szechwan, Kwangsi and Yunnan] joined hands with the Central Government. All three having been opposed in the past and all three have large armies and are quite wealthy....So it looks like to me serious business is ahead. Because one of the main reasons why these provinces have held out on the Central Government is because they wouldn't fight the Japanese. Now draw your own conclusions why they have come across.

Mac, August 6, 1937

Bomber Versus Pursuit

Italian General Giulio Douhet theorized that the "bombers would always get through" and that pursuit aircraft would be ineffectual against them. Many influential military men in the U.S. agreed.

Interestingly, in 1934 Mac replaced Haywood Hansell in the "Three Men on the Flying Trapeze." Hansell left to devote himself to bombers, graduating from the ACTS, then becoming ACTS' youngest faculty member (1935-1938). Hansell was a primary member of the Bomber Mafia, and a main advocate and architect of U.S. air policy. He later admitted that overlooking the role of pursuit craft had been a mistake. He retired as a Major General.

Significant technological advances in aircraft design and construction occurred in the 1930s. Equipped with advanced higher power engines, large, heavily armed bombers flew higher and faster than existing pursuit aircraft. From this, Italian General Giulio Douhet theorized that the "bombers would always get through" and that pursuit aircraft would be ineffectual against them. Most military experts in the U.S. agreed that bombers would prevail, but advocated directing them against strategic military and industrial targets rather than terrorizing civilian populations. An increasing number of the instructors at the ACTS at Maxwell Field belonged to this so-called "bomber mafia." These men were highly influential within U.S. military aviation.

Lt Col Peter R. Faber, in his monograph "The Development of U.S. Strategic Bombing Doctrine in the Interwar Years: Moral and Legal?" states that "80% of the Army Air Forces's senior leadership, including 11 of its 13 three-star generals and all three of the four-star generals in service" were heavily influenced by their training in this doctrine at ACTS.

Chennault fought a losing battle against this doctrine in the U.S., but China needed a strong air force to defend itself against Japan bombers and fighter planes. Chennault was eager for an opportunity to prove his theories on aerial warfare. Unlike the majority of U.S. military strategists, Chennault believed that pursuit planes and an advance warning network could prevail against bombers. Bombers were vulnerable to attack, and pursuit planes could defend a position given adequate warning. He also believed and taught strategies that avoided one-on-one combat and emphasized teamwork among two or three pursuit planes against a single bomber. Mac was well-schooled in these theories, and believed in them, and in Chennault's leadership, whole-heartedly.

Chennault would pursue these strategies in China, making it the proving ground for his theories. His work in China with the Chinese Air Force, the American Volunteer Group (Flying Tigers) and the 14th Air Force ultimately disproved the Bombers-Only theories that were disastrous in the initial stages of World War II, both for the Allies and for the Japanese.

The Effect of U.S. Neutrality Acts

World War I left the United States strongly isolationist. U.S. participation in "Europe's war" had been costly. However, international business increasingly bound much of the world together.

In his well-researched book *War Wings*, Prof. Guangqiu Xu argues persuasively that the U.S. had conflicting interests in China which resulted in deeply inconsistent policies. In 1932 and again in 1937, Japan's aggression and growing military power altered official and unofficial U.S. policy toward China, while commercial interests resisted cutting trade in war goods such as scrap metal and oil.

A Series of Neutrality Acts

The Neutrality Act of 1935 placed a general embargo on sales of arms and war materials to all belligerents. American citizens traveling on ships from countries at war would not be protected by the U.S.

The Neutrality Act of 1936 renewed the 1935 Act and disallowed loans or credits to belligerents.

The Neutrality Act of 1937 renewed the previous Acts without expiration date. U.S. ships could not transport passengers or material to belligerents, and citizens were forbidden from traveling on ships of belligerents.

Officially, the U.S. government disapproved of Americans serving in the military of a foreign power, and the Neutrality Act of 1937 was the most restrictive.

When Japan invaded China in July 1937, Japan carefully referred to it as an "incident." Because the parties hadn't declared war, Japan could continue to buy metal and fuel.

The Neutrality Act of 1939 was passed after Roosevelt argued that the previous Neutrality Acts gave "passive aid" to an aggressor. Under a "cash-and-carry" provision, the President might allow the sale of materials and supplies for cash. President Roosevelt had lobbied for this provision to aid France and Great Britain if war broke out in Europe.

The Lend-Lease Act of March 1941 allowed the U.S. to sell, lend or give war materials to nations favored by the administration, among other provisions, effectively ending the strict isolationist policies.

> *Stung by their initial losses over Nanking, the Japanese officially demanded that all American airmen leave China. The State Department seemed only too happy to comply with the Japanese demands by trying to oust not only my group but the American pilots that worked for CNAC. When the first request for American flyers to leave China reached me, I noted in my diary, 'Guess I am Chinese.'*
>
> *Chennault, Way of a Fighter*

Effect of Neutrality Acts on Americans in China

On August 19, 1937, the Japanese ambassador to China approached the American Ambassador to China, Nelson T. Johnson, alleging that American advisers were acting in violation of the Neutrality Act. Johnson told the Japanese ambassador that if he could provide specific pilots' names, U.S. marshals from the embassy in Shanghai would arrest and remove the pilots from the country.

When the Generalissimo and Mr. Donald received notice that U.S. marshals were traveling to Nanking to arrest Mac and Chennault, Donald commanded Chinese troops to surround the Nanking office. They had orders that no one should be allowed to see the pilots.

Chennault confronted Ambassador Johnson, who informed him that the aviation personnel were not being singled out, but anyone who chose to serve in the military for a foreign power could not expect protection.

Mac commented in a letter that Williamson and the other Americans with wives in Shanghai were in a tough spot. They had evacuated from Nanchang to Shanghai's French Concession, presumably safe from direct attack by the Japanese. The married pilots were understandably eager to get to Shanghai to ensure the safety of their wives and children.

Sebie Smith's manuscript contains information from Aimee May's Shanghai diary. Her entries talk about their last few days in China. They left their homes in Nanchang suddenly, and in Shanghai, they were unable to get gas, electric, phone or sanitation.

Once the pilots were in the French Concession checking on their families, U.S. officials were unwilling to offer any protection unless they all were headed out of China.

Luke Williamson asked Clarence Gauss, the American Consul General in Shanghai, if he and the other American aviation instructors were now in violation of the Neutrality Act, as they were expected to advise and instruct the CAF in combat. Gauss said that they would be in violation.

Williamson refused to confirm or deny the rumor that unmarried men might be asked to serve as squadron leaders. He was willing to go home if advised to do so and asked Gauss to provide his colleagues with the same advice.

U.S. Secretary of State Cordell Hull advised Gauss that Williamson and his colleagues did "reasonably come within the purview" of the statutes and should be advised to leave China.

American Compromise

Madame Chiang complained to Ambassador Johnson, but Johnson explained that aviation instruction would now be considered military service.

On August 21, 1937, American pilots for the commercial airline China National Aviation Corporation (CNAC), as well as one of Madame Chiang's personal pilots, were detained in Hong Kong by the American Consul there, Merritt N. Coots. Coots did not believe they could avoid direct or indirect military service if they were allowed to enter China.

In a compromise, U.S. Secretary of State Hull directed Coots to endorse their passports, but with a disclaimer that the passport was "not valid for travel to or in any foreign state in connection with entrance into or service in foreign military or naval forces."

American officials used persuasion and threats to suggest that they all leave China. If any individuals chose to stay, they explained, they were doing so at their own risk and, more importantly, reserve officers might be forced to forfeit their commissions. This particular threat was aimed directly at Williamson and Mac, as well as a few other advisers.

The married pilots choose to leave under this pressure. Williamson returned to China in 1943 to become Chennault's personal pilot in the 14th Air Force.

ABOVE Ambassador Nelson T. Johnson, center in suit with white shirt, at aviation school graduation.

LEFT Ambassador Johnson addressing graduating class. Photos by Frank Higgs.

) I had also heard about this and was on the roof of the Hongkong Shanghai Bank Building where the RAF Flying Club held its meetings. The first attack was by only 3 airplanes. This is not for publication but it is strongly rumored and believed that the lead man was Col. Chenault, later General, with W. C. McDonald and "Red" Williamson as wing men. It is also

rumored they got $1,000 cash. None of them has denied these rumors. Of the three aircraft on the first days attack none was hit by fire from the "Idzuma".

ABOVE Chuck Sharp, in response to a question from author William M. Leary. BACKGROUND the *Idzumo* in Shanghai.

Idzumo Incident: The Rumor

Showing tremendous confidence, the Japanese had moored the cruiser *Idzumo* at the dock in the Huang Po (Wang River) opposite the Japanese consulate. The *Idzumo* was headquarters for the Japanese Imperial forces in Shanghai. Damage would hurt the Japanese forces which were superior in number, training and equipment.

What is undisputed is that on August 14, Chinese planes attacked the *Idzumo* and that Mac and Chennault were there.

What was rumored and could be true is that Chennault sent his best-prepared pilots in on the first wave of attack. That would not have been the barely-trained Chinese pilots but instead the team that had practiced these same maneuvers for years, the "Men on the Flying Trapeze." In response to questions from author William M. Leary, CNAC Captain Chuck Sharp voiced these rumors. None of the bombs hit directly.

The rest of the attack plan was carried out by nervous Chinese pilots on their first combat missions. The inexperienced pilots had to come in from a lower altitude than planned due to cloud cover, and failed to correct the bombsight settings. Bombs landed in a crowded street near the water in the International area, reportedly killing nearly 1000 Chinese and wounding over 900.

The Battle of Shanghai
August 13, 1937 – November 26, 1937

On August 13 at 9 AM, over 10,000 Japanese troops entered the outskirts of Shanghai. By mid-afternoon, Chinese troops were shelling the Japanese. By 4 PM, the Japanese navy began bombarding the city. The Japanese also had a heavily-fortified position in the International Zone. Thousands of Chinese civilians and soldiers were killed in the onslaught.

Chennault and Mac were summoned to meet with Madame Chiang. She asked Chennault for his advice on air strategy. Despite having never commanded during wartime, he was confident. He recommended dive-bombing and high-level bombing attacks on the Japanese warships.

Without a Chinese officer who could plan such an attack, she asked Chennault to plan the aerial counterattack.

Chennault had prepared twenty years for this moment. Mac and Chennault drove to the Chinese Air Force headquarters and stayed up until 4:00 AM planning.

That same day, Japanese aircraft began bombing the city, which were challenged by Captain Gao Zhihang's 4th Flying Group. They shot down six Japanese aircraft without losing a plane. Nevertheless, Chinese aircraft were few in number, and lacked proper replacement parts for repairs.

By the end of the campaign, even though the Chinese aircraft shot down 85 Japanese aircraft and sank 51 ships, the Chinese lost nearly half of China's total available combat aircraft. The remaining aircraft were not capable of forcing the retreat or destruction of the *Idzumo* or other warships. The bombardment by Japanese warships contributed significantly to the eventual fall of the city.

> Madame Chiang told those present simply, "They are shelling the Shanghai Civic Center. They are killing our people."
>
> Chennault asked, "What will you do now?"
>
> "We will fight."

Described in *Ding Hao: America's Air War in China, 1937-1946* by Wanda Cornelius

BACKGROUND The *Idzumo* in the harbor at Shanghai.

McDonald gets mission instructions from Chennault while the Hawk Special is being prepared for flight in the background. They are at the Nanking Airdrome at the base of Purple Mountain. Photo by Frank Higgs

Built for Speed & Fitted With Guns

Chennault had the new Hawk stripped to allow it to fly faster and higher. At 280 mph, the stripped-down Hawk Special was the fastest plane in China, 20 mph faster than a standard Hawk 75 and 40 mph faster than a Hawk III.

Chennault ordered guns for the Hawk Special. With some difficulty, Sebie Smith, Pete Brewster and Rolfe Watson installed two free-firing 0.300-inch (7.5-mm) caliber Colts with 600 rounds per gun in the wings, one 0.50-inch (12.7-mm) caliber gun with 200 rounds, and one 0.300-inch (7.5-mm) caliber gun with 600 rounds in the upper nose, synchronized to fire through the propeller.

The Hawk Special roamed freely through the skies of China for ten months, a long time for a combat plane. It upset the Japanese enough that the U.S. Ambassador informed Mac that a bounty had been placed on the pilots flying Chennault's Hawk. The Americans were also told that two to three squadrons of Japanese planes were tasked with bringing the plane down.

But the Hawk Special met its end on the runway during a landing. Whether we believe Chennault when he says it was another pilot, or if we believe Mac and Smith when they say it was Chennault himself, the Hawk Special didn't fall to an enemy.

The Hawk 75 Special
Fast, armed and allegedly dangerous

On August 12, 1937, just before the outbreak of hostilities, Pete Brewster, a test pilot for the Curtiss Wright Company, was demonstrating the Hawk 75 Special to Nanking. Delivered in a crate, it was assembled and tested before being turned over to the Chinese. The plane was solid green with a large "75" painted on the side.

Modifications made at Chennault's request included stripping everything unnecessary and adding guns. The ship flew faster than anything in China.

A film available on the internet shows Chennault taking off in the Hawk Special, smiling. With his head sticking above the canopy. He looked tall in the cockpit.

Mac was the first person the Colonel trained to fly the plane. At five foot three, Mac fit easily into the cockpit. Mac flew the plane for speed and fuel consumption tests several times, then took it on numerous tactical missions. Mac said in his journal entry of August 17, "Hawk very fast—fastest ship I have ever flown."

Unarmed Observation Flights

The Hawk's speed and altitude were used in observation missions around Shanghai. Mac had a great deal of training in high altitude flying due to his time at Selfridge Field and Maxwell Field earlier in his career, and his flight book documents early observation flights.

Chennault explained, "As the Jap armies surged toward Nanking, the Hawk Special was the principal source of information on their progress, making daily patrols along the railroad that guided the enemy advance." The anti-aircraft shells always blew up behind the Hawk as it flew over Japanese lines.

As noted in his air journal, many of Mac's flights involved attempts to locate the Japanese fleet in the Yellow Sea. According to Chennault, on one occasion, Mac located the Japanese carrier *Ryūjō* off the Yangtze estuary. Mac may have led the Chinese dive bombers which then attacked the carrier.

Armed "Observation" Flights

Mac was first to fly the Hawk Special after the weapons update. Mac and Smith both report that he returned from that first flight with bullet holes littering the tail. Mac complained that only one gun fired.

After his flight, Mac told the ground crew, "I suggest you fix those other three guns before the Skipper takes it up." They all worked very hard to make sure the guns fired before Chennault flew again. While several pilots flew the aircraft, Smith indicates that Mac flew the bulk of the flights.

Madame Chiang, Mac and Chennault appear to have promised never to speak of their direct combat. Everyone had a great deal to lose if such information became public. China could be criticized. Even after the war, Chennault and Mac could face criminal charges and penalties, including the loss of a military pension or even citizenship.

Chennault's Kills

Many stories exist regarding the number of planes Chennault shot down. Like a good fish story, the more times the story was told, the larger the fish got. The largest number of planes Mac read in print was 72 kills. However, his position remained unchanged over the years. Even when asked in 1983, he shook his head and simply refused to utter a word.

In a letter to the historian of the 14th Air Force in 1976, Mac wrote that "to my knowledge Chennault never shot down a single plane, but I wish he had."

Were American Advisors Flying as Squadron Leaders in Combat?

On his first flight, Mac noted in his diary that the Hawk 75 Special was the fastest plane he had ever flown. During the early days in the battle for Nanking, he made contact with Japanese aircraft at least twelve times before the Hawk was armed.

Sebie Smith reported that during air raids, Mac took the Hawk Special up, presumably to avoid bombs. They called this a "Mac Off."

Smith also strongly implied in his manuscript that Mac did not necessarily fly away from the incoming Japanese. Mac also took the Hawk up at other times, and Smith says he knew better than to ask, but he assumed that Mac had found what he was looking for.

Mac would not discuss what happened to the pilots who shot at him, but he felt strongly that enemy pilots were convinced that engaging the Hawk Special was a bad idea.

Revenge of the Squadron Commander

Some speculate that Mac led his Chinese squadron into action, as it was rumored that unmarried American advisors were asked to be squadron commanders. The following story supports that speculation. Mac himself told this story, being careful not to mention

how he escaped the Japanese net.

In 1937, Mac offended a particular Chinese colonel by replacing him as squadron commander. Later, the squadron met a Japanese formation, and Mac signaled the planes to attack. The colonel in Chinese instructed the squadron to turn left and return to base instead. This left Mac alone with the enemy.

Despite this treachery, Mac was able to fight his way clear and landed safely at the base in Nanking. He called his pilots in for a private meeting.

At a reunion after the war, Mac told Roy Farrell that he had not reported the incident to the Generalissimo. Mac was aware he would need these pilots as the war would soon wear down their air assets. He knew most, if not all, of these pilots would die in combat. He also knew that the Generalissimo would execute officers and pilots for such behavior.

At the 1964 reunion in Formosa, a Chinese Lt. General walked by and acknowledged Mac with a nod. The Lt. General looked quite pale as though he had seen a ghost. Farrell heard Mac mutter under his breath, "That's the son of a bitch that almost got me killed."

perfect. Poor visibility, low ceiling, intermittent showers, and a strong wind failed to interfer with the mission. The general impression from experienced pilots that saw the approach and formation (diamond) was that the job was excellently planned and carried out. Direct hits on shops and hangars and one hit on the line at outside ...ed showed immense accuracy ... low altitude with a strong wind. ...aking advantage of the low ...onds, they made it extremely ...fficult for anti-aircraft and ...und fire to hit them. One thing ...inutely was proven and that was fact the Pursuit airplane single

...seater is the most formidable of all the weapons against bombardment. The mission was rather expensive from the Japanese viewpoint - while publicly claiming themselves as 'Kings of the air', rulers supreme, they lost at Nanking, definitely six Bombers - 36 in crews and possibly one more ship - yet unconfirmed. The machines with the latest devices of radio, Bombing and with information so thorough that it is almost unbelievable. The work and ability of the sqdn leaders in both attacks showed years of experience and much wisdom. Their biggest mistake was underestimation of Chinese Pilots to fight

A Coded Journal?

In 2012, the author received a call from a Marine Corps Lt. Colonel, who was returning from Afghanistan. He was writing a Masters thesis and had traveled to the museum in order to study Mac's wartime journal and inquire about a transcript. In passing, the officer said, "I have been unable to break it or prove it, but I am fairly certain there is a personal code throughout the flight book."

In a letter to General Marion Cooper, who was a former Chief of Staff to Chennault and was working on a movie script, Mac commented that the flight book had more information than meets the eye. Sometimes words are blurred or do not fit in sentences. Some entries seem to suggest that Mac was in combat.

The journal is on display at the Enlisted Men's Heritage Hall on McDonald Street at Gunter Annex, which is next to Maxwell Air Force Base in Montgomery, Alabama. The Heritage Hall is an award-winning museum and has won many honors among military museums.

From the British Archives

30.

44.   That night I had dinner with Colonel CHENNAULT and an American instructor named McDONALD. The latter is credited with having brought down a large number of Japanese but he was reluctant to talk about his combatant activities. The story (for what it is worth) is that he was paid so much per hostile aircraft crashed. He was making so much that the Chinese reduced the payment to ₡1,000 gold when McDONALD said that "on those terms they could go and shoot the blankety things down themselves." The conversation was of a general character but both said that the Japanese had made a great mistake by concentrating on bombing Chinese aerodomes.

British Naval Attaché Robert S. Aiken Intelligence Report on March 7, 1939

That night I had dinner with Colonel CHENNAULT and an American instructor named McDONALD. The latter is credited with having brought down a large number of Japanese but he was reluctant to talk about his combatant activities. The story (for what it is worth) is that he was paid so much per hostile aircraft crashed. He was making so much that the Chinese reduced the payment to $1,000 gold when McDONALD said that "on those terms they could go and shoot the blankety things down themselves."

46.

RUSSIAN ASSISTANCE

I have already referred to the difficulty of obtaining information about the activities of the RUSSIANS. Such information

Mac & the Blankety Things

The number of planes shot down by Chennault or Mac remains a mystery. It seems clear that they encountered Japanese planes while flying a plane equipped with guns. It seems unlikely that they did not put the guns to use.

Did Chennault shoot down any Japanese planes? Mac claimed he did not. Yet Chennault's own book claims that Japanese pilots who tried to trap him paid "the ultimate price."

McDonald would not confirm or deny kills. In later years, Mac stated that Chennault did not want anyone to know and that was the end of the discussion.

It seems likely that, as widely reported, Chennault, Mac and Madame Chiang made a pact whereby none of the three would ever discuss the topic with others.

Did Mac shoot down Japanese planes? It seems likely. How many? A researcher suggested that Mac's journal contains a code. Perhaps it will tell us.

For now, here is the evidence and logic which suggests that Mac shot down many planes during his time in the Hawk Special.

Both Chennault and Mac were outstanding pilots, well-trained, well-practiced. The combat techniques perfected during years with the Flying Trapeze were used to great effect with the Flying Tigers just a few years later. The skies were filled with Japanese planes. Neither man claims a single kill, which seems very suspicious, as Smith claims that Mac in particular came home with bullet holes in the Hawk after "observation" flights, implying very close "observation."

An entire group (not just a single squadron) of Japanese planes were tasked with finding and destroying the Hawk Special. There was a widely-reported rumor that Hawk pilots had a large bounty on their heads. Would the Japanese trouble themselves that much over an observation plane?

Chennault credits John Wang, who also flew the Hawk Special, with shooting down thirteen Japanese planes in far fewer flights than Mac made. Unlike the other Hawk flyers, Wang was a Chinese citizen.

Military attachés of several nations reported that the Hawk Special participated in aerial combats.

No confirmed kills by either Mac or Chennault exist in the Chinese war records. In 1976, Mac asked Col. Shu to look through the records in Taiwan for any record of kills for either Chennault or himself. Strange to look for records that couldn't exist…

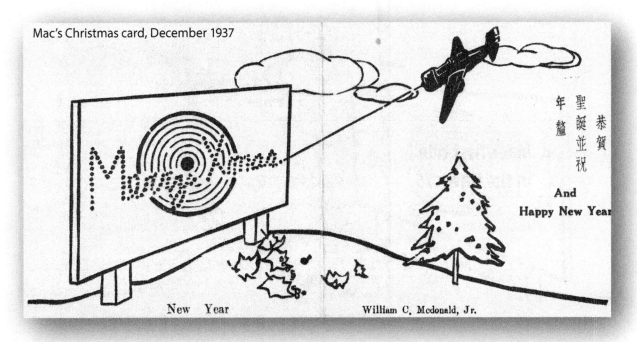

Mac's Christmas card, December 1937

恭賀
聖誕並祝
年釐

And
Happy New Year

New Year   William C. Mcdonald, Jr.

Mac's Logbook Entries
August–September, 1937

Mac flew the Hawk 75 Special extensively during this period, as documented in this logbook. All entries are consistent with events described in his letters. Neither letters nor this logbook make any mention of combat, which would be evidence of a serious breach of the Neutrality Acts.

Mac's first ride in the Hawk 75

From Mac's CAF journal, August 17, 1937

> Aug. 17
> To-day has been a little too quiet – possibly the lull before the storm.
> Tried new Hawk 75 – had to take off in a hurry – more Japs headed for Nanking – did not last long – Hawk very fast – fastest ship I have ever flown. Made a short xc flight to Yangchow 60 miles away – up in 20 minutes – back in 15 minutes – Mr. Paxton American Consul for dinner said last boat for evacuation to-morrow at ten – going to Hankow – only two alarms to-day – Japs don't seem so cocky

日 期 Date	飛機式様 Type of Plane	任務記號 Mission (Code No.)	任 務 概 A BRIEF STATEMENT	略 OF MISSION	飛 行 時 間 FLYING TIME				飛行次數 No. of Flights
					任飛行員 As Pilot		任觀察員 As Observer		
					點 Hrs.	分 Min.	點 Hrs.	分 Min.	
1937 August									
1	Hawk III	rj	Nanchang	Radio Test	✓	4			1
3						30			"
4	Northrop	t-a		Flight Test		40			"
"						20			"
12	Douglas	X-c	Nanking to Shanghai & return	Cross-country		310			2
17	Hawk 71	t-a	Nanking	Test & Familiarization		130			1
"		X-c	Nanking to Yangchow & return	Cross-country		4			2
18	"	1-h	Nanking	Reconnaissance		410			1
20	"	X-c	Nanking – Hangchow – Nanking	Cross-country		344			3
"	"	"	Nanking – Kaishing – Nanking			240			"
22	Hawk III	rj	Nanking	Radio Test		100			1
"	Hawk 71	X-c	Nanking - Shanghai return no	landing cross country		314			1
24	"	1-h		Reconnaissance Raffles Island		244			"
28	Hawk III	rj	Nanking	Radio Test		34			"
30	Vultee	t-a	"	Flight Test		4			"

Found naval base & carrier

Folmar, Watson, Smith and myself got up at four, went to the field and I took off at 5:58, flew 2:30, found a regular naval base on Raffles Island 100 miles east of Kashiang. Very uneventful but was lucky to find the carrier again. Big plans to take care of the base. Arrived back in Nanking 8:30.

From Mac's CAF journal, August 24, 1937

Nanking
August 22, 1937.

Dear Dad,

Business has certainly picked up. I think the last letter I wrote was from Nanchang. On the 12th we all came here and have been here ever since. Luke, Tatum, Holland and Jack May are in the French Settlement at Shanghai. The rest of us - Colonel Chennault, Watson, Smith, Folmar and myself are here at the Metropoitan Hotel.

The Japanese have been carrying on intensive raids and I know the papers back home have been playing the situation sky high. One advantage of being in the interior of China is that you are only subject to raids from one force while in Shanghai both Japs and Chinese are dropping bombs and the fighting there is rather fierce. The Chinese had hoped to take the Shanghai area but the Japs have put up a stubborn resistance although a loosing one. I can't see how they can hold out much longer because they have really been at war there.

The Jap Bombers have reached Nanking three times. The first was on Sunday 16th and two more times since then. From a Chinese viewpoint the raids were not very successful. Simply because the Japs failed to do a hell of a lot of damage. Although their tactics and strategy were OK they didn't expect the Chinese to fight them so hard. All I had better say is that the Japs lost more planes than the Chinese.

It has all been exciting and interesting. We are of course not taking active part in the affair but are continuing with our jobs as if nothing was going on.

Madame Chiang has been marvelous. She visits the fields at least twice a week and possibly more, Cheering and encourageing her boys. We have pointed out the manner that American people go about assisting the boys that are defending the country that is of sending food and drinks and anything that would be comfortable to the pilot. The Women have jumped at the oppertunity to help and there is a real spirit evidant in the results.

There appears a long war - In the North and possibly it will break out in the South.

I am going to stay here with the Colonel as long as it isn't too dangerous. I am sure there is no need for you to worry over this business at all. However, since you are so far away I am sure you can't help it. Because letters are going to be few and far between.

As soon as the mails are open again I will write once as usual.

Address my mail now to me - % Commission on Aeronautical Affairs, Nanking - Please forward.

Love to all,

Business has certainly picked up.

It has all been exciting and interesting. We are of course not taking active part in the affair but are continuing with our jobs as if nothing was going on.

I am going to stay here with the Colonel as long as it isn't too dangerous. I am sure there is no need for you to worry over this business at all.

Mac, August 22, 1937

A Close Call for Mac and Chennault

Chennault, Watson, Smith, Folmar and Mac, the remaining members of the American group, first stayed at the Metropole Hotel in Nanking. They then moved into one of H.H. Kung's homes for a few days.

On the third night of staying in the palace, it was attacked by the Japanese.

Mac and Chennault were flattened by a blast of flame and flying steel. In the morning, they noticed the wall was pockmarked with shrapnel. They'd had another close call.

It seemed the Japanese had discovered the palace was used during the day for the Generalissimo's meetings, but did not know that at night the Generalissimo slept in a modest cabin nearby.

By August 31, 1937, Mac and Chennault were living on Purple Mountain at the Nanking Country Club which overlooked a golf course, airdrome and valley. He and Chennault watched air battles from the mountain and occasionally endangered their lives doing so.

Reported by Sebie Smith, unpublished manuscript

Not reported by Mac in any letter home

There probably is one of the greatest Wars coming up in this part of the world that can be imagined...and it is practically impossible to guess what is going to happen. It is quite possible that a World War will be the outcome.

...we have had a few scares but no one was hurt other than a few skinned knees running through briars to bombproof shelters.

Mac, September 1, 1937

Nanking
September 1, 1937

The first mail that I have received from home and or the States finally caught up with me yesterday. Letters from Malcolm and Lucie and several people in Montgomery.

Glad that Lucie is feeling so much better and that Malcolm is getting along O.K. Also the report that Mother is hail and Hearty and working in the gardens every day signifies all is well. Also that you are pretty busy means something too.

Mail service is certainly terrible in this part of the world at present and from all evidences it looks asmif it will be sometime before things get back towards normal.

There probably is one of the greatest Wars coming up in this par of the world than can be imagined. At present the situation looks seric one day and calmed down the next and it is practically impossible to guess what is going to happen. It is quite possible that a World War will be the outcome - naturally we are hoping for the best and hoping that our Diplomatic Corps can take care of the situation by weilding the pen. Excitement ran High several days ago when Chinese Flyers dropped bombs of the Dollar Liner, The Pres. Hoover, by mistake. It is regrettable and it was a mistake and not deliberate. The pilots have all been punished. It was a shame and real hard luck.

Most of our crowd, especially the Married ones have all gone to Manila. However, Cecil Folmar is still here. His wife aslo is in Manila. Col. Chennault, Watson, Smith, Myself and several others that you don't know are here and we are still acting purely in the role of Advisers and Non-combatants. However, we have had a few scares but no one was hurt other than a few skinned knees running through briars to Bombproof shelters. Lot os joking about it after it was allmover.

Remember I will try and take care of myself as long as I can and if things get toodangerous well I will get out of here the best way that I can. If mails don't reach you. Don't worry. I will get in touch with you every once in a while regardless.

"IF THINGS GET TOO DANGEROUS..."

Remember I will try and take care of myself as long as I can and if things get too dangerous well I will get out of here the best way that I can. If mails don't reach you. Don't worry.

Mac, Nanking, September 1, 1937

Madame Chiang made a speech to America over the radio this AM that I hope everyone in the States heard. She covered the conditions here very clearly and was very mild in describing some of the atrocious things that the Japs have done. They have bombed passenger trains, buses, private motor cars, defenseless areas of all kinds.

Their war machine is running amuck and it may take some other great Nation to help stop them. Because if Japan wins here – Lord knows what ideas will come into their alert brains then. They naturally have been planning this war for many years and are going to exercise everything in their power to win it.

The Chinese are fighting and fighting hard. The Japanese did not expect opposition so strong. They had planned on capturing all of China in just a few weeks, but their plans have gone a little astray. One of the fiercest wars in history is being fought around Shanghai. The outcome is impossible to predict at this time, but we do know that the Japanese thought that they would be in possession of a lot of China by this time."

All of us are working like the very devil – they need us now more than ever…

Nanking,
September 12, 1937.

Dad,

Well the War is still going on and in a big way., The Japanese raising hell everywhere. I imagine that the papers cover the real ation fairly well in a general way so will not say much about it.

Madam Chiang made a speeech to America over the radio this AM I hope everyone in the States heard. She covered the conditions very clearly and was very mild in describing some of the atrocious s that the Japs have done. They have bombed passenger trains, buses te motor cars, defenseless areas of all kinds. Their war machine ning amuck and it may take some other great Nation to help stop Because if Japan wins here – Lord knows what ideas will come in alert brains then. They naturally have been planning this war for ears and are going to exercise everything in their power to win

The Chinese are fighting and fighting hard. The Japs did not opposition so strong. They had planned on capturing all of China a few weeks. But their plans have gone a little astray. One of rcest wars in history is being fought around Shanghai. The out- impossible to predict at this time. But we do know that the Japs that they would be in possession of a lot of China at this time y really are not. There are – or were nearly 500,000,000 Chinese and there is only 75,000,000 people in Japan. So it looks like y can just hold here own for a long war that Japan will just cave

if China can just hold here own for a long war that Japan will just cave
in from census hunger.

ll of us are working like the very devil – they need us now ever and we are really putting our shoulders to the wheel ng. Time is flying by and we are having plenty of excitement.

Japs are past masters at spreading propaganda. Their official re a great laugh to us. From the reports that you people are ck in the States according to Japanese spokemen – the Japs sful and superior and supreme in everything that they do and the Chinese that are doing all the dirty tricks and blaming The English papers make plenty mirth in their daily papers. re the targets of many jibes and jokes and on the side plenty ass cussing, too.

or me – I am feeling great and not a bit alarmed over my so I don't think you should be. There are four of us here and we have a large House of the certain Club and our servant so everything is OK.

ecieving much
st letter

C.S. Wu,
Aeronaut

I am feeling great and not a bit alarmed over my own safety so I don't think you should be. There are four of us here in Nanking and we have a large house of the certain Club and our servant and guards so everything is OK.

Mac, September 12, 1937

> Their object was to wipe out the Chinese planes…our air force is still working.
>
> Mac, September 21, 1937

Until this time, biplane fighters of the competing air forces possessed roughly similar performance. However, the Japanese found far more resistance than they expected. They sent in their "first line planes," the Type 96 and 97 monoplanes which were much quicker than the Hawk II and III biplanes. Only the Hawk Special was faster than these new types. The Chinese Air Force no longer fought on equal terms, and losses mounted quickly.

Nanking
September 21, 1937.

…is past week I have recieved your and Mother's note written …e. I was indeed glad to hear from you. The first time I have …from you in over two months. I know you and Mother are really …in the devil Altoona was – I can't place it. Lucie must be visit- ing some of here friends in North Alabama. Glad to hear that she is bet ter.

Now for the war ;- I guess the most startling news is that from previous news and official reports put out by the Japanese so called spokesman is that the Chinese Air Force has been completely destroyed. The Jap airmen evidently made a lot of false reports to their Commanding officers about victories and hits on objectives. One thing that the Japs have done and that is they have dropped a lot of bombs. They have bombed almost every field in China. But their accuracy has been lousy. From first reports they were supposed to have the best air Force in the world and were afraid of kno one. But they lost plenty of face when China's small Air Force locked horns with them and slowed them down plenty. The Japs began burning the cables for reinforcements. So they have sent their first line planes and pilots to bust us and completely destroy the Chinese Air Force AGAIN.

On the night of September 18th Chinese Airplanes appeared in the sky at 7:40 PM and successfully bombed the Japanese wharfs and depots along the Whangpoo in the Yangtsepoo area. A great deal of damage was done by the Chinese raiders. Numerous fires were started from their incendiary bombs. Distruction was rather severe to the Japs. The Chinese Air Force continued the attack until after midnight and I imagine that the Emperor was aroused in his sleep when after he was informed that the Chinese Air Force was no more they suddenly appeared and busted hell out of an important supply position. One Chinese airplane was brought down by Japanese anti-aircraft guns. It was later reported that two Jap ships were hit by bombs an d one sank. And from last nights papers it appears that the Japs have departed from this area all ships. Was the Emperor mad about this ? So the next morning the Japs sent every airplane avail- able to Nanking to destroy our Air Force again. They arrived about nine in the A.M. and the air above Nanking was full of airplanes spitting lead at each other. From where we live (At the Country Club – at the foot of Purple Mountain –7 miles from the city) we could see everything The Japs were desperate. They bombed the city(Chinese section), little damage. Their object was to wipe out the Chinese planes. After calling the roll at night fall we were all even with them – and our air force is still working.

I guess most of this is in … …to all … …pers but not details. Love …n busy as the devil.

…[from] official reports put out by the Japanese so-called spokesman is that the Chinese Air Force has been completely destroyed. The Jap airmen evidently made a lot of false reports to their Commanding Officers…

On the night of September 18th Chinese airplanes appeared in the sky at 7:40 PM and successfully bombed the Japanese wharfs and depots along the Whangpoo in the Yangtsepoo area. A great deal of damage was done by the Chinese raiders…

I imagine that the Emperor was aroused in his sleep when [the destroyed Chinese Air Force] suddenly appeared and busted hell out of important supply positions.

Mac, September 21, 1937

Sept. 19th

As the Colonel predicted:—

"The Japanese will come to Nanking with pursuit supporting Bombers"

日 期 Date	乘機式樣 Type of Plane	任務記號 Mission (Code No.)	任 務 概 略 A BRIEF STATEMENT OF MISSION		FLYING TIME				飛行次數 No. of Flights
					任務航員 As Pilot		任觀察員 As Observer		
					點 Hrs.	分 Min.	點 Hrs.	分 Min.	
1937 Sept.									
1	Hawk III	1j	Nanking	Radio Test ✓		44			1
2	"	1-e	"	Dive Bombing Demonstration		30			"
3	"	x-c	Nanking-Anking + return	Cross-country		330			2
"		1j	Nanking	Radio Test		30			1
7			"			100			
9	CR-19	t-a	"	Flight Test		100			
11	Hawk III	1j	"	Radio Test		34			
18			"			20			
20	Hawk II	t-a		Test		30			
21			"			44			
22			"	Practice		14			
24		1-h	"	Reconnaissance		310			
27	CR-19	1j	"	Check Flight ⓒ		30			
"	Hawk II		"	Practice ✓		44			"
28			"			30			

Night Dive Bombing

It was the first time in the History of Aviation that Dive Bombing has been used at night.

They all came back OK. Several boats were hit.

Mac's CAF journal, Sept. 7–8, 1937

Sept. 7th Monday

Out to the f...
...

so far abo...
When ...
Col. "C" an...
waiting there ... found out
that the special mission was
in progress —
   I had had no tiffin so
Col. C and I returned for
early chow and we were
back at the field at 7³⁰ to
see the boys return — It
was the first time in the
History of aviation that
Dive Bombing has been
used at night —
   They all came back OK
several boats were hit. We
were elated and later displeased
to learn some started dive show...

Sept. 8th

Results — and damned good
ones — "Special mission" was sent
out and all came back — and
best of all — Two Destroyers were
sunk and one Cruiser badly
damaged — The Japs were
hurt by this — So early
this a.m. They sent planes
to Bomb — Kashing — Hangchow
and Kwangteh — 6t Bombers

and 4 pursuit — were intercepted
and a nice battle took place
in the vicinity of Tai Ho —
   Results — Two Jap
Bombers shot down
and China's first official "ace"
Lt. Lui — however he had
a close call in this fight —
Shot the wingman and
filled the leader full of
holes when Jap pursuit
shot him — he was
shot in the Buttocks and
the bullet traveled about an foot
down his leg — but he fought
on and chased Japs off —
back — Then he found that
his landing gear had been...

Logbook & Journal Entries

日期 Date	飛機式樣 Type of Plane	任務記號 Mission (Code No.)	任務概略 A BRIEF STATEMENT	OF MISSION	飛行時間 FLYING TIME				飛行次數 No. of Flights
					任飛航員 As Pilot		任觀察員 As Observer		
					點 Hrs.	分 Min.	點 Hrs.	分 Min.	
1937 October									
1	Hawk 7A	1-2	Nanking	Reconnaissance	1	10			1
2			:			44			
	Hawk III	4	:	Radio Test		20			
6	Hawk 7A	1-2	:	Reconnaissance		24			
2/	:	:	:			20			
2/	:	4-a	:	Test		110			

Sept. 22 —

To-day I may have been a damned fool for more than one reason — but then one leads their life — and I reminisce.

Another raid to-day — I flew the 75 " to keep it out of danger from bombing."

A couple of holes in the card and vicinity.

Practiced golf — played cribbage — I lost at it, too.

Sept. 29th

— I have asked the Colonel time and time again to express himself regarding the employment of bombardment and pursuit. He has done so vigorously. Quite naturally we feel that all we learn in this war should be brought to the attention of our own countries air force. Definite proof that so much of the omni-pilot doctrine of Bombardment has been wrong will cause some one to back water.

The power of pursuit in every phase that the Colonel used to teach has been clearly brought out. Let alone the several additional tasks he has taught

---

Oct. 1st

" Reconnaissance to Shanghai took-off at 2:30 landed 4:15. Japs have about 30 planes on a field near Point island."

Col. made plans to destroy same but we have a weak commander and I am afraid they didn't go out.

---

and assigned to them.

In China we are faced with two vital factors to a real competent pursuit force:
1. Lack of equipment
2. " of experienced pilots.

If China had had only 200 pursuit planes alone — with their pilots as they are — Japan would not be anchoring their navy in a river or envading the interior daily.

The supremacy of the air is what counts — and pursuit is the answer — without pursuit you cannot operate your other branches of military aviation. I hope we can make our own country see the light.

Oct. 2nd

" Reconnaissance to Shanghai" took-off 2:10 land 5:05. Found several Buckets - two filled. Mission # 2.

Filling Buckets

October 2nd "Reconnaissance to Shanghai" took off 2:10 landed 5:05. Found several Buckets – two filled. Mission #2.

Mac's CAF journal, Sept. 19, 22, 29, Oct. 1 & 2, 1937

September 28th
Nanking

Dear Dad,

I hope my letters are reaching you O.K. because I don't want you people back home to worry too much. I know you are troubled by all of the newspaper reports etc., therefore I intend these letters of mine to clear things up considerable and to ease your mind.

The most interesting experience of my life is in the making. Day by day and many times at night. Since my last letter the Japanese have become more than bold. They informed all of the Foreign Ambassadors to move out of Nanking and to take their Nationals with them by the 21st of Sept. because the Japanese Air Force was going to bomb Nanking until it was level with the surface of the earth. What a furore this caused. Immediately the wires were hot back to London,Washington,Paris, Russia, and the rest of the Capitols. The answers of most of the Countries to the Japs was that they (the Japs) would be held responsible for damage to foreign property and life. The biggest joke of the affair was our own American Ambassador, Mr. Johnson. He took his staff and left the Consulate to seak refuge aboard the Luzon, American gunboat stationed here. He was severely criticised by everyone. The next day he returned and offered an explanation. It was a fool move and not very smart on his part. He saw his mistake and corrected the best he could.

The Japs came with their bombers and have been coming ever since. Their attacks have been fierce. They began dropping bombs on the city the 23rd and have been killing several hundred non combatants (civilians) daily. A great deal of damage to property but nothing extremely serious. They are attempting to cut all channels of transportation and communication by bombing the Light Co., power plant, railroad stations and docks. Their marksmanship in bombing is even poorer than the Chinese. Soon the Japs should get better because they have been doing lots of work. We are still fighting them with pursuit and anti-aircraft guns.

Sept. 25th, Many news reel men were in Nanking and got some good pictures. They were, in fact jubilant, saying that they got better shots here than in Spain. On this day, the Japs sent 5 waves of attack, the first starting at about 9:30. The scene was all set. Cameras were ready. Guns were ready, pursuit was ready and the Japs came in on time. Their first objective was the RR station. They used dive bombers - and at this time one of the most spectacular raids that probably has ever been witnessed took place - down the bombers came - in more or less chain formation - motors roaring - machine guns wide open - suddenly the sky was literally filled with anti-aircraft shells - eager eyes and cameras watched the diving ships when - it happened ; one ship in the dive was hit by a shell, the plane busrt into flames and continued the dive leaving a blazing, smoking trail to mark its path to destruction. Before this ship hitnthe ground, another plane was hit and down it came, the same way. The fire visible for miles. One of the two ships did not drop its bombs and when it hit the ground - well the bombs went off and there was nothing left. Thats the story and you may see it on the screen.

For myself, I am getting fatter and feeling great. Be sure and answer by air mail because regular mail is stopped by the Japs.

Until next week, Love to all , Wm

I hope my letters are reaching you O.K. because I don't want you people back home to worry too much…I intend these letters of mine to clear things up considerable and to ease your mind.

The most interesting experience of my life is in the making. Day by day and many times at night.

The Japanese have become more than bold. They informed all of the Foreign Ambassadors to move out of Nanking and to take their Nationals with them…because the Japanese Air Force was going to bomb Nanking until it was level …with the surface of the earth.

Our own American Ambassador, Mr. Johnson…took his staff and left the Consulate…He was severely criticized by everyone. The next day he returned…"

The Japs began dropping bombs on the city the 23rd and have been killing several hundred non combatants (civilians) daily. "

September 25th, many news reel men were in Nanking and got some good pictures. They were in fact jubilant, saying that they got better shots here than in Spain."

Cameras were ready. Guns were ready, pursuit was ready and the Japs came in on time."

…down the bombers came – motors roaring – machine guns wide open – suddenly the sky was literally filled with anti-aircraft shells – eager eyes and cameras watched…

Mac, September 28, 1937

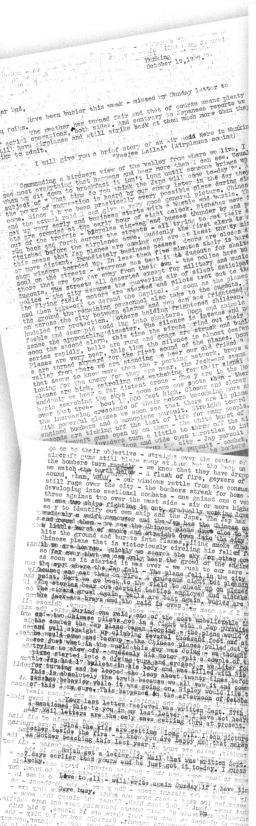

STORY OF AN AIR RAID—OCTOBER 12, 1937 NANKING
"Feejee Lailai" (Airplanes Coming)

The weather has turned fair and that of course means plenty of aerial operations, both sides. And contrary to Japanese reports we still have airplanes and still strike back much more than they like to admit.

Commanding a birdseye view of the valley from where we live, I can see most everything that happens and hear more than I can see. Usually when we sit down to breakfast it isn't long until someone brings up the subject of "What time do you think the Japs will come to-day?" As if the power of suggestion is heard by our enemy later in the day they do come.

Since I have been practically every possible place during alarms and the actual raid I can give a very good general picture. Chinese all get up very early and business starts with a hustle and bustle. The streets are crowded at the early hour of eight o'clock. Rickshaws move in and out of the traffic—bicycles zig-zag and busses thunder by and people run back and forth across the streets—all trying to get their chores finished before the airplanes come.

Suddenly the first alarm is sounded, this means that Jap planes are coming and are at least thirty minutes or more distant. Immediately business ceases, doors are closed and the show windows boarded up. In less than five minutes there is hardly a soul on the street—everyone has beat it to dugouts for shelter. For those that are too far away from their own—the police have built public dugouts. The streets are all deserted except for military and municipal police—the city assumes the quivering air of silent anticipation.

At the Flying field, motors are started and pilots trot out to their planes and then take-off to defend the Capitol. As soon as the planes clear the ground the remaining personnel also take to the dugouts. I have ridden across the city between alarms and you can see the frightened groups huddled for protection. Mothers holding frightened children. Old men feeble and decrepit toddling into shelters. Dogs and animals of all kind sense the approaching disaster. The silence is intense and nerve wracking.

Soon the second alarm, this time the sirens grind out their pulsating series rapidly, bells are rung and gongs are struck and bugles blow, the Planes are very near, this time the silence is almost deafening—all ears are turned skyward for the first sound of the planes.

Down in the valley from where we are standing we hear our old friend "a Jack-ass" that seems to know more than the reporting network, brays and we begin looking for the enemy for they are near, the Jack-ass seems to know. Our planes are high, patrolling and watching for their signal to close in – suddenly we hear a far distant drone – they are in the Northeast – we begin searching the skies – soon someone spots them – there they are over that tree – about 12,000 feet high. Closer and closer they come – the increasing crescendo of their motors becoming more and more audible.

With powerful glasses we soon see that there are 15 planes, 9 big twin engined bombers and 6 monoplane pursuit. Straight toward the City – the seconds are ticking off the last of life for many people. Closer, now our Anti-aircraft guns open up on them – the white bursts of smoke high in the sky makes the invaders turn a little to throw off the aim of the gunners. Our pursuit sees the Japs and wide open throttles to intercept – it is a race to keep the bombers from the city – Jap pursuit streak to halt the Chinese planes – pursuit against pursuit – combat, high in the heavens, motors now roar, round and round, the bombers have escaped and go on to their objective – straight over the center of the City.

Anti-aircraft guns still blaze away at them but they keep on – suddenly we see the bombers turn rapidly – we know that they have dropped their bombs and we watch the earth below – a flash of fire, geysers of smoke, then the sound, wham, WHAM – our windows rattle from the concussion – dogfights still rage over the city – the bombers streak for home – the battle is developing into sectional combats – one against one over the east side, three against two over the west side – six or more higher, then suddenly we see two ships fighting it out, gradually working lower and lower, it is easy to identify our own ship and the Japs. The Jap has the upper hand, suddenly a swift maneuver and the Jap has the Chinese on his tail, round and round then – we see the Chinese plane draw close to the Jap and then a little burst of smoke and straight down into the city – the Jap plane hits the ground and bursts into flames, piling smoke almost as high as the Chinese plane that is victoriously circling his fallen foe. We cheer until we are hoarse.

Quickly we search the sky for other combats – some are so far away that we can only hear the growl of the engines – then almost as soon as it started it was over – we rush to our cars – and drive to the spot where the Jap fell – the plane fell in the city on several small houses and set them on fire. A gruesome sight but pleasant from our viewpoint. Next we go back to the field to check up on planes and pilots. The stories bear out certain tactics employed and mistakes committed. The sirens growl again, bells are beat again, bugles are blown again, the jackass brays and the raid is over.

During one raid, one of the most unbelievable things happened – two Chinese pilots got in a fight with a Jap pursuiter and during the combat the Jap plane began looping – the plane would dive very low and pull straight up climbing several thousand feet and stalling – down he would come and back up – the Chinese planes pulled out to the side to see just what in the world this guy was doing – we thought the bird was trying to show off – suddenly his motor spit a couple of times and the plane started into a diving turn and crashed – we later found out that the Jap had 17 bullets in his body and was killed with his controls set for turning and he looped the loop about twenty times before crashing.

This is absolutely the truth because we all saw it and commented on the strange behavior while it was going on. Ripley would like to get a hold of this I am sure. This happened on the afternoon of October 12th. (Mac, October 19, 1937)

Nanking
October, 31, 1937.

Dear Dad,

It doesn't seem possible that it has been over 4 months since I left Hangchow with the Colonel and Smith on our Inspection trip. As you remember we were in Sianfu when ordered back to take care of rapid preparations. Arriving here about the 9th of August and have been here ever since. Time hasn't flown - it has whizzed right passed us.

This week I recieved your letter mailed and one from Uncle James mailed the fifth. Glad is going along O.K. back home. I think I have al Mr. Roosevelts speech. It went over big on this Now the Nine Power Treaty is being watched close Japan has absolutely refused to discuss peace or erence. They have definitely decided to conquer to her knees. And believe you me the Japs are gc tough time doing it. They may kill and destroy n must be remembered that for the first time - Chi Japs are at this war business right now simply l that China is getting stronger and that if they will never have another chance. The one big mist the underestimation of the Chinese resistance a Personally I cannot help but feel that if with a at all, China will become victorious in driving China though China will suffer collosal loss in And it will take many years to recover. But Chi China is going to fight it out.

Chinese are mainly pacifists and they Nation or interfere with the progress of any ot great leaders, Generalissimo and Madame Chiang of the outstanding figures of the world to-day. their work can continue unabated. I cannot say admiration for them.

I know that the newspapers have been Japanese victories in China. It 5 explain Japanese capture, a small village, 5 cross a soldires is killed, or wounded, or train is wre thing that the Japanese did, their brilliant mo Agency" plays it up to the skys." apan the inv The Rising Sun". I guess they thin that their country that the sun rises . Well - collective so hot. I think that this fact has been brough world. They have bombed practically every hosp China regardless of what flag was flying over have bombed and killed defenseless women and c every front. They have even ruthlessly machine eigners while they were out(horse-back)riding. killed just out of savage impulse. They think and no one will be the worse off especially th " So sorry ", " Regrets ", all that sort of nc masters at the art of lying and playing in dip there will come a day - and woe is me - somethi worm might turn.

the boys did a marvelous job in getting

Don't worry about me as to danger. One has this country. Dodging richshas and what not Chi really is an art. But as for War danger - so fa 66 Air raids all mostly aimed at the field. Of beat a hasty retreat to a haven of safety and to count the bomb holes in the flying field. Th dropped plenty bombs at the field. But for resu I would say practically nothing. It was a grand many planes - much more than the Chinese. Beari the deeper an offense goes into enemy teritory.

Don't get alarmed at any so called hot nev wife heard through some agency that Cecil had h to catch a boat for Honolulu to sooth her - esp are expecting another child.

That's all for this week.

Love to all,

China is unified…and she is going to fight

Mac, October 31, 1937

It doesn't seem possible that it has been over 4 months since I left Hangchow with the Colonel and Smith on our Inspection trip. As you remember we were in Sianfu when ordered back to take care of rapid preparations. Arriving here about the 9th of August and have been here ever since. Time hasn't flown - it has whizzed right past us.

This week I received your letter mailed about October 14th and one from Uncle James mailed the fifth. Glad to hear that all is going along O.K. back home. I think I have already mentioned Mr. Roosevelt's speech. It went over big on this side of the pond. Now the Nine Power Treaty is being watched closely by everyone. Japan has absolutely refused to discuss peace or attend the conference. They have definitively decided to conquer China. Beat her to her knees. And believe you me the Japs are going to have a real tough time doing it. They may kill and destroy many people but it must be remembered that for the first time - China is unified. The Japs are at this war business right now simply because they know that China is getting stronger and if they wait any longer they will never have another chance. The one big mistake so far has been the underestimation of the Chinese resistance and "Esprit de Corps". Personally I cannot help but feel that if with any degree of luck at all, China will become victorious in driving the Japs out of all China though China will suffer colossal loss in both men and property. And it will take many years to recover. But China will recover and China is going to fight it out.

Chinese are mainly pacifists and they desire to invade no

Nation or interfere with the progress of any other people. The two great leaders, Generalissimo and Madame Chiang Kai-shek, are two of the outstanding people of the world to-day. Our prayer is that their work can continue unabated. I cannot say enough in praise and admiration for them.

I know that the newspapers have been playing up the many Japanese victories in China. It can be explained that every time the Japanese capture a small village, or cross a creek, or one of their soldiers is killed, or wounded, or train is wrecked or just anything that the Japanese did, their brilliant mouthpiece "Domei News Agency" plays it up to the skies. "Japan the invincible." "The Land of the Rising Sun." I guess they think that their country is the only country that the sun rises. Well - collectively the Japs are not so hot. I think this fact has been brought out in the eyes of the world. They have bombed practically every hospital and school in China regardless of what flag was flying over the buildings. They have bombed and killed defenseless men and children on practically every front. They have even ruthlessly machine gunned Shanghai foreigners while they were out horse-back riding. Many people have been killed just out of savage impulse. They think they can do anything and no one will be worse off especially themselves. Apologize, "So sorry", "Regrets", all that sort of nonsense. They are past masters at the art of lying and playing in diplomatic red tape. But there will come a day - and woe is me - something tells me that the worm will turn.

Don't worry about me as to danger. One has to take chances in this country. Dodging rickshaws and what not Chinese drivers. It really is an art. But as for War danger - so far we have had only 66 Air raids all mostly aimed at the field. Of course we always beat a hasty retreat to a haven of safety and then rush back to count the bomb holes in the flying field. The Japs have certainly dropped plenty bombs at the field. But for results in their favor I would say practically nothing. It was a grand show - the Japs lost many planes - much more than the Chinese. Bearing out a theory that the deeper an offense goes into enemy territory the weaker it becomes.

Don't get alarmed at any so called hot news - Cecil Folmar's wife heard through some agency that Cecil had been killed so he had to catch a boat for Honolulu to soothe her - especially since they are expecting another child.

Mac, October 31, 1937

> Don't worry about me as to danger. One has to take chances in this country. Dodging rickshaws and what not Chinese drivers. It really is an art.
>
> But as for War danger - so far we have had only 66 air raids...
>
> Mac, October 31, 1937

Nanking
Nov. 28 1937

Dear Dad,

Wham- just like that things have picked up to where we are so busy and activity is so condensed that it is darned h ard to keep track of everything that is going on.

Several days ago the Japs broke the Chinese lines near the strategical positions and news of this leaked out by "Grapevine Telegraph " resulting in a wholesale rush for boats and trains and cars to evacuate into the interior. The entire city has been upset and it looks bad when you don't know the real facts. Naturally the people only hear a lot of rumors and that is all that it takes to get them going so maybe it is a good thing. At least the streets are not so crowded and there arn't as many crazy drivers on the streets.

We have had plenty of excitement ourselves. You know the story about the man that started a   rumor about a gold mine and he heard it told again so much that he began to believe it too. So we have had a time controlling things.

Our gang still intact here - and the plans are if we get caught by some freak of luck we will go aboard the US Gunboat in the Yangtse about a mile from where we are staying. Of course we have plans for going into the interior ourselves - possibly Hankow. So don't worry.

The Chinese still have a fighting chance and I can't help but believe that in the course of time that China will come out of top.

Mail has practically been severed. Our mutual friends in the Aeronautical Commission have already moved to Hankow and since we are here chances for our mail reaching us promptly is not good so we are carrying on the best we can.

We have had a few cold spells lat... ...othing to compare
with what is in store for us. Pl... ...rwear and sweaters
have been purchased to ... ...nd when I get all
dolled up to g... ...ve gained about
50 po...

...- but if you don't
...e it hard for the

Wham – just like that things have picked up to where we are so busy and activity is so condensed that it is darned hard to keep track of everything that is going on.

Our gang still intact here – and the plans are if we get caught by some freak of luck we will go aboard the U.S. gunboat in the Yangtse about a mile from where we are staying. *[ed. note: The gunboat was the USS Panay.]*

The Chinese still have a fighting chance and I can't help but believe that in the course of time that China will come out on top.

Mac, November 28, 1937

The Fall of Nanking
Early December, 1937

Shanghai fell in early November, and the Japanese continued to attack the capital, Nanking. The Chinese made a gallant effort to hold Nanking but by mid-November 1937, the American group began planning for their escape, and Chiang Kai-shek's government made plans to move as well.

The Japanese believed that taking the Chinese capital would result in the end of the war. Instead, a fake retreat to Hankow masked the government's move to Chungking, which was 2000 miles in the interior of the country, out of the range of carrier attack from the coast. The troops were ordered to defend Nanking as long as possible, to buy time for this retreat.

As the fighting intensified, Mac went on more reconnaisance missions. They provided a clear picture of the current situation to the Chinese High Command. Despite the outstanding capabilities of the Hawk 75 Special, these missions were some of the most dangerous of Mac's career. He doesn't bring that up in the letters home.

The bombing of the air field near Purple Mountain left thousands of craters. "Coolies were up to the task of filling the bomb craters in a matter of hours and keeping the field in action." Mac had a high regard for the hard work they did, very often with only hand tools and muscle.

In a letter from December 6, 1937, Mac described the details surrounding the ensuing fight for Nanking. After piloting numerous recon missions over Nanking, his knowledge of the region is evident:

> Since the river curves around the city, this means that the Jap gunboats can bombard the city from the river. The ground troops can approach from the East and the Southeast.
>
> The Jap plans to flank Nanking via Wuhu Southwest have received a setback. Chinese troops in the sector around Kwangteh and south of Lake

> The Japs in Shanghai are making things pretty miserable for the foreigners there. They are beginning to get bold and brazen, and it looks like trouble is ahead. I only hope that the other countries interested will not wait until it is so late.
>
> Mac, December 6, 1937

Tahu have counter-attacked, recaptured several important towns and are at present driving the Japs back. In fact, a very cagey flanking movement by the Chinese has cut off over 7,000 Japanese soldiers in this sector.

On the other hand, the Japanese troops are driving fiercely forward on the North of the line near Chinkiang.

The isolationist policies reflected in the various U.S. Neutrality Acts of the 1930s would not provide protection from Japan's ambitions, but as Mac comments, this seemed like common knowledge in China - everyone knew this likely outcome except the American government.

> The Japs in Shanghai are making things pretty miserable for the foreigners there. They are beginning to get bold and brazen, and it looks like trouble is ahead. I only hope that the other countries interested will not wait until it is so late.
>
> They desire to control the entire Orient. The Philippines, French-Indo China [Vietnam], Hong Kong, Java, Sumatra, and the Islands and possibly India. Australia is alarmed and I know so many other people that are able to see through all this realize that, if Japan is allowed to continue this conquest, it will only be a matter of years before she will try to take the Hawaiian Islands.

Mac and the other Americans planned to stay in Nanking as long as possible, and to return if they could. Chennault made the call to get out on December 4. They escaped only a few days before the city was overrun by Japanese troops.

Prince Asaka, a member of the royal family, became temporary commander of the forces during the

Hankow
December 6, 1937

Dear Dad,

I came to Hankow last Friday the 3rd for two reasons. For about one week now I have been suffering from a pretty bad head cold. In spite of long underwear and what nots I came in with a beaut. I immediately went to bed but I couldn't shake the thing loose. So on Wednesday night after having my usual trouble of an earache I called in a Doctor. He took one look at the ear and got his knife out and lanced same on the spot. I felt relieved immediately. However, the cold still remained in the upper story and my sinus began to bother me too much so I mentioned to the Col. the status of the cold and he told me to pack up and go to Hankow were I could get better medical attention and be in the clear if they had to evacuate Nanking suddenly. So I came up in one of the Generalissimo's plane, the Boeing and called a doctor. There were no rooms at the Hotels orthe YMCA so the Doctor suggested that I stay a couple of days in the Hospital so I took him up on the matter. Just jumped in his car and came down as a guest would ordinarily. I still feel stuffed up in the head but expect to be up and about in a couple of days. Don't know where I will stay. Probably get a cot and move in with about 4 other fellows.

The Chinese are making a determined effort to keep the Japs out of Nanking and I believe that it will go down in history as one of the major battles of the world. Defense directed by the Generalissimo himself. The mornings paper says that the advance Jap vanguard is only 22 miles from Nanking. This means that the real fighting for the defense of the City will start in a very short time. It is going to cost the Japs plenty of lives to capture the Capitol but I am almost positive that they can do it. They have three approaches. Since the river curves around the city this means that Jap gunboats can bombard the city from the river. The ground troops can approach from the East and the Southeast. The Jap plans to flank Nanking via Wuhu Southwest has received a setback. Chinese troops in the Sector around Kwangteh and south of Lake Tahu have counter-attacked recaptured several important towns and are at present driving the Japs back. In fact a very cagy flanking movement by the Chinese has cut off over 7000 Jap soldiers in this sector. On the otherhand the Japs are driving fiercely forward on the North of the Line near Chinkiang. So the scene is all set, the orchestras tuned up and we are ready for the curtain. We were planning to stay in Nanking to the last moment but because of my illness and the difficulty of evacuation getting more serious we decided to move out. None of our crowd is there now. We may go back if the tables are turned. In fact we will go back.

The Japs in Shanghai are making things pretty miserable for the Foreigners there. They are beginning to get bold and brazen and it looks like trouble is ahead. I only hope that the other countries interested will not wait until it is so late that they will have a real job of exterminating the Japs. It is a shame that they are allowed to go on in the present manner. Because this is only the beginning. They desire to control the entire Orient. The Philipines, French-Indo China, Hongkong, Java, Sumatra and the Islands and possibly India. Australia is alarmed and I know so many other people that are able to see thru all this realize that if Japan is allowed to continue this conquest it will only be a matter of years before she

...the real fighting for the defense of [Nanking] will start in a very short time. It is going to cost...

So the scene is all set, the orchestra's tuned up and we are ready for the curtain.

...this is only the beginning...if Japan is allowed to continue this conquest it will only be a matter of years before she will try to take the Hawaiian Islands.

Mac, December 6, 1937

final assault (December 2–6, 1937) while its aging commander, General Matsui, was ill. Asaka allegedly issued the order to "kill all captives." The Battle of Nanking, given as December 1 through December 13, 1937, ended when Chinese defenses collapsed. Following from December 13 through February 10, 1938, the occupation by Japanese soldiers is generally known as "The Rape of Nanking" or the "Nanking Massacre."

Estimates of the final number of deaths in Nanking range from 50,000 to 300,000 to nearly 500,000. The savage behavior of the soldiers, directed against both civilians and military personnel, included widespread looting, torture and rape.

The few surviving aircraft in the pursuit squadron were relocated to Hankow, only 150 miles away. Not particularly safe, but for now, it would be a temporary refuge for the American air advisors.

will try to take the Hawaian Islands.

Japans conquest is not unlike a fire. Fanned by the breezes of victory and kindled by firewood domination it is likely to spread the world over.

In the North Japs preach to the Chinese that if the Chinese will only join hands with them - the Whitemans yoke in the Orient can be broken and thrown away for ever. This is only used as propoganda but it does weigh something.

Of course most all foreigners knew that the Nine power treaty would be another first class wall-walla and it was. So as we predicted from the very first it would be necessary for two nations to join hands and Navies and police the situation as it should be.

China is in no way to blame. Under her present leadership much progress has been made and The New Life Movement has accomplished worlds of good and had the movement been given a chance it would have taken only one generation fro China to become abreast of the world in the March of Progress and civilization. Now - ??

I have given you an address temporarily. I don't think I will stay in Hankow long. I most likely will be stationed at Nanchang but I don't know yet. So use this address with please forward on it.

I haven't heard from you folks in about a month. I know the mail is somewhere in China but Lords knows where. Post Offices have moved from Nanking as well as the Commission so you can see why.

Japanese Sink American Gunboat USS *Panay*

The most sensational news concerning Americans broke Sunday afternoon and we are still picking up fragments of the real issue to date. Sunday afternoon, the Japanese began bombing everything on the river around the Nanking area. The USS Panay and three Socony [Standard Oil Company of New York] boats in the Convoy were all bombed and sunk 29 miles [upriver] from Nanking.

The Japs seem a little out of control of their own command.

Higher Japanese authorities regret the affair very much. But, the Japanese have continually endangered non-combatants, both Chinese and foreigners. They have bombed towns and cities, hospitals, and schools.

I am surprised that this has not happened before.

Mac, December 14, 1937

December 4: A Japanese bomb landed in the water 100 feet from the USS *Panay*.

December 10: A collection of intelligence on the Japanese gathered by Chennault and Mac—notebooks detailing the capabilities, strengths and weaknesses of planes in combat, pictures and film showing individual combat performances, observations of all kind—were placed on the *Panay*.

The cache also included several lockers full of parts and other material taken from downed Japanese planes. These were to be taken to various agencies in Washington, D.C. Chennault believed that the film and notebooks contained valuable information on Japan that the other branches of the U.S. military likely did not have.

December 12: Despite being clearly marked as a U.S. ship, the Japanese attacked and sank the USS *Panay*. Mac and Chennault always wondered if the Japanese knew they had placed the compromising information on the boat, but they were never certain.

December 13: Nanking had fallen.

On the *Panay*, two U.S. Navy crewmen and two civilians were killed. Forty-three Navy crewmen and five civilians were wounded.

It seems unlikely to have been a mistake. Survivors watched from the shore as the crew of a Japanese powerboat raked the *Panay* with machine gun fire.

The boat sent a boarding party onto the deck for a brief visit. Did they retrieve something? Did they set a charge? Were they looking for survivors?

Five minutes after they left, the ship rolled to starboard and sank.

…in regards to the crude and wanton bombing of American boats including the sinking of the *USS Panay*…We feel almost certain that the Japs did this to feel out the Americans and I now think that they are darned sorry that they did it so boldly.

…there were too many eye witnesses that escaped…

Mac, December 18, 1937

PHOTOS The United States gunboat *Panay* sinking on December 12, 1937, after Japanese planes attacked it and other boats on the river. Several Americans were killed or injured. They might be considered the first American victims of Japanese aggression in World War II.

One theory, and a theory Mac believed, says that the Japanese used incidents like these to gauge the will of a country to fight. Mac believed prior attacks on British and French citizens were such tests.

High Wages Attracted Many, Some Qualified

During an interview with Chennault, a young man displayed a stack of his log books listing twelve thousand hours of flying time. Chennault had just short of ten thousand hours after twenty years of extensive flying. Winking at Mac, Chennault asked him to check the pilot on a basic trainer. Mac, grinning reassuringly, said to the young pilot, "Don't worry, it's easy. As a matter of fact, these planes are so easy to fly that I won't even bother to give you a check ride. Just climb in and take it up solo." The pilot stopped at the cockpit, turned pale, and confessed, "I guess I better not. I've never flown a plane before." The high wages had been too tempting.

Mac in center of the International Squadron photo, resting his arm on a bomb. Chennault to his right.

1938
International Squadron

In January 1938 in Hankow, less than ten Chinese fighters were left and many of the best pilots were dead. The Generalissimo wanted to hire an international squadron and Chennault reluctantly agreed. Foreign pilots were hired but they proved to be a rowdy bunch.

Through CAMCO, Bill Pawley sold the Chinese several slow yet long-range Vultee bombers. After a few months of ineffective bombing attempts, the squadron lost nearly all of its planes in a single raid by the Japanese. Unwilling to arise early to fuel and arm their planes as ordered, they prepped their planes before going out for the evening. The Japanese, alerted by their spies at the bars the International Squadron frequented, staged an early morning bombing raid. One hit set off a chain reaction that destroyed the entire fleet.

Chennault disbanded the group as a failure.

FROM UPPER left Russian Pursuits
I-15; I-16; SB-2 Bomber.
Photos by Frank Higgs.

Chennault, the Chinese & the Russians

Chennault calculated that the Japanese would conduct a large raid on Emperor Hirohito's birthday. For the first and only time, he persuaded the Russians and the Chinese to fly a combined mission, planned with great care.

Martha Byrd in *Chennault* told the story like this:

By assembling nearly every plane in China, Chennnault formed a respectable force of sixty-five fighters. He sent a large group of planes in the direction of Nanking and ordered the pilots to make a lot of noise during departure. The Japanese spies saw this and called in an air strike.

On April 29th, 1938, the Japanese attacked with 15 bombers escorted by pursuit planes. The warning net worked perfectly and provided time for the defending forces to get into position.

The Chinese surprised the Japanese over Hankow and forced them to expend fuel reserves performing maneuvers. When the Japanese retreated, they were ambushed by the larger force of Russians poised to intercept the fleeing planes.

With insufficient fuel to maneuver or escape, the Japanese suffered significant losses. According to intelligence reports, 21 planes were shot down. Only 6 returned to their base.

It was an uncommon victory for the Chinese and badly needed for morale.

A Few Months in Hankow
December 1937 to June 1938, Hankow

> "...don't worry. I am as safe here as anywhere else in China. There are quite a few foreigners here in Hankow. I don't know where we will go next – maybe out through Russia.
>
> Mac, December 14, 1937

Late November: *Mac had a cold and sinus infection for a week. Chennault told him to pack up and go to Hankow to get better medical attention and to be in the clear if they had to evacuate Nanking suddenly.*

Mac ended up in a hospital, where he met the U.S. Admiral in charge of the American gunboats on the Yangtze.

December 4: *With the "difficulty of evacuation getting more serious," Chennault decided to evacuate his team to Hankow. Chennault flew the Hawk. Royal Leonard picked up Sebie Smith in a Boeing. Mac assumed the rest came on the Panay. A Japanese bomb landed in the water 100 feet from the Panay.*

December 8: *Mac is out of the hospital and rejoins his group at Roy Leonard's apartment.*

Mac and the other American air force advisors regrouped in Hankow, using Royal Leonard's apartment as a base. Fewer than 10 of their fighter planes were left. Many of the best Chinese pilots were dead. Mac believed that it would take two years to produce a pilot with only the basic skills in place. China didn't have two years.

The Chinese Government had already moved to Chungking, protected by a ring of mountains. The Generalissimo had bet that Japan's attacks in Shanghai and Nanking, cities with large international populations in concession areas, would draw in other nations to help. Official support did not come. Without an air force, China was helpless against Japanese bombing. Without supplies, the army could not fight and expect to prevail. One Chinese general explained the desperate circumstances as "using blood and bone to fight metal."

At the Generalissimo's behest, Chennault set up an International Squadron with volunteers from Germany, France, the Netherlands, the United States and China. This desperate effort wasn't successful militarily, and the pilots spent a great deal of time carousing. The group was disbanded.

Mac witnessed both the fall of Shanghai and the fall of Nanking, and knew first-hand how outmatched the Chinese were.

> The possibilities of a war on a much larger scale seems to be growing daily. There is a rumor that China has signed a military pact with Russia. This may mean something and again it may not. But most everyone feels that Russia wants to take a crack at the Japs. One thing is definite and that is that China must have help in order to repulse the Japanese.

The Russians did come, bringing everything a fighting group needed to survive in war. Unlike the Americans, who were there as individuals and volunteers, the Russians came officially and brought equipment and manpower. Like Roosevelt, Stalin wanted to keep Japan's resources focused on China. The war in China served as a great training ground for Russia's fighter pilots and Air Force.

Mac and Chennault also had great admiration for the Russian pilots. Chennault described pilots who sat ready in their cockpits for 12 hours at a time and then partied all night.

> "It does not seem possible that so much has happened since I left Hangchow last June…"

Hankow, China,
December 18, 1937.

…pretty hard to tell. Nanking has fallen. It does… happened since I left Hangchow last June. As I… is only a short time until another Christmas… writing 1938 on our letters I can hardly keep from… home almost two years. Time is surely flying.

The present situation is pretty much about what the United States is going to do in regards the crude and wanton bombing of American boats including the sinking of the USS Panay. As a matter of fact we cannot help but feel the immediate change of action by the Japanese. We feel almost certain that the Japs did this to feel out the Americans and I now think that they are darned sorry that the did it so boldly.

First, the English were the targets of Japanese atrocities in many ways. The attack on their Ambassador and military Attache, the killing of English troops at Shaghai, the attacks of British boats in the Yangtse and near Canton, the encroaching on British property and many smaller incidents. All incidents were met by the Japs with a courteous answer to British protests with "So sorry". British people here are getting pretty sore about the bold way the Japs are going along. They don't like it one bit. But one thing is that the Japanese found out that the British were not ready to fight over the present situation. Their next move was to see just how the French felt so they arrange several incidents and tried to encroach on French property but they were met with a strong rebuff and they had to back water or else - The French mean business and they don't want the Japs to mess around them as they did the British and therefore the Japs have ceased making things miserable for French subjects. Apparently one thing that was bothering them more than anything else was just how much the United States was interested in this Far East affair. So they (Japs) tried a sample incident on the US Marines in Shanghai and were met with similar treatment as from the French but they wanted to know a little more so they evidently planned a little river Bombing thus the Panay Bombing and attack from the Air and the Army. The Jap planes bombed the Panay and 3 Standard oil boats and then machine gunned the escaping life boats. Several sailors were seriously wounded. Then a Japanese Officer boarded the Panay while the American Flag was still flying and I hear that the crew were also raked by rifle and machine gun fire from the shore. Several parties had to run like the devil for their lives after they reached shore. A pretty cold blooded attack and there is no question as to the identification of the boat because the Flag was flying and also one was painted on the awning especially for airmen to see. The Jap planes came very low and the attack was continued for at least 10 minutes and possibly more. I had planned to leave Nanking by this boat if I had not left earlier but fortunate I did not take it.

The Japs are using every means of trying to smooth the matter over but to no avail The use of Japanese School Children to raise funds to replace the boat is darned near an insult to the injury. Since the beginning of the war the Japanese have very pointedly bombed schools, Hospitals, Missionary controlled property and organizations wantonly. I have seen with my own eyes just how dastardly they have been.

One of the best stories regarding this unauthordox and cruel type of attacks was about an experience that a Chinese Nurse had in the Central Hospital in Nanking. A Japanese pilot had been shot down but he was not killed. He was rushed to the Hospital and while interned there the raid alarm was sounded and the Nurse noticed that the Jap pilot was unusually nervous. She asked him what was the matter and he said that he wanted to leave the hospital " TO GET TO A PLACE OF SAFETY ". But you can bet your bottom dollar that he didn't leave the hospital - and his nervous nature certainly justified because the Central Hospital was bombed that same day. No - I don't think the Jap was killed. …llow to escape being shot down and bombed by his fellow men while

One of the best stories regarding this unorthodox and cruel type of attacks was about an experience that a Chinese nurse had in the Central Hospital in Nanking. A Japanese pilot had been shot down, but he was not killed. He was rushed to the hospital and, while interned there, the raid alarm was sounded and the nurse noticed that the Jap pilot was unusually nervous. She asked him what was the matter, and he said that he wanted to leave the hospital 'TO GET TO A PLACE OF SAFETY.' But you can bet your bottom dollar that he didn't leave the hospital - and his nervous nature was certainly justified because the Central Hospital was bombed that same day. No - I don't think the Jap was killed. A very lucky fellow to escape being shot down and bombed by his fellow men while convalescing in the hospital.

Mac, December 18, 1937

Mac's letters home from Hankow seem a little darker and more introspective. He flew very little, and he had several sad losses. In early January, Mac wrote, "This week has been a rather tragic one for our crowd here." In one incident, attempting to bomb airdromes near Hankow, the Japanese hit huts instead and killed about fifty women and children. In another, Sterling Tatum, one of those who came over on the *Empress of Russia* with Mac, had returned to the U.S. and begun working as a test pilot. He died during a test flight. Three other Americans died in China that week.

In the midst of struggle and uncertainty about his future, Mac still noticed the coolies who worked in the city in weather and war:

> Today has started off trying to be one of those miserable days. Of course, I mean the weather. It has been trying to rain and snow all at the same time and this has made the streets all wet and a general gloom has been cast over the city. I guess the reason I feel this way is because when you go outside and see the [rickshaw] coolies patrolling around looking for fares. Most of them are barefooted and lots of them are barelegged. Lord knows they must be cold.

> But they just toddle along. A human beast of burden is the best name one can give the [rickshaw] coolie.

> We had another raid this week. 12 bombers came over and unloaded about 100 bombs on the airdrome. All they do is dig a lot of holes in the ground which gives the coolies a job filling them up.

One of the largest air battles of the war occurred in Hankow on February 18, 1938. The Russian government provided new planes for the Chinese Air Force. Shortly after 1 PM, fifteen twin-engine Japanese bombers flew in from the East at around 10,000 feet. Chinese pursuit planes circled the airdrome waiting their arrival, alerted through the early warning network. The Chinese won the aerial contest, and it provided "a Chinese Victory, one of the biggest and the best." The Chinese pilots handled their new planes quite nicely and the morale of the entire air force was never higher.

Mac was re-assigned to Kunming in March 1938. While he came back to Hankow a few times, the Japanese military forced the Americans to evacuate Hankow entirely near the end of October 1938.

The Japs are making it well understood that their purpose is to wipe out the white man's interest in the East.

Mac, December 26, 1937

Hankow,China,
Jan. 22,1938.

Dear Folks,

    After my feeble letter in longhand I feel like I should have a lot to write about. Things have been so tame here for the past 10 days that I sometimes wonder if there is really a war going on.

    Hankow of course is in a very congested condition. People from the Japanese occupied areas have literally flooded this city. The local City Gov., is cautiously suggesting that they move on further west so as to relieve this place. It is so crowded that when a batch of ten thousand leave you can't even tell it. There is no expectatnt food shortage but there is some talk of coal shortage and that the power plant will have to cease operating on sundays. This has not started yet but it will soon.

    Cecil Folmar is not renewing his contract and is on his way back to the States. He left here by train yesterday or the day before and will leave Hongkong on the President Taft. His wife and family will catch the same boat at Honolulu. I imagine he will try and get back in the Army,too. He showed me a letter that stated that Reserve Officers could get active duty until they were 35 years of age. That gives me three more years before that is over anyway. However I don't see the point in leaving China now. Because it is now when they need us most.

    I have been reading a great deal what other people write and think about the situation here in China. And in spite of the fact that Japan has China outnumbered in trained personnel. In spite of lack of war supplies and war plants, I feel that " There will come a day " when China will be the victor. According to me world statistics there is one chinese to every four people. Now it seems to me that it will take a long time and a lot of killing to wipe out a nation with a population that is 1/4th the population of the world. These so called authorities quote statistics and bring forward reasons and facts that there apparently is no answer other than that Japan is going to win. Personnally I can't see it yet.

    Japan rather expected China to surrender from pure panic and fear after the downfall of Nanking. But alas and alac, China didn't. The Central Gov. of China is firmly entrenched in their new location and business is being carried on in spite of all kinds of hardships. And speaking of hardships that is just what the Chinese like. I guess the best example is to see some of these Chinese coolies trotting along under a load that would stagger the ordinary horse. But they chant their song, trot along, smile and get to where they are going because it means that there is a bowl of rice waiting. One cannot help but admire a race of people that can carry on like these people have been doing since the Japs have come along and messed their lives up. But they don't seem to mind. They still carry on.

    Admiral Marquart and his Chief of Staff, Lieut. Commander Goode, were here for about an hour this morning. We had quite a bull session. They have known the Chinese for many years and they too feel the way that I do. The Admiral is being transferred back to the States about March and we all hate to see him go because he has been awfully nice to all of us here. He is reponsible for the cable that reached you on Xmas day. I told him that you had recieved it.

    I got a letter from you folks yesterday that was mailed in August. It mentioned about getting a card or something from Sian. I guess the other letters will reach me someday.

        Love to all,

                                              William

I don't see the point in leaving China now. Because it is now when they need us most…One cannot help but admire a race of people that can carry on like these people have been doing since the Japs have come along and messed their lives up.

Mac, January 22, 1938

I have been reading a great deal what other people write and think about the situation here in China. And in spite of the fact that Japan has China outnumbered in trained personnel, in spite of lack of war supplies and war plants, I feel that 'There will come a day' when China will be the victor…it seems to me that it will take a long time and a lot of killing to wipe out a nation with a population that is 1/4th the population of the world.

Mac, January 22, 1938

Hankow,
Feb. 19,1938.

DearDFolks,

Yesterday one of the biggest air battles of the war was fought here. Starting near the airdrome and progressing in almost every direction. Shortly after one oclock in the afternoon with the City all prepared for the raiders 15 large bi-motored Jap Bombers appeared coming from the East at about 10,000 feet. Chinese pursuit planes were circling our airdrome waiting for them and when everyone thought that the pursuit planes would drive the bombers away. Our planes suddenly turned to the north and we heard the drone of diving motors and knew that the Japs had brought along their own pursuit support. Down came the Japs and the Chinese pilots turned to meet the attack. Like cavalry meeting cavalry they charged into the fight. They met - formations broke up and Chinese pilot picked a Jap pilot and round and around they want. First a Chinese plane was shot down, the pilot jumped, then a Jap plane burst into flames, another Chinese plane went down and another Jap. In the first five mintues of the fight four planes had been shot down. In the meantime the bombers heading straight for the airdrome were almost ready to release their bombs, the anti-aircraft shells were bursting very near and you could see the planes waiver a little from nervousness, then they dropped their bombs with a terrific roar and turned quickly and headed back to their base. But the fight between pursuit and pursuit was still going on. The planes were out of sight but you could hear the roar of the straining motors and the bursts of machine gun fire. about 1:30 the all clear signal was sounded and the battle was over. From our observation station we rushed to the field to count noses and planes. As the planes landed and the pilots jumped from their cockpits we could see the happy smiles and the thrill of victory on their faces - and believe you me it is a pleasant sight and mighty contageous - the pilots ran to each other, shouting and patting each other on the back - It was a Chinese Victory. One of the biggest and the best. The score at this writing not entirely confirmed but almost, is Three Chinese killed, one wounded, one jumped out in his parachute and one was forced to land with bullets in his engine. The Japs lost 7 Planes and all of their crew. WHO SAID THE CHINESE PILOTS COULDN'T FIGHT. They fought a fight that the Japs will have a hard time forgetting.

The Hankow Herald Headlines this morning were " CHINESE AIRMEN SHOOT DOWN 11 JAPANESE PLANES NEAR HANKOW " and THRILLING DOGFIGHTS WITNESSED WHEN 38 ENEMY MACHINES ATTACK CITY; ONLY 22 RAIDERS SUCEED IN RETURNING TO BASE IN SAFETY ". This may be true but we only saw 28 planes and it is possible that some were wounded and had their gas tanks pierced and failed to get home. This I hope to be true. Because the Japs when they come here have to go a long ways to get back to friendly territory.

The Chinese pilots have new planes and handled them very nicely. The fight brought the moral of the entire Air Force to a high pitch and every one in the City was happy.

Either the Japs will bring in 100 or more planes to wipe out the place or they will pull in their necks. Will let you know the results

... something really important
... Well it looks like it is
... thing is that the Japs are
... hy ??? Maybe Russia is going
... hat the Japanese will have
... out of thier invasion. It

... week and February will
... and time just skips by.
... ay home. His contract
... o far away.

... It was mailed Jan. 28th

... ing this coming June.
... on.

... r so. Still waiting
... chance that I will

... ere hasn't been
... had few snow
... y we had a scare
... weather between

... vicinity of the Huai River, north west
... the Japs a nice fight. Chinese planes have been
... tions and this has given the Chinese a better heart
... The Japanese are being harassed in all sections by small Chinese guerilla
units. The other day between Kashing and Hangchow on the Shanghai-Hangchow
RR a Chinese guerilla unit opened fire on a small truck and killed 7 Jap
flyers that were en route from the Kashing Field to the Hangchow Field. Also
Chinese planes have been raiding the former location of the Central Aviation
School at Hangchow. The Japs are using this field as a base of operations.
Strange as it may seem. They are dropping bombs on their own houses and
hangars. But this is war. I guess ??

Owing to the fact that the Japanese have forcebly sent a great number
of Formosan women to China to " COMFORT " the Japanese troops and have also
demanded foodstuffs and supplies several uprisings have occurred and the
whole Island has developed with Anti-Japanese atmosphere. This item appeared
in to-days paper.

Well, Folks hold the fort until next week. Will sure be glad when I
start recieving your letters regularly.

Live to all,

Wm.

"Boycott of Japanese Goods"

The subject for this week's letter shall be 'Boycott of Japanese Goods' and refusal of American manufacturers to sell supplies to Japan. Most of all the Chinese return students naturally are very familiar with the situation and waste no time or words in explaining to the Americans here that the U.S. is supplying Japan with materials that is enabling Japan to continue her aggression in China…

The world knows that if the United States would curtail selling of supplies to Japan that they would soon fold up. Big Business is solely responsible for this - and naturally they don't desire to give up million dollar accounts just to avert a world catastrophe. However, with the [U.S. Government] behind a move to cease business with Japan, it could be done very easily…

Mac, February 6, 1938

China is still valiantly fighting. The world has been surprised at the way China has fought and the world is pulling for China to win...

Dear Folks,

Hankow, China,
March 6, 1938.

Although this week has not been as exciting as last week we have had some astonishing things to break out in the open. One of the most important to me and the other Americans here was the re-organization of the Commission on Aeronautical Affairs. This was not a complete surprise but we all guessed wrong as to the Number One of the organization. Madam Chiang as Secretary General of the Commission was forced to turn her job over to some one else because of three or four things. Two of which are;- She just had too much work to do for any one person. Now she can devote more of her time to matters of more importance. And - her health hasn't been any too good. Nervousness more than anything else. The other factors - well never mind. Anyway surprise was awaiting and did appear when Madams brother T.V. Soong was appointed as the Number One. It will take time to change the organization into a more efficient machine but we all have high hopes because of the business ability of Mr. Soong. He also isn't lined up with any "clicks". So ─── a toast to the new helmsman and luck to him.

Last night a reception given by the Officers of the Yangtse Patrol, U.S. Navy was given held at the French Club. The occasion was the departure of Admiral Marouart and the arrival of his replacement Admiral Lebretton. A very nice party and it made one forget that there was a war anywhere. However, I might as well tell you the wild rumor that was stirred up by one gentlemen who said that his Chinese House Boy told him; " That the Japanese were gathering a sky fleet of 700 planes to send to Hankow and destroy the Chinese Air Force AGAIN". Of course we discount the rumor entirely but I grant you that it would be an undertaking have that many airplanes but on the other hand Japan does requiring much effort. The greatest thing the Japs have done is to show us how not to operate an Air Force. Their tactics and stratagy has been rather poor but I must say that it is improving. From a practical view-point I can say that the energy and expense expended by the Japs has not in any way been justifiable to them. They have met with some success but not a great deal.

The fighting has now practically centered around the area in Northern Honan Province and SouthEastern Shansi Province. Bitter fight-ing is being waged by the Chinese to prevent the Japs from Crossing the Yellow River and so far the Japs are still North of the River. The objective of the Japs is to cross the river and sever the lines of com-munications and supply coming in from the Northwest by rail, Air and road. The Hangchow area is quiet as is the Wuhu area near Nanking. The Chinese are harrassing the Japs from the rear with small units and just this week the Japs had to use airplanes to get supplies to their troops in Northern Honan.

...y Mary Woodall that I have
...waiting. Sometimes it takes
...r from Lucie arrived that was
..., August 13.

Love to all,

The greatest thing the Japs have done is to show us how not to operate an Air Force. Their tactics and strategy have been rather poor but I must say that it is improving. From a practical standpoint I can say that the energy and expense expended by the Japs has not in any way been justifiable to them.

Mac, March 6, 1987

Hankow, China,
March 12,1938.

Dear Dad,

The weather has been on a rampage this week. Monday night we had a regular thunderstorm and plenty of lightning. It rained for a couple of days and then all of a sudden it turned cold as the devil and then snowed. The entire week has been pretty bad. One of the strangest things happned -- while it was snowing one night we had an electrical storm. Lightning and thunder when it snows. Well it just don't seem right. We all commented on it the next morning but nothing was mentioned in the papers about it.

The re-organization of the Commission is still going on and nothing definite has taken shape for me. But I expect to be transferred away from Hankow to the new location of the Central Aviation School. I must keep the location secret for military reasons at present. Later if I am transferred I will let you know how to address me.

Yesterday marks the contract day. I have four months to go before my contract expires. Of course I plan to stay with this thing until the war is over. In fact I like being in China very much. About the only thing that I don 't like about it is that it is so far away from home. But when the war is over I will come home for a little vacation

Some of our boys have enough and are planning on going back but I don't think I can make this amount of money in the States and I am going to hold on if the want me.

The Chinese have a lot of good traits that I like very much. It takes a foreigner a long time to realize that their civilization is so much older than ours and that the foreigner should go out of his way to aclimate himself to China rather than visa versa.

No letter in two weeks. It certainly makes life miserable when you know that you are not getting letters that you know have been mailed to you. Patience - that is the key word here and sometimes the mail just taxes the system too much.

I have written to Uncle James. I was so sorry to hear about William Ailshie. When you wrote me about it. There was only one sentence to tell all. Please go more into detail on these things. Also Tatums accident. Surely you must have heard some things about it. At least you could have called the field and asked them there and they have been glad to tell you.

Love to all

P S

Tell Mother and
never bothered with
I don't mention same.

> It takes a foreigner a long time to realize that their civilization is so much older than ours and that the foreigner should go out of his way to acclimate himself to China rather than vice versa.
>
> Mac, March 12, 1938

                                        Hankow, China,
                                        March 12,1938.

Dearest Lucie,

          I have an oppertunity to-day to write you and Malcolm
seperate letters. I know you have been reading my letters that I
write to you all. But I just wanted to write you and tell you how
glad I am that you are well again and doing well in school. I am
mighty proud of you and I hope that you are so happy because when
you are happy then I am happy,

          Just the other day I recieved a letter from you that
was written last summer. In fact it was written on the day that the
Shanghai battle started. Little did you know at the time that their
was starting an undeclared war in the Orient. You were in Altoona
visiting one of your girl friends. The date was August the 13th and
you addressed it to me in Nanking. The letter probably has traveled
a lot. Late though it was I was so glad to get it. I am keeping it
as it will be a pretty memory piece someday.

          I wish you could see me now. I weigh about 175 pounds.
The old "Beer Muscle" is about 35 inches in circumference. I feel
great now but during December and January I was suffering from a nice
cold that just about wrecked my sinus. In fact they wanted to cut part
of the bone out of my nose but it finally cleared up.

          The Chinese Air Force has been strengthened lately and on
the 18th of Feb. the Japs raided Hankow and met with the Chinese pursuit
planes and one of the largest air battles of the war was fought with the
Japs losing heavily. In fact they haven't been back to Hankow Since. I
expect them to some here next time with a larger force and then the fur
will fly and I hope the Japs lose again.

          This past week we had a nice 3 inch snowfall. It seemed
like home. The kids were out in the streets having snow battles and
making snowmen. But their models were mostly of snow Buddhas. And very
good work, too. It is all about gone now and I hope that spring is just
around the corner.

          Here is your name in Chinese written by my good friend,
Major Poyen Shu who, by the way, is a graduate of the University of
Michigan. Your name, as you see calls for 5 characters. The first two
are "Loo See", the last three, Ma - Don - ah. " Loo See" means, literally;
"The dew on flowers" - Many Chinese girls use this name - it sighifies
the clear drops of the dew and freshness. Fresh or bright and clean.Nice?
          Be a swet girl, study hard, but not too hard. Enjoy your
friends and give them my regards.

                                        Your brother,

Moving the Flight Schools
1938 - Kunming

Following the losses of Shanghai and Nanking, the CAF retreated to Hankow. Due to Japanese air raids, the training schools had to move to safer locations. By February, the Primary and Basic schools were assigned to Liuchow and the Advanced school to Kunming. Chennault was again asked to take charge of training in the CAF.

Changes were also in store for the Commission on Aeronautical Affairs. Madame Chiang resigned as head, and months of political infighting ensued which affected Chennault and the American instructors. Chennault stayed in Hankow to deal with this reorganization while McDonald went on to take temporary charge in Kunming.

Kunming was a city of about 100,000 located in the province of Yunnan and bordering Burma. Situated at high altitude, Yunnan consisted mainly of brown mountains, green fields, and blue lakes. Mountains provided natural protection from the north, south, and particularly the west.

The French had constructed a railroad from Hanoi to Kunming, and during the summer, people travelled to Kunming for the climate. This left a distinct French influence on everything from food to architecture.

Mac arrived on March 28. He loved the weather, with lows in the 60s and highs hovering around 80. Vegetables and flowers grew abundantly, and Mac particularly loved the beauty of the wisteria and cherry blossoms. Mac thought it would be an improvement over Hankow, though he was worried that he'd need to learn French.

The city was crowded with refugees fleeing the war so housing was short, with many living in tents. Mac first lived in a room in a hospital next to the hotel. Eventually he moved into a house with three bedrooms, a dining room, living room, and a downstairs bath, and he looked forward to having his own cook. He shared the house with one of his best friends, master mechanic Sebie Smith.

Mac remained confident that China would win the war, optimistically thinking this might happen within the year. He was thrilled when three Chinese pilots flew along the western side of Japan, dropping propaganda sheets instead of bombs. All of the planes returned safely, "a remarkable flight performed solely by Chinese pilots."

By this point, the Chinese Air Force was filled with young, inexperienced pilots who were poorly equipped and outnumbered in most fights. Most of the pilots had been flying for less than seven years.

Mac felt "the boys have done the best that they know how and that is all one can expect from them." But he hoped that Russia would eventually declare war on Japan and assist China because "China must have help from someone." He retained his optimism, saying "...though things look dark, I can easily remember when things looked darker. So maybe the cloud will suddenly take on a silver lining."

Kunming training accident. Photo by Frank Higgs

…from the looks of things I am going to have to learn to speak French. Woe is me.

GRAND HOTEL DU COMMERCE

MADAME VEUVE RAZNATOVITCH Propriétaire
Yunnanfou (Chine)

Maison Française recommandée par le Touring Club de France

Yunnanfou le   March 29   193 8

Dear Folks,

        I left Hankow the 26th but was delayed in Chengtu until
yesterday. Arrived here yesterday afternoon about 5:40 P.M. Shanghai
time.

        The French influence here in the City proper is tremendous
and from the looks of things I am going to have to learn to speak
French. Woe is me.

        I am writing this rather rapidly because I am going to give
it to one of the pilots that is leaving here for Hongkong via Chengtu
Hankow. So the letter may catch Thursdays Clipper.

        Can't tell you much now except that Chinese currency took
a terrific drop in value yesterday and all business men are terribly
 upset. I don't know whether or not it will mean the end of China or
not. I do think that it is a smart move on the part of the financial
heads to place the situation back in their favor.

        My love to all.

        You can address my letters via Hongkong-Hankow-Chengtu-
Kunming or Hongkong-Hanoi-Kunming.

        By the way I hope you are filing all my letters away. Someday
I may want to read them and recall some of the things that I have experienced.

Wm

By the way I hope you are filing my letters away. Someday I may want to read them and recall some of the things that I have experienced.

Mac, March 29, 1938

On the positive side, Mac and the others were training a new breed of pilot. According to Jack Samson in *The Flying Tiger*, these pilots were not from elite Chinese families and would not be passed automatically like those in the earlier Italian-based training. They had grown up with war, had lost family and left communities, and knew they would give their lives to protect their country.

The students were sometimes uncooperative, and the American instructors lacked the ability to discipline them for this. Training wasn't going well.

In late May, Mac flew from Kunming to the Primary and Basic schools at Liuchow, a 3-hour flight over rugged mountains. He saw just four towns in 450 miles and compared the area to a slightly less populated south Alabama. He spotted caves honeycombing the mountains to explore in the future.

Mac continued on to Hankow to meet with Chennault and report on the difficulties at the training schools. The primary issue was of authority—were the Americans merely advisors or were they in charge? Without authority, supplies or Madame Chiang's ear, Chennault took his resignation to the Commission. Eventually his authority was reestablished and Chennault relented.

He also told Mac that several of the Americans planned to go home when their contract expired. Of the group who had come over on the *Empress of Russia*, Williamson was already in the States, a pilot for Delta. Smith and Watson left on June 19. Smith was going to marry a girl from Montgomery, perhaps visit Mac's parents, then return to China.

Mac thought that people should try to stay until the end of the war. His second year in China nearly complete, he hoped to stay longer. Mac wanted to travel home for a vacation, but "only after the war." He and Chennault had that in common.

Chennault finally arrived to take charge in Kunming on July 11, and Mac was pleased. Mac and Chennault were now roommates, and probably for the first time

I have learned from Colonel Chennault that some of the boys plan on coming back to the States when their contract expires in July. I hate to see them go back because the war hasn't finished and I think we should stay until it is finished. (Pardon use of word finish.)

Mac, April 25, 1938

KUNMING, Yunnan,
May 25,1938.

Dear Folks,

Your letter dated May 9th arrived here this morning. It
looks as if our communications set-up is beginning to function along
normal lines once again.

On the 19th the Generalissimo ordered Chinese troops to
retreat from Hsuchow. The Japs had planned that once Hsuchow fell
that they would just walk right on into Hankow but they have again
been stopped at Lenfeng,East of Kaifeng. The Japs lost thousands of
troops and it cost them plenty money and effort to capture this point
which is strategic in one way yet in another it just means another
Chinese town. The Chinese don't seem at all discouraged.

They still have no idea of giving up. On other fronts the
Chinese have been knocking the tar out of the Japs. Especially at a
point some 15 miles East of Taiyuan in Shansi Province and then along
the Hankow-Peiping RR near Paoting. So even though the Japs are getting a lot of publicity they are also getting their share of bullets.
Paoting is the capitol of Hopeh Province.

One of the greatest flights by Chinese pilots was made
on the 19th and 20th of this month when three planes were flown to
Japan. They flew along the western side of the Island and dropped
propoganda sheets instead of bombs. All planes returned safely to
their base. A remarkable flight and done by Chinese pilots alone.

To-day we are a little startled by the news that Germany's
Madman Hitler, has started a little trouble between Czechoslovakia
and themselves. France has issued an ultimatum that if Germany invades
the Checks they will declare war on Germany in 24 hours. Looks bad.

Yes, Colonel Chennault is still here in China. In fact he
is in Hankow. I miss him very much because we had a good time to-gether
talking about the war and different things but of course we couldn't
always be to-gether.

Yes, I guess business is a little bad in the States and I
don't plan on coming back there unless they do not offer me another
contract. However, according to the job they have assigned me to now
it looks as if they will give me one. I was more or less assured of a
renewal when I left Hankow but anything can happen in China and I can
remember when I was assured of a regular commission on the Army back
there but something went wrong so I am not ever putting faith in anything until it's on the dotted line.

To-day is the first real day of sunshine since May 8th
and we are beginning to feel a whole lot better.

Sorry Malcom must go to Summer School but I want him to

I guess business is a little bad in the States and I don't plan on coming back there unless they do not offer me another contract. However, according to the job they have assigned me to now it looks as if they will give me one. I was more or less assured of a renewal when I left Hankow but anything can happen in China and I can remember when I was assured of a regular commission in the Army back there but something went wrong so I am not ever putting faith in anything until it's on the dotted line.

Mac, May 25, 1938

since landing in China, had a little free time. In addition to working hard, Mac and Chennault had numerous adventures over the next couple of years, including some adventurous flying and many hunting trips.

Chennault, a country boy, was determined to go hunting as much as possible. Shortly after Chennault's shotgun arrived in China, he asked Mac to find shells. Mac flew to a British base and traded whiskey for shells. He joined Chennault and they went shooting for sand cranes, which were abundant.

On another trip, they drove about twenty miles west of Kunming. The two friends killed two teal, two yellow beak, two snipe, a goose, and a dove over fifteen miles of walking. Hunting for the abundant game seems to have given both men time away from the intense struggles they faced.

Flying was another of their shared loves. Most biographers mention how happy Chennault seemed when he was flying. Once, flying a two-seater trainer with Chennault from Kweiyang to Kunming, the cockpit canopy blew off. Attempting to keep their heads out of the slip stream blast, Mac and Chennault lost their bearings. Only after flying an hour in a general westerly direction did the men spot what appeared to be a swarming ant heap of an airfield still under construction. Buzzing the area, Mac located a portion of the field completed just enough for a "safe" landing. Chinese workers hauled gas from a cache six miles away to refuel the plane, allowing Mac and Chennault to return to Kunming.

Another time on the same route, a distance of roughly three hundred miles, the plane's compass stopped working. Mac and Chennault flew nearly two hours before seeing a single town. Finally, Mac spotted a small village with an airdrome and landed for gasoline. He noticed that there were no roads or rivers in or out of the village, yet there were several nice buildings and, of course, the airdrome. It required sixteen days to transport ten gallons of gasoline to the field, traveling by train to Mengtseh and then by pack train to the airfield. The name of the village was secret. After gassing up the plane, they returned to Kunming shortly after dark.

Training wrecks at Kunming. Photos by Frank Higgs.

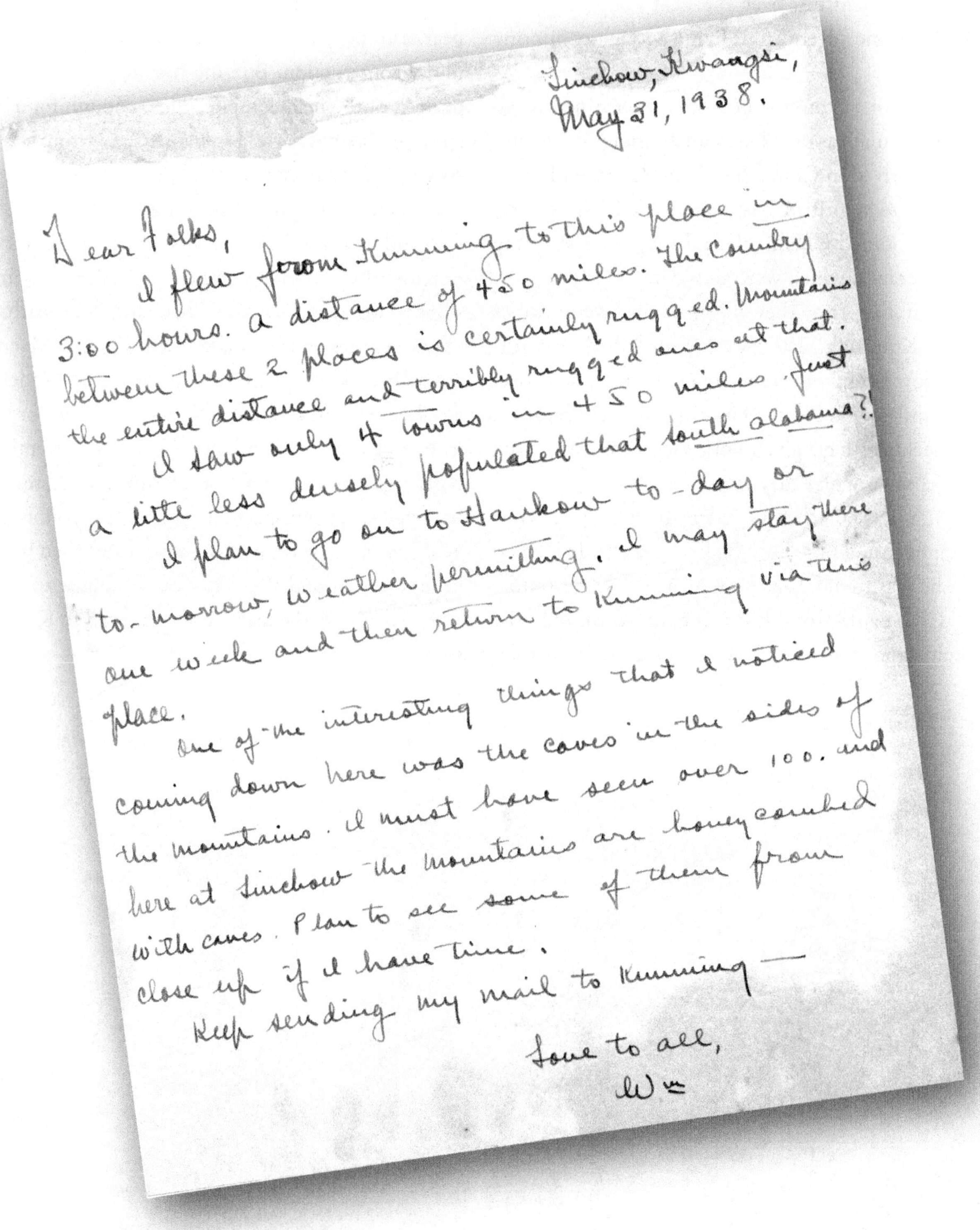

Tinchow, Kwangsi,
May 31, 1938.

Dear Folks,

I flew from Kunming to this place in 3:00 hours. A distance of 450 miles. The country between these 2 places is certainly rugged. Mountains the entire distance and terribly rugged ones at that.

I saw only 4 towns in 450 miles. Just a little less densely populated that South Alabama?

I plan to go on to Hankow to-day or to-morrow, weather permitting. I may stay there one week and then return to Kunming via this place.

One of the interesting things that I noticed coming down here was the caves in the sides of the mountains. I must have seen over 100. And here at Tinchow the mountains are honeycombed with caves. Plan to see some of them from close up if I have time.

Keep sending my mail to Kunming —

Love to all,
W—

Mac traveled regularly without Chennault too, taking several trips to Hankow and visited the CAMCO facility in Hengyang to get a plane repaired. Staying in Hengyang for a few weeks, Mac lived with some old friends on the banks of the Kiang River. He complained that they didn't have the right kind of bait for fishing!

In August Chennault was gone again, working for a couple of months at the school in Liuchow. Mac planned to visit in late September.

When Chennault left for Chungking, he left Mac in charge. While he seems to have done a good job, Mac was very happy when the Colonel got back.

Kunming was his first test of being in charge, but it would not be his last.

Chennault's Joe

Mac loved telling a story from Kunming which showed the legendarily combative Chennault in a different light.

Just before Chennault and I left for Kunming I found a man with some Dachschund puppies. I bought one and gave it to Colonel Chennault. He became extremely fond of this puppy and they were constant companions. Joe slept at the foot of the Colonel's bed and the Colonel taught him numerous tricks—sitting up, barking on command.

Joe also became a great hunting dog. He would retrieve any kind of game on command. One day at Kunming the Colonel and I went Sand Hills Crane hunting and after bagging two of them we saw several ducks on a pond. We fired and killed several but one duck was wounded. The Colonel sent Joe out to retrieve the wounded duck but Joe got in trouble and even though it was in the winter time when Joe had been slapped to almost unconsciousness by the wounded duck and began to drown. Colonel Chennault shed his outer heavy garments, dove in, swam to Joe and brought him ashore. No greater love could be expressed in this unusual rescue.

Mac, speech notes

> The Japanese now have what they set out to get, but after they have it, they don't know what to do with it. Rather like having a bear by the tail.
>
> Mac, June 3, 1938

MAIL

Hankow, China,
June 9,1938.

start on what is going on in China I desire to
Movie film to the Eastman Kodak Company at Rochester New York for
processing and I have asked them to mail the finished films to you.
When they come take them down to the Eastman Representative there
in the Magic City and ask them to run the pictures for you and then
let me know just how good or bad the scenes are so that I will know
how to correct my mistakes later. I hope they are good and that they
give you some idea of what things look like overhere. (Keep Them There)

The war situation is beginning to take on the same tone
in Hankow as was in Nanking last Fall however at the moment it is
not quite so serious.

Many people are speculating on whether or not Hankow will
fall into the Hands of the Japs and just how long it is going to take
before they arrive. Naturally with this kind of chatter going on it
tends to cause uneasiness among those that are not in close touch with
the situation.

Chengchow is more or less the next objective for the Japs
and at this time they are very close and should capture the place in
a week. Chinese will retreat down the railroad toward Hankow and dig
in where the terrain is more suitable for them to fight. The Japs
have much better mechanized outfits and it would be foolish for them
to try to stop the Japs on level ground. I believe that
plan on giving the Japs a real battle for Hankow. Anyw
the Japs are going to try and take the place.

The day after I arrived here we were able t
air battle just north of Hankow. The Japs evidently go
crossed because the pursuit boys got mixed up and came
Bombers turned and went back. Our pursuit intercepted
and knocked down 13 of them while we lost 4 planes and
of our boys jumped out. So again the Japs were whipped
Hankow. The next time the Japs come here we expect the
the city as the objective. This will of course be very
Hankow is terribly crowded and many lives will be lost.

For the past two weeks the Japs have been bo
indiscriminately and have caused much damage and loss o
too bad that we can't do anything about it just now. Ma
from foreigners in Canton have gone out and respective
have warned Japan but warnings will not stop Japan it t

n the next

ly wish that she could
the circumstances it

William

> ...aviators consider home as the place where they last left their baggage.
>
> Mac, June 20, 1938

> For the past two weeks the Japs have been bombing Canton indiscriminately and have caused much damage and loss of life. It is too bad that we can't do anything about it just now. Many protests from foreigners in Canton have gone out and respective governments have warned Japan but warnings will not stop Japan – it will take LEAD.
>
> Mac, June 9, 1938

Kunming, Yunnan,
July 21, 1938.

Dear Folks,

Your letter dated July Fourth arrived to-day. Am trying to get this letter away in time to catch the plane going to Hongkong to-morrow.

First, I have sent a letter with check for Twelve dollars to Madame Chiang Kai-shek. I told her from where it came and asked her to mail the reciept and letter of thanks to Mother.

The Japs are trying to reach Hankow by the 14th of August but at the moment they are not doing so well. However, they are now starting a wholsesale bombardment of the City proper at Hankow. Last few days they have bombed Wuchang, across the river from Hankow and Hankow and Hanyang, which is just across the Han River. All three cities suffered. Many civilians were killed. The Japs say they are going to continue bom bing in this ruthless manner because Hankow area is a real military objective.

Here in Kunming we are experiencing some real excitement. One day last week 16 soldiers attached to the Field here as guards went AWOL and they took several machine guns and plenty of ammunition. When they were located they had managed to join a band of bandits about 200 strong. The local soldiers tried to capture them and heavy fighting took place. Finally the deserters escaped. To-day we have just heard that more soldiers have deserted and joined this renegade outfit. It may turn into something serious and then it may blow over. The peculiar thing about the whole affair is that the local Governor left this week for Hankow to see the Generalissimo regarding the local situation. We understand that he is not in good grace with the Central Government officials and that he has been asked some months ago to come to Hankow but he refused. Now that he is gone it may be a ruse on his part to hurry back here and straighten matters out. Funny things go on and it is hard to cover the matter on paper. The best way is to say - " Never a dull moment".

In your letter before this one you sent a clipping saying that Americans were thru in China. The Germans have left. We are still here but we don't know how long. Personally I am ready to come back.

My contract has not been renewed. But I have been ordered by Dr. Soong to remain here. As a matter of fact an investigation is going on and in a week or so - I should know something. Colonel Chennault is here and is taking my place as No. 1 of the Schools, IF HE STAYS. And if he goes I will go also. At least I think I will.

Don't worry - I am going to try and be home for Xmas anyway.

Love to all,

PS
Special greetings to Franch
Always send snapshots girl

My contract has not been renewed. But I have been ordered by Dr. Soong to remain here. As a matter of fact an investigation is going on and in a week or so – I should know something. Colonel Chennault is here and is taking my place as No. 1 of the Schools, IF HE STAYS. And if he goes I will go also. At least I think I will.

Mac, July 21, 1938

Kunming, Yunan,
August 1, 1938.

Dear Dad,

...from the front yesterday. It seems that our ...who became famous for his work at Taerchwang, ...time at Hwangmei (Yellow Plum) just north of ...ons with him and has captured Yellow Plum and ...Jap lines. The Japs have lost heavily and it ...inundated ranks of the Yangste and the cont-...in the rear from Chinese Guerilla forces ...and their offensive stopped. You remember ...Headquarters had promised the Emperor and ...they would capture Hankow before August ...said that they will start a drive in October.

...thought the war would be over in three months ...long drawn out affair with no pleasant outlook ...g. captured Jap soldiers have expressed ...fighting. They have enough. Also ...urge of desease, pestilence and lack of ...tion. The Chinese are use to it but the Jap ...the war will last. I am sure ...the Generalissimo wants the Japs, not ...Manchuria as well.

...month it rained 24 days and this month it has rained 14 so far. So we here had a very wet 6 weeks.

> Several days ago I went to a very official Chinese dinner. There were 16 dishes on the table from start to finish. I have eaten lots of Chinese food since I have been here in China but never have I before had these dishes:
>
> Elephant trunk - with mushrooms
>
> Deer tendons and ham
>
> Bear paws (Fat part) and bean sprouts
>
> Fungus (a sweet dish), the jelly-like clear stuff that grows out of our fruit trees at home. Not a bad dish either. The Chinese called the first item above elephant nose. How would you like that for dinner?

Several days ago I went to a very official Chinese dinner. There were 16 dishes on the table from start to finish. I have eaten lots of Chinese food since I have been here in China but never have I before had these dishes;

    Elephant trunk - with mushrooms
    Deer tendons and ham
    Bears Paws (Fat part) and bean sprouts
    Fungus (a sweet dish) This is the jelly like fungus, clear stuff that grows out of our fruit trees at home. Not a bad dish either.

The Chinese called the first item above - elephant nose. How would you like that for dinner?

I am going to Hankow on Monday via Eurasia Airlines for a week or so and will be back here by the first of the month, I hope. I know that it is going to be not as the very devil and I hate to leave here because it is so comfortable. Even have to wear a coat when it is cloudy.

...smith should be there by now. Write him and invite him up ...week end and ...show him ...you our movies ...took. His address ...aym...Mis...

...ove to all...

P.S. Wrote Ailchito.

San Francisco in Kunming

The isolation in Kunming was difficult for Mac, and he was thrilled when the radio he purchased picked up music from Manila, Hong Kong, Hanoi, Rome, London, Berlin and thrice-daily news. In a moment fit for a movie, Mac describes one evening when he and Chennault suddenly hear an American radio broadcast from Treasure Island in San Francisco, California.

Three nights ago I was tuning around and listening for new stations when all of a sudden I heard an American Voice and when the announcer gave the station identification my hair just stood on end. Chennault and I got up and cheered mightily. We got a thrill out of it and particularly the news program. The station comes in clear and strong. It almost sounds like it is located in Yunnan.*

I have this day written to W6BXE telling them that their programs are being received and I asked them to play "Is it true what they say about Dixie" for you folks at 9:15AM the 31st so listen in.

It is touching to think of these two men, in the midst of war, with so many young lives in their care and entwined in the fate of a nation, being so happy just to hear a voice from home.

Socializing

Photos by
Frank Higgs

Hugh Woods & the Japanese Attack on CNAC Plane

In August, Mac's friend H.L. Woods came to dinner. The next week near Canton, a Japanese pursuit plane attacked the China National Aviation Corporation plane that Woods was flying. The plane was forced to land in the Pearl River. Woods, the radio man and one other person escaped by jumping into the river and swimming ashore. The Japanese continued dive bombing and strafing the helpless passengers with deadly machine-gun fire. Several people were killed, including women and children.

The Japanese may have thought the President of the Yuan legislature, Dr. Sun Fo, was aboard as well as several prominent bankers. The plane was plainly marked for proper identification and could not have been mistaken for a bomber.

Mac was outraged by this attack on a plane clearly marked as civilian, bombing defenseless towns and villages, and using poison gas behind the Yangtze front. He thought that their "main objective [was] the complete terrorism of China."

Woods returned to the States shortly after this, but eventually returned to China and CNAC.

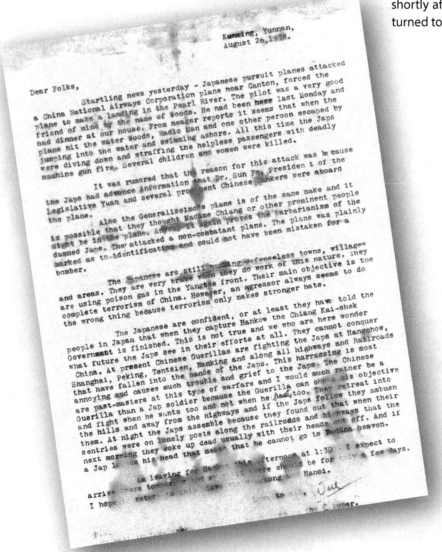

...an aggressor always seems to do the wrong thing because terrorism only makes stronger hate.

Mac, August 26, 1938

AIR MAIL

Hengyang, Hunan, China,
September 13,1938.

Dear Dad,

I have been careless again and haven't written since I left Kunming on the 28th last month. I came to Hankow, stayed there a week and came on down here. For your assistance in locating it on the map it is down the RR from Hankow toward Canton and 100 miles south of Changsha.

I expect to be here about a week longer and then will return via Hongkong, I hope. I desire to pick up my baggage there. It has finally arrived from Shanghai and I am anxious to check up and find out how much I have lost.

It sure is hot here in comparison with Kunming. It took me all this time to become acclimated because of my sudden change in temperature and altitude. Feeling ok now.

Well the Chinese are stilling fighting the pants off the Japs. On the North bank the Chinese have recaptured a place called Hwangmei (Yellow Plum) and the Chinese are counter-fighting all along the lines in that area. Right now the war looks very rosy for the Chinese and the Japs are having a hard time. It looks like they will be more than a month capturing Hankow and I don't believe they ever will and even if they do they haven't won the war by a long shot.

Hengyang is a pretty small place but fortunately I ran into old friends and am living with them in a nice house located on the Banks of the Kiang River.

We have had a lot of fun on the river but the fishing is not so good for some reason we don't seem to have the right kind of bate or bait.

The Japanese have paralized air traffic as far as the airlines are concerned. Woods, the pilot of the C.N.A.C. passenger plane that was shot down several weeks ago near canton was a very good friend of mine. He has enough of China and the war and is returning to the States. Two Eurasia planes were forced down but there were no casualties. Anyway traffic has ceased to Honkong. All mail should be routed via Hanoi.

Love to all,

Mysterious Flight to Burma Border

I have just returned from one of the most interesting flights that I have ever made. Naturally I cannot reveal the purpose but I can tell you about the flight. Assigned to an airplane with a lot of gas I took along one passenger. Friday afternoon at three o'clock we took off from Kunming and headed northwest. After flying over high mountains for an hour and a half we landed at a little village called Yunnanyi.

On this first leg of our flight we sighted many snow-capped mountains to the north. It was a beautiful sight. Although we were flying at an altitude of 12,000 feet above sea level and only 2000 feet above the ground at times, we were not cold. After we landed we walked almost 2 miles to the village where we spent the night with an official. A very primitive arrangement but nevertheless, more than welcome. We retired early and rose early but due to the walk back to the field we were a little late taking off. However, it was our own schedule and it didn't make any difference.

About 30 miles distant in the early sunshine we saw Tien Chang Mountain and Talifu Lake. Without a doubt this was the most beautiful sight I have ever seen. The Lake, blue as the sky and the rugged mountain rising from almost the water's edge to over 10,000 feet toward the sky. Tien Chang means pointing to the Heavens. The mountain was snow-covered along the top of the entire range. We took pictures and I hope they came out O.K.

On reaching the lower end of the Lake at a little town called Ksis-kuan we turned to a course of Southwest and flew 200 miles over territory very much unsettled and very rugged. Very much like the terrain in Kwangei Province but rougher. About one hour and fifty minutes after leaving the Lake we arrived at the Burma Border. Being careful not to cross it we circled around looking things over for about 30 minutes. The nearest large town from the spot where we were in Bhamo and the Burma town of Namhkam was just across the river from where we were circling. Namhkam is 60 miles Southeast of Bhamo. So get out your map and take a look.

I am fairly positive that I flew further west in China than any other pilot. I feel that I blazed a new trail and it was a lot of fun. It was easy because I had very good maps.

We started back to Yunnanyi at 10:30 and reached the snow-capped mountain and Lake again at 12:00 then landed Yunnanyi at 12:15. Gassed up and took off to arrive at Kunming at 2:15. A round trip in less than 24 hours. We could have been months if we had been forced down.

Namhkam is 320 miles straight southwest of Kunming.

Mac, November 21, 1938

> I am fairly positive that I flew further west in China than any other pilot. I feel that I blazed a new trail and it was a lot of fun. It was easy because I had very good maps.

30 Degrees Against That Mountain

Bill Pawley, on flying with Billy McDonald

William "Bill" Pawley

- Provided planes to China
- Ran CAMCO, which hired and supplied the Flying Tigers
- Ambassador to Peru
- Had access to Presidents
- Involved with clandestine work for U.S. government and outside governments
- Active in behind-the-scenes politics during and after the war

Bill, I guess we've had it.

Mac, while lost in the Himalayas

My trips in and out of Loiwing were almost invariably by air. Whether these flights would be uneventful or hazardous was always unpredictable. Over these high mountains instant changes in the weather, some of them ominous, were frequent. Gales would sweep down unexpectedly from the high Himalayan massifs of Nepal and Tibet; we could be flying in clear weather and suddenly find ourselves wrapped in impenetrable mist or fog.

On one of these occasions, when we had flown in from Hong Kong to Kunming with two American test pilots just arrived from China and with Billy McDonald as pilot. Mac had been relying on visual recognition for navigation, but the mountains are so numerous and so much alike, particularly when fog and overcast partially shroud them, that this can be tricky. After failing to reach an expected landmark, we realized that we were lost. We kept on flying with the gas supply of the Vultee inexorably trickling away. We were still in the midst of a wilderness of icy mountains with no sign of human habitation visible anywhere.

Mac checked his fuel gauge which was almost empty, then turned to me and said,

"Bill, I guess we have had it."

We agreed to try a forced landing on one of the mountain slopes around us. The maneuver consisted of lifting the plane's nose at the last moment for a pancake landing on a rock surface, generally at a gradient of anywhere from thirty degrees up. Assuming the plane didn't crash on impact, the next gamble was whether it would start sliding down the slope or be blocked by one of the tremendous boulders on the mountainside. If these two hazards were surmounted, the only one remaining was surviving in this mountain waste and making one's way out of it, generally by going down to the valleys scoured between the mountain chains. These were usually jungle with malarial mosquitoes and primitive tribes.

We tied everything down and stowed whatever we could under the seats. The two test pilots were horrified at the prospect of losing their lives on their first air trip in China. Then the fog lifted slightly and, at that moment, I pointed to a clear patch directly ahead. Mac headed for it and came down safely in a rice paddy. We were only thirty miles from Loiwing, on the other side of a 15,000-foot mountain range.

Flight from Loiwing to Kunming

Site of CAMCO Airplane Factory

Kunming, China,
December 15,1938.

Dearest Mother,

"Just 10 more Shopping Days until Christmas." Th i s
is the remark that we are making in a place where it is impossible
to buy a single thing of any value. So with this condition we are
planning a very mild Christmas.

Not only the above condition exists but it is impossible
to mail packages from Kunming because of the heavy mails the past
six months. Bags of mail are stacked sky high around the P.O. and also
inside. Someday people will recieve this mail (probably 2nd class)
because it won't be lost unless the Japs come here which I dou bt.

I was pleased to learn that you are having another nice
journey. I know how happy you must be to see Aunt Lucie and al l the
other Ailshies. Recent letters from Dad say that everything is unde r
control and all is well. Even Aunt Virginia. I am glad to hear this
good news.

I don't think that you recieved my last letter where I told
of my flight to the Burma Border. On the 18th of Nov. I flew f rom
Kunming to Talifu about 170 miles then the next day I flew 200 more
miles to the Burma Border. I believe that I was the first pilot to
fly over this particular terrain. The course was over very mou ntainous
country and the people are all tribesmen. I have been told that they
are not very friendly either so I was mighty glad that the en gine did
not fail me. When we got to the Border we flew along looking for a
place to land but could not find one so turned around a flew b ack. Snow
covered mountains were visible around talifu and northward. A beautiful
sight. The flight back was uneventful. Several weeks later we got a
little excitement when we recieved a report that a Chinese pl ane had
flown across the Burma Border on the Date that we were there. The
British protested mildly. Some joke. I was very careful not to fly
over the Border but have been told since that there has been a dispute
over the exact Border since 1000 B.C. or some years ago.

Have been doing a bit of Duck Hunting. Last Sunday we wen t
out and killed enough duck and goose to have a dinner for 18 p eople.
It cuts the grocery bill down, too.

Colonel Chennault has gone to Chungking. I don't know how
long he will be away. This leaves me holding the fort at the House.
He and I (is that proper english) live to-gether and have been
enjoying life here in Kunming for sometime. The life now is rather
tame in comparison with our earlier exeriences at Nanking.

News last ... ... hru
giving in to Hitler. T... ... ...hat
the USA will also fall ... ...ion.
take the starch out of ...

Mail this ... ... write
him one before the pla...

Love to al...

W

> Colonel Chennault has gone to Chungking. I don't know how long he will be away. This leaves me holding the fort at the House. He and I…live together and have been enjoying life here in Kunming for sometime. The life now is rather tame in comparison with our earlier experiences at Nanking.
>
> Mac, December 15, 1938

On the 18th of Nov. I flew from Kunming to Talifu about 170 miles, then the next day I flew 200 more miles to the Burma Border. I believe that I was the first pilot to fly over this particular terrain. The course was over very mountainous country and the people are all tribesmen. I have been told that they are not very friendly either so I was mighty glad that the engine did not fail me. When we got to the Border we flew along looking for a place to land but could not find one so turned around and flew back. Snow covered mountains were visible around Talifu and northward. A beautiful sight. The flight back was uneventful. Several weeks later we got a little excitement when we received a report that a Chinese plane had flown across the Burma Border on the date that we were there. The British protested mildly. Some joke. I was very careful not to fly over the Border but I've been told since that there has been a dispute over the exact Border since 1000 B.C. or some years ago.

Mac, December 15, 1938

"WE WILL PROBABLY MOVE WEST AGAIN, ON TO TIBET "
THE WAR NEWS

On October 25, 1938, the Japanese captured Hankow. Mac had hoped that the Chinese could hold out, or even stop the Japanese assault. However valiant the Chinese effort, Japan had the upper hand in training and equipment.

The Chinese had stopped the Japanese north of Changsha and were pressing hard on Canton. If Changsha fell to the Japanese, they would acquire better lines for communication and supplies farther in the interior. They would have the river and the railroad, and could now attack the airdromes around Kunming.

By December, Mac believed England and France would soon go to war with Germany, and speculated that the United States would fall in line. Mac felt strongly that something needed to be done in order "to take the starch out of Japan" as they were "a menace to all civilizations." He was excited to learn that the United States and England had loaned China money.

Mac believed that Japan knew they had lost the war, but wanted a major power to force them out of China. This would avoid a loss to the lowly nation of China, which would call into question their standing as a world power.

Hearing that the war would be over by the summer, Mac looked forward to a return home for a visit. He didn't know that it would be over three years later before he went for a visit, in late 1942, and that the war would not end for another seven years.

In late December, Japanese war ships began shelling Pakhoi, only five hundred miles from Kunming. If they established a base to operate bombers, they could "bomb the hell out of us here," Mac worried. "If they do this, we will probably move west again, on to Tibet."

News from Kunming

Perhaps due to the quieter life and his growing sense that he wanted something else, Mac's letters from Kunming end up filled with news of other people's lives, though with a few recurring themes.

Crashes

Crashes and the deaths of fellow pilots served as regular reminders of the nature of his work, the fallibility of machines and the unpredictable nature of flying in China. A January 3, 1939, letter described a crash in detail:

> One of our fellows, Lowell F. Johnson, from Lafayette, Ind., flying a Boeing 247 Transport ship belonging to the Generalissimo's Squadron, crashed into a mountain in very bad weather on the 27th of December. He was above clouds and from radio reports it seems that Johnson's radio operator could not make the Direction Finder work. We think the operator told Johnson he was over Kunming and to let him down thru the clouds. Instead they were 150 miles Southeast of Kunming. Johnson was married and his wife was living here. She plans on returning to the states at an early date. The place where Johnson crashed is 95 kilometers from the French RR and it is impossible to bring the body out so he has been buried there. Carney, one of the boys stationed at Mengtseh went by Donkey over trails to reach the spot. He hasn't returned yet.

Mac received a letter from Julius Barr, a pilot who had spent more than six years in China but had gone back to be a test pilot for Boeing. A week later, the Boeing Stratoliner that Barr was flying crashed near Seattle. "Fate is a funny thing, isn't it."

AVG Foreshadowing

Mac could not directly tell his family that he and Chennault discussed what would become the AVG, but there are several comments that in hindsight mention it.

There's also a suggestion that might be the first mention of the AVG in Mac's letters, on January 10, 1939:

Chennault is in Chungking to answer a summons by the Generalissimo. We may get more Americans out here, but I don't know. Keep that under your hat.

Everyone is predicting the war will be over next fall. I think it may last much longer. The Generalissimo has no intention of giving up. As long as his excellency feels this way we will stay and help him.

> *Chosen as the new location for the school precisely because it was far from the action, Chennault felt that being stationed in Kunming was a form of exile, with only the fine hunting there to recommend it.*

Thursday Colonel Chennault and I flew to Yunnanyi to see some of our boys there. In a previous trip I had landed here on my flight to the Burma border. We stayed there all day and came back about dark. The country is certainly wild. There are thousands of duck and geese there. We brought back a few for our larder.

A letter of April 24, 1939, sounded quite like Chennault's ongoing advocacy for something like the AVG:

> Colonel Chennault left again this past week for Chungking and there is a strong possibility that he may be ordered to the States to inspect certain equipments and to investigate a few things. His address will be Waterproof, La. Wire or write him there if there is anything you desire to talk to him about or send back to me because he will return in two months, if he goes?

World Politics

Mac also watched Japan closely, and thought about world politics (February 15, 1939, letter):

The Democracies must stick together against Facism and Hitlerism. There is no question that Germany and Italy influence the Japanese Policy in a big way. I personally believe that if the United States and France and England would back Russia that Russia would come in and wipe the Japanese off the map. It should be done because the Japanese have their eyes on the rest of Asia. With such a barbaric people directing the destiny of Asia a war unsurpassed in magnitude will be the outcome. It will be the yellow race against the white race. Fires should be extinguished before they get out of control.

"Local War Business"

Paying close attention to war news, Mac noted that their war experience supported Chennault's theories:

Now for the local war business….Recently the Japanese have raided Lanchow, northwest of Sianfu, in an attempt to wipe out supplies coming from Russia. The last time the Japanese raided with 30 bombers and the Chinese shot down 8 of them. This will cause them to hesitate about raiding that place again. One thing this war has proved and that is that bombers are not invincible to pursuit attack as spread by our bombardment theorists there in the states. They have a lot to learn about warfare in the air.

He'd also heard about a shocking discovery made near Lanchow. On March 6, 1939, the Chinese reported discovering a horrifying thing about Japan's air force:

A rather interesting thing has been reported and verified. More than a dozen Japanese heavy bombers have been shot down over Lanchow in the Northwest. And the amazing thing is that it was discovered in the crashes that the entire Japanese crew were chained to their stations in the airplanes. Only the pilot has a key. Each gunner, radio operator, bombardier, co-pilot and pilot were wearing chains around their necks and the other end fastened to the airplane. It proves that the Japanese were having a hard time making their bombers fly into China and bomb. The main reason is that they are afraid of Chinese Pursuit planes and if they chain the crew they will lose all hope of living and, like a cornered tiger, they will fight without flinching. The Japanese send out reports almost every time a Jap pilot is shot down that the pilot, mortally wounded, would dive his burning plane into the Chinese objective. City or airdrome, wherever they were bombing. I wonder if the Jap pilots are not tired of this kind of tommy rot.

By May, the Japanese were bombing the capitol of Chungking. Chennault was there on business, and Mac wrote about how it affected the Chinese people:

It is a strange thing that the Chinese cannot seem to understand this war business after over a year and a half of experience. In Spain a city digs in and although raided and bombed as many as five times in one day the casualties are extremely low. But here in China the people just carry on – day after day and they dig a few holes but not enough for the population and when the Japs come the results are terrible.

Tuesday morning – 9th of May. Colonel Chennault just got back from Chungking and described the terrible bombing there.

Another Crash

Sadly, Mac mentioned crashes all too often. Another pilot had died, but Mac may be adjusting to the losses of war:

…George Weigle, test pilot for one of the airplane factories here in China was killed last Friday at Chungking. It was announced over the Nanking Radio Broadcast Station that Weigle was a graduate of the Army Flight School in the States and was a Reserve Officer. This is not true – I don't know where the dope got out that he was one of our crowd. He was from Fort Myers, Fla., and he had very little training. We were sorry to hear of his death but things will happen sometimes.

Christmas Holiday with the Colonel

Chennault went back to the States in October 1939 for a vacation of several months. Over the 1939 Christmas holiday, Chennault wrote a sweet letter to Mac's sister to invite her to spend some of the Christmas holiday with his family. The McDonald family took him up on his offer and spent a week with the Chennaults in Louisiana.

> Randolph Field, Texas.
> Dec 15, 1939.
>
> Miss Lucie McDonald,
>   Birmingham, Ala.
> Dear Lucie :-
>   I haven't replied to your appreciated letter sooner because I hoped to be able to visit you — as requested — at your home. I would have loved to do so but now it looks like it will be impossible to do so. I have so many places to go and so many things to do.
>   Next week, about Dec. 19, I am going back to Waterproof — and will remain there through the holidays, probably until Jan. 10. Would it be possible for your father to drive you and your mother down during the period Jan. 1 – 10? We would be glad to have you and know you wont mind being a little crowded at night.
>   Hoping that you can come down and with my very best wishes for a merry Xmas for your whole family, I am
>   Most sincerely,
>   C. L. Chennault.

GONE TO THE U.S. FOR FOUR MONTHS
Chennault Puts Mac in Charge

When Chennault returned to the U.S. for several months in October 1939, he turned his duties over to Mac, who took them in addition to his other duties. He was already working from 5:30 AM to evening every day. The pressure was growing, and the war was coming closer again.

Chennault had been gone just over two months when Mac wrote home, "I wish that it was time for the Col. to come back, and that he was here. I am really overloaded with work" and that rumors held the Japanese "will really bomb the devil out of us."

Even with Chennault gone, he took a brief break for the holidays. Writing December 22–25, 1939:

> Today is the day. It is now 9:30 AM and in 3 more hours, I will be on my way to Hanoi for Christmas vacation. All this week we have been a little worried because of Japanese activities. This alarms me in that they might cause a delay or even canceling of my flight. But this morning the weather is too bad at least for the Japanese to interfere. So I feel greatly relieved. I had an Air Mail Christmas card from Colonel Chennault…
>
> Have just had a mighty fine turkey dinner here with the Greenlaws. They are mighty nice and have had more than 14 Americans around their house this Christmas.

Other sources report that many of the Americans were pilots who flew planes there and landed them at the Greenlaws, so that their yard looked like an active airfield.

By January of 1940, Mac reported some good news, "[Colonel Chennault] will be back in a little over a month. No need to mention that I will be extremely glad to see him. I am anxious to come home as soon as Colonel Chennault gets back."

On the other hand, it is clear that he really doesn't want to miss a thing.

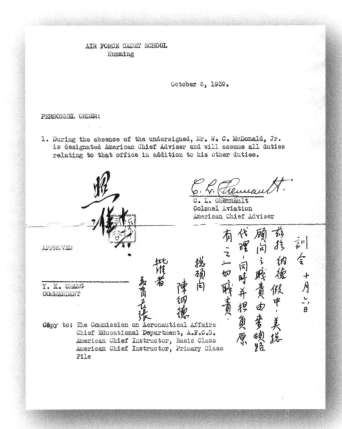

There is only one thing that worries me – I am afraid that if I go home, I will miss something exciting. Possibly, the war will terminate, and I would certainly hate to miss the end since I have been here from the beginning.

Mac, January 1940

AIR   MAIL

Kunming, China,
Feb. 15, 1940.

Dear Dad,

Colonel Chennault arrived in Hongkong on the 12th and will come here in another week or so. He must first report to the Madame and Gissimo. I am so anxious to see him, especially after you folks drove down to see him in Loiusiana.

Last night my table was graced with three letters from you folks. I was delighted no end. I was certainly glad to learn that you all had received my Christmas presents. I can see both Dad and Malcolm busy with those razors. I certainly like mine and wouldn't go back to a wet razor again for anything. Must have patience.

On the 13th the Japs tried to raid the Railroad again. We sent our lads down to see if they could prevent them from doing so and darned if they didn't stop them cold. One Jap bomber was shot down and the rest dropped their bombs hurriedly without aiming and turned and flew back home PDQ. The city was jubilant and gave $5000 dollars to the pilots along with alot of wine and food. Needless to say, we Americans were so happy we almost screamed.

I had a letter from Mildred Adams. I was awfully glad to hear from her. She is a nice girl and I was afraid she was a little mad at me for missing a date with her or something while she was in Manila. But all is well and she is herself again.

I am as anxious to come home and see you folks as you are to see me. The only thing is that I am afraid I would be away when this war would finish and I would certainly be dissappointed if that happened. Anyway, as soon as I see the Colonel I will be able to make some plan and I will let you know as soon as I know.

I think our winter weather is over. All this week it has been nice and warm. Even in the mornings it isn't necessary to wear a topcoat. This makes me feel very good because if there is any one thing that I don't like it is cold weather. When I leave this place I think I will settle down on some warm and balmy south sea island.

I know you must have enjoyed your trip to La. to see the Colonel. It is too bad that the weather was so rough. That always make traveling bad. Anyway

All letters
me from any suspense.

I am as anxious to come home and see you folks as you are to see me.

The only thing is that I am afraid I would be away when this war would finish and I would certainly be disappointed if that happened....

Mac, February 15, 1940, Kunming

China Has Lost Its Air Force

The war dragged on. Many of China's best pilots were dead and few Chinese fighter planes survived. Japanese planes roamed freely over China, wreaking havoc in cities.

U.S. companies continued to sell the building blocks of war to Japan, particularly aircraft materials, scrap metal, machine tools and metal ore and oil, in spite of strong isolationist policies intended to keep the government and its citizens out of "foreign entanglements." Mac continued to feel strongly that doing business with Japan endangered the U.S. and the world.

Despite that, Mac believed that China would resist and that failure awaited Japan in the long run. In June of 1938 he had wriiten:

> Japan is committing national suicide. No matter whether Japan wins or not she cannot recover from the great damage that the military organization has done. Greed and thirst for power coupled with poorness of vision has put them in a most desperate position. No great victory awaits Japan. China is unified and China cannot be crushed now. Japan waited too long and now her back in one sense is up against the wall.

The American advisors at Kunming continued to train new pilots for the Chinese Air Force but Mac estimated that it took two years to give the young Chinese pilots a reasonable chance of surviving against the well-trained and well-equipped Japanese. While the Chinese pursuit pilots that he and others trained in these tactics could sometimes beat far superior Japanese forces, Chennault expressed deep regret that these pilots went into battle "knowing so little."

Mac was thoroughly trained in Chennault's aerial acrobatics, tactics and flying techniques during the Flying Trapeze years. Chennault, Mac and Williamson spent many hours practicing and perfecting their techniques, and they had far more flying hours than most American pilots. But they proved it was possible to perform these maneuvers, flying in formation. By 1940 in the skies over China, Chennault had proved that his strategies and techniques were effective in combat against superior forces of bombers. But few of China's pilots, however well-trained, survived long enough to gain the flying experience they desperately needed.

Early in 1940, the Japanese introduced the A6M Zero fighter which was distinctly superior to any of the CAF pursuit planes. Even if CAMCO could have supplied Hawk 75s in sufficient quantity,

Japan has lost most of her best pilots as have the Chinese. This is expected in war in the air. Training now is the important thing. And believe you it is a tough job.

Mac, July 1938

Kunming, China,
Feb. 29, 1940.

Dear Folks,

Last week I wrote a letter and for some reason or another I failed to mail it. So I am sending it straight mail along with some more small snap shots for Lucie. Please accept my apology for failing to mail my letters.

For the past three days we have had some rather chilly weather. A little snow, a little sleet and a little rain and plenty of cold wind. To-day the sun has come out and we are getting back to normal temperature. The mountains all around us have had little snow caps for decoration but to-day after several hours of sunshine the caps have all dissappeared.

Colonel Chennault has arrived back in Kunming. I was so glad to see him. He gave me the Hankies Mother sent. Thank you very much Mother.

General conditions here in China are similar to the inside of a haunted house. One can feel that there is something present but just what it is - well, I don't know. The radio reports from the Japs say that they are mopping up the Chinese everywhere and that they are preparing to lauch large scale activities on this front and that front. The Chinese radio reports just the opposite. So !!

If America would pass the embargo bill aginst the Japs I am of sincere belief that the Japs would fold up in less than three months. I can't see why it isn't done. The Japs are certainly detremental to all American interests and if Japan could be stomped into the face of the earth without sending froces to do so - it seems to me that this way would be best. Of course - I am only one among many.

I wish you would write and tell me more about the House. Will you loose all you have invested in the old house ? What kind of a deal are you making ? Why don't you buy a small farm so I can come back home and learn to plow or something?

I don' know anything yet about my leave to come home. We are having a conference on the 7th of next month and possibly I will have something definite to tell you after that.

Hope you are still using your razor Dad !!

Love to all,

> The radio reports from the Japs say that they are mopping up the Chinese everywhere and that they are preparing to launch large scale activities on this front and that front. The Chinese radio reports just the opposite. So!!
>
> Mac, February 29, 1940

> General conditions here in China are similar to the inside of a haunted house.
>
> One can feel that there is something present but just what it is—well, I don't know.
>
> Mac, February 29, 1940

the new Zeros outclassed them. The available equipment and pilots couldn't stop the Japanese Air Force.

According to Sebie Smith, the idea that American planes, pilots and crews would most help China was first suggested by "someone" at a breakfast meeting in 1937. In a letter to ex-Trapezer Haywood Hansell in 1937, Chennault had suggested that China needed 100 American pilots and planes. However, at the time the Neutrality Acts prevented the U.S. military from providing planes and pilots to any belligerents.

Later Chennault declared confidently that if he had 100 American planes, pilots and crews, he could defeat Japan. After years of intense study of their pilots' tactics from the air and ground, and years of taking apart their downed planes, he believed that Japanese strategy and defense were deeply flawed and vulnerable to defensive pursuit tactics he could design. He also believed that key Japanese leaders were blinded by a belief in their inevitable triumph and an assumption of the innate superiority of the Japanese, and therefore more vulnerable

The airfield at Kunming
Photos by Frank Higgs

RIGHT Munitions bunker.

MIDDLE Dewoitine trainers.

LOWER Operations.

CAF Memories

UPPER LEFT Mac on CAF training field

UPPER RIGHT Chennault's radio man, Dr. Lee, and Mac

LEFT Chennault in uniform, Mac with camera, Higgs seated in front

to offensive attack. His audacious plans even included a way of attacking Japan's home islands.

Although Chennault's ideas were not widely accepted in the American military establishment, the Chiangs saw the results of Chennault's training and were convinced. Despite losing almost the entire Chinese air force, they believed that Chennault had proven his ideas and training methods.

In the U.S., President Roosevelt had also gotten an provision added to the 1939 Neutrality Act which would allow China to receive American planes. The president was also willing to maneuver out of the public eye to support his global agendas.

Chennault's focus shifted from training Chinese pilots to bringing over American pilots, crews and planes. The result would be the American Volunteer Group (AVG), popularly known as the Flying Tigers. The Tigers themselves gave credit for the group's singular and outstanding success against the Japanese to Chennault's training and tactics.

But when Chennault took trips away from Kunming, Mac took over command of operations at the school but also kept doing his job as Chief Instructor. He found doing both jobs very tiring. At its elevation of 6200 feet, Kunming was hard on his health and he suffered respiratory problems. Always looking for new experiences and new people to know, Mac was plainly bored.

His early flying career had been remarkable, with lots of fame and edgy flying. His first year in China was eventful, filled with constant wonder. A spy mission to Japan and working closely under Chennault as he took over air strategies to combat the Japanese incursion provided challenges and new experiences. Taking his training groups out on real missions upped the ante. Flying the Hawk 75 Special on observation missions, and perhaps engaging in combat with Japanese fighter planes, provided plenty of flying and adrenaline.

Now he'd spent three years at "constant war with the Japanese." He'd trained class after class of young pilots for the Chinese military, only to see most of them killed. He didn't mention the kind of exciting flights that filled his early letters from China.

When the CAF offered Mac another annual contract in the spring of 1940, he declined.

> The Japs have started their bombing again because now the weather is beginning to clear up. The Chinese newspaper had an article on it the other day, calling it "The Bombing Season."

Chungking San Hu Pa Airport runway

"...the Chungking airfield...is under 60 feet of water for at least two months out of the year. At the best of times it looks like a mud flat in the Mississippi."

Martha Gellhorn, *Flight Into Peril*

CNAC
Flying over enemy lines at night in unarmed transports carrying high-value goods and passengers into airfields of cobblestone packed by hand, sometimes in rivers

CNAC is a darned good company and they certainly do a lot of interesting work.
Mac

Photo of DC-2 at Chungking's San Hu Pa Airport by Mac

After years of wildly varied flying, of being wing man to the driven Chennault and of learning to fly—and especially to land—under the many conditions in China, Mac was ready for the unbelievable challenges that he and the other pilots of CNAC faced.

Mac's Story So Far

Mac wasn't a run-of-the-mill commercial pilot. There was the pesky bounty on his head, for starters. His flying resume might read like this:

One-third of the famous Three Men on the Flying Trapeze. Among the dozen men selected to take the first high-altitude flights. Pilot in the largest air armada exercises ever. Survivor of crash where plane was reduced to ashes, though staying with the plane long enough to make sure others weren't hurt. One of 250 Air Services pilots given the dangerous job of flying mail without proper equipment or training. Transport pilot during record-setting trip delivering planes to Columbia, front-page news in many countries.

Knew the planes, pilots and crews in China's small aviation world. Had a knack for making and keeping friends of all kinds.

Flew outdated and unarmed planes over a great deal of China through skies dominated by enemy fleets of modern pursuit planes and bombers. Made dangerous observation flights that resulted in bullet holes in his plane. Likely engaged in aerial combat with Japanese fighter planes.

Knew the network of large and small landing strips that continued to develop, sometimes by villagers' bare hands and feet. Worked with the Chinese military at the highest levels long enough to understand its unique culture and structure. Personal connections with the Chiangs, Gen. Mow, officials of the aviation companies selling planes to China, and others in power.

Trained young Chinese pilots. Learned about and appreciated Chinese culture and language. Moved aviation schools from Hangchow to Nanking to Hankow, and finally to Kunming. Witnessed massive destruction and suffering inflicted by the Japanese in places like Shanghai, Nanking and Chungking.

Close personal relationship with Chennault. Hunting buddies. Roommates. Golf partners.

Professional relationship with Chennault since 1934. Hired and trained for the Flying Trapeze, given leave to get his transport rating on the South American trip by Chennault. Publicly defended by Chennault when Mac and Williamson were passed over for promotion by the Army. Encouraged to go to China to work at the CAF training schools.

Still Chennault's Wingman

In China, Mac was still Chennault's wingman. They took a spy trip in Japan together, and each flew a plane on the inspection trip to review the Chinese Air Force's readiness. The two of them planned the response to the initial Japanese attack in Shanghai in 1937, and Mac flew Chennault's Hawk 75 Special on observation missions and into combat. They'd had a number of close calls together, and shared a love for China and its people that exceeded their desire for personal safety.

When his many duties and projects called him away, Mac was Chennault's regular choice as his second-in-command, entrusting him with operational details and authority in his absence. From all reports, Mac earned that trust with Chennault and with the men he commanded.

After years of conversations, Mac had an in-depth understanding of Chennault's plans for defending China using an all-American air unit.

During those long years, Mac listened as Chennault developed his ideas for the AVG, refined his ideas to defend and attack based on Japanese tactics and planes, used the information from the early-warning net to help direct the scarce resources of China's air power to best advantage. In speeches later in life, Mac spoke about planning this together though he was always careful to give Chennault full credit for it.

He had a personal and unfailing loyalty to the Colonel, and he would continue to serve him faithfully and help him defend China. But now he was ready to fly on his own and to enjoy some of the rewards available to him as one of the best flyers in the world. CNAC was a great opportunity, and one that would take advantage of nearly every kind of experience he'd had.

AIR   MAIL

Kunming,
March 28, 1940.

Dear Dad,

    I arrived here yesterday and after consulting with
Colonel Chennault I wrote out my resignation. Now I have thre[e]
more days left with the School.

    I will leave here sometime next week. More than likely
around the 5th or 6th. It may take a few days to clear up my affairs
here and there but I am anxious to get away. Once my mind is made
up I don't particularly like to tarry around.

    I hate very much to leave the Colonel but I am tired of
living back here in the sticks and too this altitude doesn't agree
a whole lot with my sinus.

    I will go to Hanoi by t[...]   to Hongkong as it is
the easiest way to get my baggag[e...]

    I may stay in Hongkong [...]
a little trip of two weeks down [...]
I am anxious to see these place[s...]

    Two letters came last [...]
in making the trip down to Liv[...]
anything that I had rather do [...]
open.

    Very little war acti[...]
it the quiet before another s[...]

    I am very busy tryi[...]
not in a very good mood for [...]
is improving and that she li[...]

    After this letter [...]
Also please write to Grover [...]
him of my change of addres[s...]

> After consulting with Colonel Chennault I wrote out my resignation…I hate very much to leave the Colonel but I am tired of living back in the sticks and too this altitude doesn't agree a whole lot with my sinus.
>
> Mac, March 28, 1940

P.S. Please notify
Union Bank & Trust of my new
address and tell them to send me
itemized statment for the past year.

Hongkong,
April 17, 1940.

Dear Dad,

    Monday I went to work for China National Airways
Corporation. CNAC has been operating successfully in China for
about 8 years. At present there are five American pilots and
two Chinese pilots that fly out of Hongkong. There are about
10 co-pilots, all Chinese. I have been employed as co-pilot and
will have to fly as co-pilot for six months. In the States a
pilot must fly as co-pilot for sometimes as much as four or five
years. The reason for that is there is no vacancies at the top.
It is differant here. An American pilot is not employed as co-pilot
unless he can be used as First pilot or Captain at the end of six
months. Right now there is this vacancy – so I am all set. The pay
for this first six months is just enough for me to live on here in
Hongkong but the pay after promotion is exceedingly good. AND WHAT
I LIKE ABOUT THE JOB IS THAT IT HAS A FUTURE.

    Pan American holds the controlling interest in the
Company and it makes me feel good to be working for an American
organization again.

    I think the China Clipper is due in Hongkong to-day. It
will leave to-morrow. I have writ6en a letter last week but it missed
the Clipper and there should be two letters reaching you at the same
time.

    I have already made my first flight into China and will
make another to-night or rather tomorrow morning at 4:00 A.M. to
Chungking-Chengtu and back to Hongkong to arrive here about 9:00 PM.
It is a lot of flying for one day but then I don't have to fly again
for two or three days.

    Well ft looks like Mr. Hitler made a rather serious
strategical error in his assumption that England was going to just
sit back and let him take Norway, Sweden and Denmark. The Danes had
no alternative but I was darned glad to see the Norwegians stand
there ground. It looks like it might have been a deliberate trap for
the Germans. Anyway they took a licking that may mean the start of
Hitlers decline.

    Guess that is about all for this time.

Love to al[l,]

"A JOB WITH A FUTURE"
Off to a Flying Start

On a trip to Hong Kong, Mac was offered a job with the China National Aviation Corporation (CNAC). In six months, he'd be a Captain with a substantial pay raise. He could leave CNAC and go to work for Pan Am, a sweetheart deal not everyone was offered.

Never one to hang around after a decision, Mac resigned from the CAF on March 31 and started with CNAC two weeks later, on April 15, 1940.

His reputation preceded him, in several ways. Captain Hugh L. Woods, CNAC's Chief Pilot, and Captain Charles L. "Chuck" Sharp, Operations Manager, were aware that the Japanese had a price on Mac's head as one of the pilots of the Hawk 75 Special. Another airline—perhaps any other airline on earth—might not have hired him because of that.

Instead, they changed Mac's call sign to "Little Joe," a reference to Chennault's famous Dachshund, Joe, to throw the Japanese off.

By April 17, he had already flown a DC-2 into China and would soon begin as co-pilot on a run that left Hong Kong at 4:00 AM, then landed at the storied San Hu Pa Airport in Chungking, flew on to Chengtu, then ended at 9:00 PM back in Hong Kong. After that long day, he expected to have two or three days off.

He seemed to take advantage of those days off. Hong Kong was a dynamic and international city with an abundance of recreational opportunities for the well-paid CNAC pilots. Mac sailed in Hong Kong Bay and swam in the YMCA pool twice a day. There were horse races, movies, clubs and a seemingly endless number of parties. Comparing it to rural Kunming, Mac was very pleased to be in a city.

By June, 1940, he had settled into a new apartment with a good radio and record player, "an excellent staff of servants, a rented Chevy and plenty of local color."

This new phase of his life was off to a flying start.

> What I like about the job is that it has a future.
>
> Mac, April 17, 1940, Hong Kong

> I sure am happy here in Hongkong.
>
> I was just about to go nuts [in Kunming].
>
> Mac, 9 days into the job

JUST ANOTHER DAY OF FLYING
The Hong Kong - Chungking - Chengtu Route

CNAC WAS AN UNUSUAL AIRLINE. A joint venture of the Chinese government and Pan American World Airways, it flew across China's vast spaces from 1929 to 1949. War didn't stop their flights. CNAC's routes were critical to maintaining communication and moving supplies into, out of and across China.

Despite valiant opposition, by 1937 Japan controlled the major cities in northern and central China and all major ports on the Pacific Ocean. They advanced, systematically cutting off supply routes and lines of communication, forcing CNAC to change routes.

Hong Kong — Chungking — Chengtu Route

CNAC's "milk runs" were unusual as well. In January 1940, CNAC's most important route connected Chungking and Hong Kong, flying four times a week carrying full loads of passengers and 9,000 pounds of freight.

In 1938 on this same route, Japanese fighter planes attacked a CNAC transport flown by Captain Hugh Woods. Fourteen people died, the first loss anywhere of a commercial airliner to hostile aerial attack.

Another airline might have abandoned the route, but CNAC pilots instead flew the route at night.

William Leary in *The Dragon's Wings* agreed:

> This air service to Hong Kong was a hazardous undertaking, and it was unique in the annals of commercial aviation. The route was 770 miles long; approaches to and departures from Hong Kong had to be flown at night—hopefully in bad weather. Japanese fighter planes were a constant menace, and a forced landing almost anywhere en route meant capture.

Leary also quotes a description by Royal Leonard, another CNAC captain:

> Airline flying by night over China has no parallel. There are no intermediate fields, and there are no airway beacons so common in America. Also no lighted cities, because planes heard at night are taken as Japanese. Radio communications are restricted, weather reports almost unavailable. There is a further hazard of running afoul of the Japanese. Approaching Hong Kong, CNAC's route then actually went over some of the Japanese bases.

Mac left that out of his early letters too.

Even the landing fields were also unusual. A new CNAC employee, Fred Pittenger, described his first landing in Chungking like this:

> San Hu Pa Airport is in the middle of the Yangtze river and is only 2200 feet long, surfaced with more or less flat cobble stones. From the river's edge a steep rocky slope raised up 1200–2000 feet. The approach is to fly down the canyon until you cross high tension cables, cut engines to idle, add full flaps and dive for the runway. Crossing the Hump impressed me but so did landing at San Hu Pa.

To handle those challenges, CNAC's pilots had to be among the best pilots in the world. They had to survive the daily challenges of flying in a non-industrial, poorly-mapped country in outdated equipment, plagued by parts and fuel shortages, while being on the lookout for sudden worse weather or enemy fighter planes hunting in packs.

China needed great pilots, and the combination of adventure, romance and money brought them. To Mac, it was a job with a future.

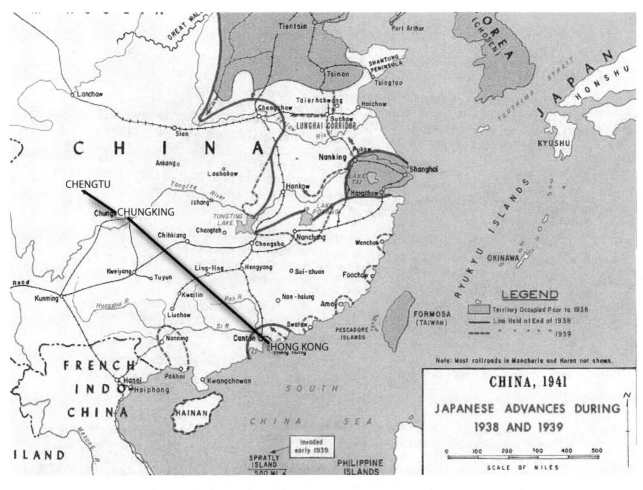

CHENGTU
CHUNGKING
HONG KONG

LEGEND

| Territory Occupied Prior to 1938 |
| Line Held at End of 1938 |
| 1939 |

Note: Most railroads in Manchuria and Korea not shown.

CHINA, 1941

JAPANESE ADVANCES DURING
1938 AND 1939

SCALE OF MILES

High tension wires and mountains

Chungking San Hu Pa Airport
runway on sandbar in river

Ned Jones

Hongkong
June 10,1940.

Dear Dad,

The darndest thing happened this morning. I got up, had a bite of breakfast, and then wrote my weekly letter. When I got ready to go down town I couldn't find the letter and I looked all over the house. I guess it is one of the mysteries of the orient.

Anyway - here goes again. I missed getting a letter off on the last clipper because I was delayed one day in Chungking on my way back from Rangoon, getting back heer the same day the clipper left.

We stopped at Loiwing, where Sebie Smith Works, on our way to Rangoon and he told me that he had just resigned and was going back to the States and plow or make traffic lights. You may see him in a couple of months.

Mrs. Watson, another fellows wife that came over here is here in Hongkong now and I am sending Lucie somethings for her friends. She leaves on the Empress of Asia next Thursday.

By the way did Lucie have here Jade ring reset ? I haven't heard much from her about it. Also are you and Malcolm still using your eletric razors ? Lets hear from you about these th9ngs.

I ha fairly reliable information to-day that Am erica would be in the war in a very short time. Possibly by the time you get this letter a lot of things will have taken place. I believe that Italy's entry into the war had better be on the side of the Allies or Russia will come in with us. Regardless the old world has certainly been torn up by this B ---- Hitler.

I have been in my apartment now for almost a week and I can tell you I am certainly comfortable. Living all alone with a good radio and victrola attachment, a good staff of servants, a new rentéd Chevy and plenty of local color.

Had a letter from Uncle James last week as well as your weekly letter and a regular letter from Lucie. My mail is very good despite my new change of address.

Will

I had fairly reliable information to-day that America would be in the war in a very short time. Possibly by the time you get this letter a lot of things will have taken place. I believe that Italy's entry in to the war had better be on the side of the Allies or Russia will come in with us. Regardless the old world has certainly been torn up by this B------ Hitler.

Mac, June 10, 1940

The Chinese Air Force, inferior in equipment as to quantity and quality, are fighting their hearts out against these great odds.

I feel that three good squadrons of Americans could really mop up with the Japs...

Mac, August 22, 1940

August 22,1940.
Kowloon, Hongkong.

Dear Dad,

The trend of events out here is not satisfied with keeping everyone in a continual state of jiterryness with the general war news and has now added the fury of mother nature. Yesterday the wind was blowing at sometimes 66 miles an hour with rain. The ferry boats were forced to run at irregular intervals as the water across the channel to the Hongkong side was quite rough. Heavy limbs and many smaller ones were blown from the trees and the streets were more or less littered with them.

The Clipper naturally has been delayed again. So I have delayed writing this letter until to-day. I leave for a regular scheduled trip to Hanoi via Chungking and Kunming to-night and will return here Saturday night.

In the bombing of Chungking the Japs have prior to this past week been using High Explosive bombs which results in great explosions and very little fire. This week the Japs changed to using incendiary bombs and they have done much damage to what was left of Chungking. The City has been bombed without any thought of danger to women, children, sick and the helpless. Fires have trapped hundred that were in Bombproof shelters. Not a single building, house or shack has escaped the relentless work of the Japs. This was true many weeks ago and now the fires. Yes, and many of the bombs were either made in America or made in Japan from parts of scrap iron bought from America.

The Chinese Air Force, inferior in equipment as to quanity and quality are fighting their hearts out against these great odds. Yesterday they brought down four Japs out of 170. And probably the Chinese had much less than 50 pursuit planes to combat the enemy. Yet some of the Japs will never get home.

The general reports we get out here from people that return or pass thru Hongkong is that America is preparing to fight Japan. I for one would rather do that than anything else. And that is the general opinion of all the pilots in the Company. I feel that three good squadrons of Americans could really mop up with the Japs in such a way that the war would make a sudden change out here in favor of the Chinese.

Guess that is about all for the time being - will see you again next week.

to all,

This week [Chungking] has been bombed without any thought of danger to women, children, sick and the helpless. Fires have trapped hundreds...

Yes, and many of the bombs were either made in America or made in Japan from parts or scrap iron brought from America.

Mac, August 22, 1940

STATE HOTEL,
JODHPUR.

June 28
1940

Dear Lucie,

Just arrived here for lunch — on to Bombay this afternoon — This is a beautiful spot the outer edge of the desert. — Love

---

Telephone 22001   Telephone 22001   Telegrams "Palace Bombay."

TAJ MAHAL HOTEL
INDIAN HOTELS CO., LTD.
BOMBAY.

June 29th, 1940

Dearest Mother,

I have just completed a flight that I wouldn't have taken a cool million dollars.

Two weeks ago tomorrow I was loaned by C. N. A. C. to a private organization to fly their plane — anywhere — anytime.

After flying around in China and Burma the "Boss" wanted fly from Rangoon day before yesterday. om Rang ..d via

---

HOTEL CECIL,
DELHI.

July 2, 1940.

Dear Lucie —

Just a note from here. I've arrived here about 12:00 noon from Jodhpur in a rather awful dust storm. The storm was more than 6000 feet high and we were unable to see the ground. I've have a new type radio direction finder on the plane which enabled us to get down very nicely.

Love,
William

HOTEL CECIL,
DELHI.

so long — here. I ce he feels the 10th

ight
— movies
of July

HOTEL CECIL,
SIMLA.

The Ho of Ju 1940

Dear Dad,

Arrived yesterday after very pleasant trip by ca To-night we leave again this time by train. The to-morrow we fly to-war Rangoon and will go as far as we can.

Simla is the most colorful spot of this kind

THE MYSTERIOUS TRIP
JUNE 16 – JULY 10, 1940

Taj Mahal Hotel, Bombay
June 29, 1940

Dearest Mother,

I have just completed a flight that I wouldn't have taken a cool million [for].

Two weeks ago tomorrow I was loaned by CNAC to a private organization to fly their plane — anywhere — anytime.

After flying around in China and Burma the "Boss" wanted to fly from Rangoon to Bombay. The day before yesterday (Thursday) we took off from Rangoon and flew to Allahabad via Aleyab and Calcutta. Then yesterday I flew a rather out of the way course to reach here. Taking off from Allahabad, we flew 540 miles to Jodhpur. There in the desert we found a beautiful airport, an excellent hotel, where we took a swim and had lunch. In the distance, we could see enormous castles and a stone fort that has been under construction since 1479 and has never been captured.

At 3:00 PM, we took off for Bombay straight south. About 30 miles from Jodphur, we encountered a sand storm over the desert. The sand was more than a mile high. I rather expected rough riding when we went over it but there were only a few bumps. It took us took 3 hours and 50 minutes, a distance of 530 miles. We reached Bombay at 6:50 just after a terrific gale had passed. Fortunately, we were informed by radio and knew what to expect.

I think we will stay here a week and make an easy trip back—stopping overnight at several places to do a little sightseeing.

Hotel Cecil, Simla
The Fourth of July, 1940

Dear Dad,

Arrived yesterday after a very pleasant trip by car. Tonight we leave again, this time by train. Then tomorrow we fly toward Rangoon and will go as far as we can.

Simla is the most colorful spot that I have ever seen. Mother would love it.

India is much more advanced than China. Good roads, nice buildings, good telephones, excellent hotels and superior radio service and airdromes comparable and better than many of our own. Will write air mail from Rangoon,

Love to all

Hongkong
September 24,1940.

Dear Dad,

We had a late Clipper in this past week – since I did not get a letter on the Clipper before I decided to wait for your letter on this one and answer to go pn tomorrows Clipper.

Well the Japs have " Peacefully " envaded Indo-China and it certainly Smells to High Heaven. It means that the Japs have just got another firm foothold out here in the East and it will mean just that much more effort to dislodge them when the time comes. Everyone one with any intelligence at all knows that the Japs can make thnigs tough for any competitor in business because of their use of cheap labor and materials. It is well known in the States by the authorities and why we are letting them carry on like this is beyond my scope of thinking. American businessmen out here are extremely despondent. Many are closing thier offices and looking for other fields. And when an office closes out here it means that associates in the States also suffe

CNAC is naturally effected. We will probably close down our Hanoi line which means the loss of foreign currency. We make most of our money in the foreign exchange ports. In China a full load of passengers will not pay for the gasoline and the hire of the crew. But the Government makes it this way because it is the only way to travel. However, the loss of the Indo China business will probably make it necessary to raise fares and rates in China to take care of the loss.

Your letter mailed on the 12th reached me on the 22nd. I say that is pretty fast work. Glad Lucie is so much better. I would like to write Malcolm a letter and I wonder why he doesn't write to me –now that he is away from home. What is his address and what not ?

I think I will be able to buy that lot or two lots for you sometime in the Spring. My idea is to have plenty of space for a lawn. Either have two lots are have more land back of a lot in order to allow room for putting the house further from the road or street. I would like to see your plans for the house. Be sure to include a bath for every bedroom. It may be expensive but it is a sure way to keep a peacefull household.

It is still as hot a s blazes here and we are all looking forward to a break. We have had a Cholera epidemic. More than 700 cases this month.

Guess that is about all for this time. Love to all,

Wm

Well the Japanese have "Peacefully" invaded Indo-China, and it certainly Smells to High Heaven. It means that the Japs have just got another foothold out here in the East and it will mean just that much more effort to dislodge them when the time comes.

Why we are letting them carry on like this is beyond my scope of thinking.

American businessmen out here are...closing their offices and looking for other places to work.

[CNAC] will probably close down our Hanoi line, which means the loss of foreign exchange ports. In China, a full load of passengers will not pay for the gasoline and the hire of the crew. However, the Government makes it this way because it is the only way to travel. The elimination of the Indo China business will probably make it necessary to raise the fares and rates in China to take care of the loss.

We have had a Cholera epidemic, with more than seven hundred cases this month.

Mac, September 24, 1940

Chungking, China,
October 6, 1940

Dear Dad,

Have not written for a couple of weeks because I haven't heard from you folks and because the Clipper has been delayed again.

Thursday morning I flew a new ship up here to be used on a spur line from here to Chengtu and I am instructing two Chinese pilots in handling the ship. I may be here for about two weeks but after all since the job is a little sour to be doing and having to live up here where the Japs are always visiting and where one looses the nice things of living that we have in Hongkong. However, since I have just been promoted to Reserve Captain with a nice raise in pay I can't complain about dirty jobs since usually all juniors are in line to get them in all walks of life.

I have another little idea that I would like to offer. Since Mother is so interested in flowers and since we have relatives that have been in the floral business why wouldn't it be a good idea for Mother to start out as a florist. If she is interested I would be willing to put up a little money to finance same. Let me know about it.

Will you send me Malcolms address and correct title etc.

The Japs have started the second and third part of a threat they made some time ago. They are now bombing Chengtu and Kunming. The last two days they have passed up Chungking and have gone on to Chengtu. Yesterday the Chinese shot down three Jap bombers. I don't think the Chinese lost any but I am not sure.

It is nothing short of Hitlerism that the Japs are dishing out to the Chinese and it is simply marvelous how they can carry on the way they do. In one town where the Japs have bombed the very heart of the City the people now just leave the City at 7 A.M. and go to the country and farm or picknick then at dark they come back to the City and most of the trading and normal life goes on at night. A siren blows the signal for the people to leave and calls them in from the fields at night. And though it is a lot trouble the Chinese smile and carry on waiting for the day when America will come to their aid.

Chungking is still a City although badly damaged. It reminds me of a badly punished boxer that keeps on fighting, though bleeding and reeling. It is uncanny how the shopkeepers still keep open. And open it is because most of them do business in a house with only one wall and some bamboo matting for a leanto roof. It is hard to believe but it is true.

It is certainly disconcerting and unpleasant when we read the remarks of supposedly intelligent people screaming for America to keep out of war when actually we are already at war. The Nazi agents are everywhere. And I venture to say there are at least 10 in the B'ham district and Washington knows it.

What does it all mean and what will the end be ? Lord only knows.

My love to all, more next week.

Wm

I may be here for about two weeks...having to live up here where the Japs are always visiting...

The Japs are now bombing Chengtu and Kunming. The last two days they have passed up Chungking and have gone on to Chengtu. Yesterday the Chinese shot down three Japanese bombers.

It is nothing short of Hitlerism that the Japs are dishing out to the Chinese, and it is simply marvelous how the Chinese can carry on the way they do. In one town where the Japanese had bombed the very heart of the City, the people now just leave the city at 7 AM and go into the country and farm or picnic, then at dark they come back to the City, and most of the trading and normal life goes on at night.

A siren blows the signal to the people to leave and calls them in from the fields at night. Though it is a lot of trouble, the Chinese smile and carry on waiting until the day when America comes to their aid.

Chunking is still a city, although seriously damaged. It reminds me of a gravely punished boxer that keeps on fighting, though bleeding and reeling. It is uncanny how the shopkeepers still keep open when most of them do business with a house with only one wall and some bamboo matting for a lean-to roof. It is hard to believe, but it is true.

It is certainly disconcerting and unpleasant when we read the remarks of supposedly intelligent people screaming for America to keep out of the war when actually, we are already at war. The Nazi agents are everywhere. I venture to say there are at least 10 in the Birmingham district and Washington knows it.

What does it all mean and what will the end be? The Lord only knows.

Mac, October 8, 1940, Chungking

Hongkong,
October 31,1940.

Dear Dad,

I haven't written to you folks in three weeks. Weather conditions have prevented the Clippers from getting here and todays Clipper will be welcome as I am anxious to hear from you.

Foxy Kent &
the *Chungking*

Last Tuesday the Japanese shot down one of our planes. Foxy Kent, Kentwood La., was flying it. I was flying another ship but not in the area he was flying. However, to prevent any attack by the Japs on my plane I landed at Kweilin and stayed there all day. We were safe there.

Kent was unfortunate in being intercepted as it was the first time this place had been visited by the Japs. We do not have the details but we think he was attacked as he was landing. The Japs strafed the plane after it landed and killed all passengers and wounded the Hostess. Foxy was certainly a fine fellow and we were all upset about it but we are helpless. Mrs. Kent is here with their three-year-old son, Peter. I feel so badly about it I can hardly write.

The result of this attack is that we shall be forced to do more of our flying at night as there is no chance at all of being intercepted.

Colonel Chennault has been my houseguest for the past week. He is here and will be aboard the Clipper with this letter. He is on his way to Washington on some very important business. It has been a pleasure having him in the house again. He is one grand guy.

When I last wrote you I was in Chungking. I have been back here two weeks.

It looks as if this old world has gone completely crazy. I can hardly believe that Hitler could have caused so much trouble. It is too bad that wars can't stop as easily as they start.

I will certainly be glad when all this trouble is over. It will be a real pleasure to work again under normal circumstances.

Mac, October 31, 1940, Hong Kong

Attacks on CNAC DC-2s: *Kweilin & Chungking*

Walter "Foxy" Kent was flying a DC-2, the *Chungking*, from Chungking to Kunming. Five Japanese planes appeared without warning from the warning net radio operators, but Kent spotted them and set down on an emergency field near Changyi.

Unfortunately the enemy planes spotted them anyway and attacked the plane and its passengers on the ground. Of the fourteen aboard, nine were killed, most of them burned inside the plane. Kent was killed immediately.

Strangely enough, the *Chungking* was originally the *Kweilin*, the plane shot down by the Japanese in August of 1938 on the route from Chungking to Chengtu. After the incident, the plane was salvaged from the Pearl River, refitted and renamed the *Chungking #39*.

Routinely carrying high-profile people and high-value cargo put CNAC planes at high risk. CNAC instituted a number of changes to try to mitigate the danger. They began to fly more at night, timing flights to leave after dusk and arrive before dawn.

C.N.A.C. AIR LINER

Corrected Casualty List Shows Nine Dead

STEWARDESS SUCCUMBS

The complete list of casualties as a result as a result of the shooting down of the Douglas airliner Chungking by Japanese military planes at Chanyi, Yunnan, on Tuesday, has now been published by the C.N.A.C. Hongkong office.

Of the ten passngers seven were killed, two were wounded and one escaped without injury. The seven killed were Mr. Chow Cheng-kang, 30, connected with the Yi Chung Co.; Mr. Sun Yu-??, 24, connected with Tien Fu Mining Corporation; Mr. Chang Chen, 26, merchant; Mr. Chien Chang-kan, 40, staff member of the Ministry of Communications; Mr. Huang Chi, 27, staff member of C.N.A.C.; Mrs. Wu Kwang-mo (nee Lin Yu-chen) and her baby about ten months old.

Mr. Wu Kwang-mo, 42, staff member of the Farmers' Bank of China, and Mr. Sun Shih-chang, 31, staff member of the Ministry of Communications, were injured while Mr. Li Chung-lin, 32, merchant, escaped unhurt.

Among the crew Mr. W. C. Kent, 37, pilot, was killed instantly, while Miss Lu Mei-ying, 26, stewardess, who was seriously injured, succumbed to her wounds on Wednesday night, Mr. Hsu Chin, co-pilot, and Mr. Lin Ju-liang, radio operator, were saved.—*Central News.*

Foxy Kent's plane #39 at a training exercise at Hangchow. Kent is the tall man at the right, with cigarette.

Hongkong,
November 12,1940.

Dear Folks,

 We have two Clippers this week and I was hoping to
get a letter from you on Yesterdays and then answer on todays.
But there is a slip even to the best of well layed plans.

 Colonel Chennault has again returned to the States.
I have asked him to call you long distance when he gets close
enough to do so with the five dollar bill   have sent Christmas presents to all of you

 Well, since my last letters I th
mention that I now have a mistress in the
was killed I was mighty lonesome for a whi
nice little Sausage dog which I have purch
with me in jam up fashion. Her name is " I
Black variety of Dachshund she is a golden
one as you ever saw. I am more than please
is only a few months old and I don't have
bathroom manners. Had to take up all my ni
as to keep her from ruining them.

 A friend of mine that used to be
been employed by CNAC and returned on the
Frank Higgs, Columbus, Ohio, and a darned
lving with me here in my apartment.

 I think I mentioned to you in my last letter that I had
been made reserve Captain. On the first of November I was again
promoted to regular Captain and have already started flying the
regular runs. I must admitt that I got as much of a thrill on my
first flight as Captain as I did when I first soloed an airplane
at Brooks Field.

 . I don't want you folks to worry about the Japs shooting
anymore of our planes down out here. We are mu
a reoccurance of " Foxy's" accident. It was ju
on a radio operators part in not telling Foxy
Now we are flying mostly at night and it is a
the Japs to intercept us.

 I guess that is about all for this
week -

 Love to a

Colonel Chennault has again returned to the States. I have asked him to call you long distance when he gets close enough.

I think I mentioned to you in my last letter that I had been made reserve Captain. On the first of November I was again promoted to regular Captain and have already started flying the regular runs. I must admit that I got as much of a thrill on my first flight as Captain as I did when I first soloed an airplane at Brooks Field.

Mac, December 3, 1940

I don't want you folks to worry about the Japs shooting any more of our planes down out here. We are much organized to prevent a reoccurence of Foxy's accident. It was just a case of neglect on a radio operator's part in not telling Foxy where the Japs were. Now we are flying mostly at night and it is almost impossible for the Japs to intercept us.

Mac, December 3, 1940

Frank Higgs
U.S. Army Air Corp
Chief Instructor, CAF
Asst Chief Pilot, CNAC

Mac's Roommate ("Rummate")

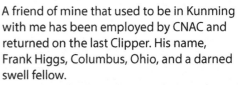

A friend of mine that used to be in Kunming with me has been employed by CNAC and returned on the last Clipper. His name, Frank Higgs, Columbus, Ohio, and a darned swell fellow.
Mac, November 12, 1940

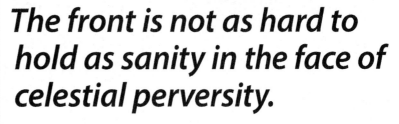

The front is not as hard to hold as sanity in the face of celestial perversity.

Frank Higgs, memo to Col. Chennault

Mac, Frank Higgs, Shelly Maydans. Hong Kong Harbor. Photo Carl Maydans.

Last Sunday five of us went for a sail. We sure had a lot of fun. Left about 9 AM and got back about 6:30 PM. We had a nice breeze and this made the trip more interesting. I wore shorts and got quite a sunburn...Hongkong weather is quite pleasant now. Mac, April, 1940

The shots are of a sailing yacht on which I am spending many weekends and lots of afternoons. It is 38 feet long and has a kitchen, bathroom, and four beds, so you can imagine how much fun it is. With Sharp's boat and Higgs at the controls it was not hard to get a date. Mac, December 26, 1940

I sure am happy here in Hongkong.

Mac

December 26,1940.

Dear Folks,

It is
over there ar
Apartments ou
tree and then
bread and we
Ronald Colema
nice. We all laughed so much. Then back to the big feed of the day at " Chuck " Sharps place (our Operations Manager). After a round of drinks we trooped in the dining room to completely destroy two well roasted turkeys and all trimmings. Then we talked and compared presents. There were twelve at the table. A lovely day and then to cap the climax - your never failing Christmas cable. Makes one feel pretty good having nice folks like you people.

Also I found out that a young Naval Lieutenant out here on the USS Tulsa is the son of Colonel Bill Porter who I used to know so well in Montgomery. So I was very happy to discover this fact. We had a long chat and today I am having tiffin with young Porter on the Tulsa.

The Clipper is due in to-day but there is no verification. I was listening to the Manila news this morning at seven and they failed to mention its arrival or departure there but nevertheless I will get this letter in the mail just in case.

Funny thing - this Colonel Porter mentioned above is now stationed at Langley Field,Va., and last night at Midnight I heard a NBC broadcast from either the Langley or Langley Field.

The Duchess is playing around my feet with an old golf ball and making me miss about half the keys on this machine. She has lost some very excess weight and is now fit as a fiddle. She certainly is lots of company. However, I am having a little trouble teaching her not to use my Nichol rugs as a bathroom.

Chuck Sharp's " Snuffy " (same breed dog) had six little pups about six weeks ago and yesterday morning chuck had them all dolled up in the nicest little sweaters you ever saw. Eacha differant color and very very bright.

I exp
The J
move
or bot

Christmas Holidays, 1940
It wasn't all flying and danger...

...sometimes there were Dachshunds in sweaters...
Chuck Sharp's Snuffy had six little pups about six weeks ago and yesterday morning Chuck had them all dolled up in the nicest little sweaters you ever saw. Each a different color and very very bright.

A Reverse Three-Point Landing
1941 version

CHESTER G. FUSON
AMERICAN PRESBYTERIAN MISSION
LINHSIEN, KWANGTUNG, CHINA
廣東連縣雙喜山崗世安
Sunday, Jan. 18,1941.

Dear Folks,

Again your wandering boy has had one of those exciting and unusual experiences. Last Wednesday night at twelve I took off from Hongkong on my way to Kunming via Kweilin. Two hours and half later I passed over Kweilin with everything running quite normal then 20 minutes later we ran into a small electrical storm. I told the radio operator to shut off his radio and we flew thru the storm without any trouble and came out in the clear above clouds in about 15 minutes. The operator turned his radio on and we tried to talk to Kunming but we were still too far away so we flew on above the clouds, sometimes flying thru the tops of some higher ones when suddenly after passing Kweilin two hours out I ran smack into another electrical storm. This time the storm was a humdinger. The radio was off and I was busy at the controls when all of a sudden a terrific flash of lightning smacked our trailing antenna, which acts more or less like a lightning rod. I then made up my mind that this condition was a little tough for me and started turning around and before I could get out of the storm, which took only four minutes, I had been hit two more times. The blue flash was so bright on one hit that I was blinded for a few seconds. Our position was some 200 (Two hundred) miles East of Kunming. Knowing the mountains there so well I started back to Kweilin and then found out that the lightning had disabled our sending set. We could hear on our reciever but not very well and could not use our Radio Direction finder so we took a reading on our situation and realized that we were indeed in for trouble. We had less than four hours gasoline left at very conservative spped and two hours and a half until daylight. Knowing that the weather conditions were not so bad some 150 miles East of Kweilin I made for this area. At 7;30, three hours after we were hit, and shortly after daylight, I saw the ground thru a rather large break in the clouds, so I began to circl down and as I was going down the hole began closing up but I managed to get under the clouds safely and spotted several fairly large sized towns with a nice river and a highway which was under construction. The town named Sing Tse, located 20 miles NorthEast of LinHsien and 155 miles ESE of Kweilin, is surrounded by rather high mountains and we flew over the entire valley for an hour looking for suitable places to land then when we had only ten minutes of gas left I selected the newly constru cted road for the spot to land. Picking a straight stretch, I landed nicely but the road was soft because of the rain and we ran along for about 200 yards and then slowed down too fast and slowly nosed up but down safely. The airplane was not even scratched and we were all pleased at getting down so nicely under such rotten conditions. We were 8 HRS 42 MIN IN the AIR- I think that is A Record of some sort.

It was quite a feat, even though I am forced to say so, in landing on the road as it is only two to three feet wider than the tread of the tires. So narrow that it is impossible to take off and we will make the road wider and surface harder before attempting the take off. But all is well and another experience ahs rolled under my bridge.

After landing I was lucky in finding a bus that was leaving Sing Tse for Linhsien that same morning so I arrived here about 2 P.M. and found Dr. Chester Fuson, Presbyterian Missionary, waiting at the District Magistrates office, as he had heard we were down at Sing Ste.

A good landing is when you can walk away from it.   Mac

Mac checks out the undercarriage. Notice the road drops off precipitously to water, and those wheels are sunk in mud.

He envited me to stay w
was not quite as good a
bridge to the Mission C
looking the Lin River a
nicer Missions in China,
which include a Hospital

The valley here is
cotton comes from the li
great pride in showing me
than other Chinese citie:
when I told him so.

Dr. Fuson and his w
has three boys and they a
at Berea College, Ky.

. . . . eaching in the States. One

The Fusons are unusual Missionaries. They are more like good old
Southern folks than anything else. They are very cordial and friendly
and not in the least boring. The Doctor has been of valuable assistance
in helping me get communications thru to Hongkong and Kweilin and we
have had many laughs out of the whole business.

There are three foreign couple here. Dr. Bradshaw and wife have
been here eleven years with the hospital and the Fusons who have been
here only two years having moved from Canton because of the Japanese
and a Canddian couple that do their work on a the River. Traveling her e
and there spreading the Gospel among the river folk.

Being slightly Christian myself they seem to think I am not such
a terrible person and have not tried to get me to join the church or
something. Anyway I am certainly lucky to havelanded so close to people
that can be of comfort when needed because I did feel bad about having
to land the plane away from an airdrome and cause it to be out of use
for weeks to come but it is much better than having lost the plane, th e
crew and one passenger - oh yes, I forgot to mention that my cargo was
some $5,000,000.00 Chinese, which the passenger was guarding . He was
certainly upset but pleased as a puppy when he got his money safely in
the bank here.

Just had a telegram last night that a car and a radio mechanic with
gasoline is on his way and should be here today. I will in the meantime
go back to Hongkong and go on other schedules until the highway is fixded
and I can fly this plane back to Hongkong.

Just wanted to write this letter under the environment of this
place as I find it difficult to retrace the thoughts and feel the
environment after getting back to Hongkong.

This place is very scenic. Mother would certainly like to visit
here. A very fertile valley and the Kwangsi - Kwangtung Mountains make
a rare setting for the valley. Sharp peaks and strange awe inspiring
effects at sunset make it a very beautiful spot. Even though the Japs
fly nearby causing an alarm almost evry sunshiney day but they have only
bombed here three times.

I hope that newspapers didn't get out a story that I was lost or
hurt or something so as to cause you unneccessary worry.

Love to all,

William

A Reverse Three-Point Landing
1978 version
by Bill McDonald

Pilots often have premonitions. On the night of January 15, 1941, I had one. My cargo was ten million dollars in Chinese banknotes and a bank messenger. I was scheduled to fly a DC-2 with Co-pilot Chen and Radio Operator Wong from Hongkong to Kunming direct. We departed Hongkong at midnight with seven hours fuel aboard. Our route was over Kweilin and west to Kunming.

About 4 AM, we were flying at 10,000 feet when I noticed a rather severe lightning display with huge build-ups dead ahead. I called to Wong, who was busy sending a message, to roll in his trailing antenna to keep the lightning from hitting us. As I saw him start to wind in the antenna, I began to plan a route through the storm ahead. When Wong had finished his job and was attempting to complete transmission to the ground station at Kunming, we suddenly entered the storm to find the lightning vicious and everywhere around us.

I heard a great crash and knew we had been hit. Lightning struck the antenna and came up through the aircraft, burning out all electrical equipment, radio receivers, transmitters and direction finder. Before I could turn back, the lightning hit us twice more.

After heading back east, we broke out into the clear, but we were flying above an overcast. I decided to head toward daylight and keep to an easterly course. Fuel was running low, so we throttled back, leaned the mixture to the utmost, and reduced our RPM until we seemed to be just floating through dark skies.

My Co-pilot was so frightened that he could neither fly nor give me any assistance. Radio operator Wong took over as Co-pilot. He was alive at least and was of some help.

Daylight came, but we couldn't see the ground. At 8 AM, exactly eight hours after take-off, I did some tall praying. Suddenly I saw the ground through a hole in the clouds and down we went through the hole. I knew we were near Kweilin because of the cone-shaped hills everywhere, but I could find no place to come down. With our fuel dangerously low, we had to land quickly, so I selected a newly constructed but unfinished road and landed. The road was only a few feet wider than the landing gear. Large clods of clay on the surface caused the DC-2 to nose up at the very end of the landing roll, but there was no damage.

Fortunately, we were in Chinese-held territory so our bank messenger was able to get the money into a local bank. Our Co-pilot simply disappeared. Coolies used clay and water to camouflage our plane. During the days we were forced to stay there, Japanese bombers passed overhead, but they failed to make an identification and didn't attack us.

Meanwhile, a thousand coolies worked to tamp down the surface of the road so we could take off. A week later, we had righted the DC-2 and a radio mechanic from Hongkong had partially repaired the electrical system. We loaded with 100 gallons of fuel and took off with no Co-pilot. We arrived in Hongkong safely, mission incomplete and Co-pilot missing. As far as I know, he has never been heard from by anyone in CNAC. Perhaps he too had a premonition.

Another view of the Reverse Three-Point Landing.

A REVERSE THREE-POINT LANDING
1941 NEWSPAPER VERSION

Not much has been told of the American airmen who are flying commercial transport planes for the Chinese government, but their work has a heroic quality that is not surpassed by aviators in war areas anywhere. Here is an example of skillful piloting by Capt. W.C. McDonald, who set his plane down on a narrow road in China's interior with his radio gone and a heavy storm raging. The pilots, volunteers in the service of the China National Aviation Corps, fly unaided and unarmed. Exposed to hurricanes, high water and Japanese bombers, they wait for nights when heavy storms prevail and conditions are unusually difficult.

1941 Los Angeles Examiner

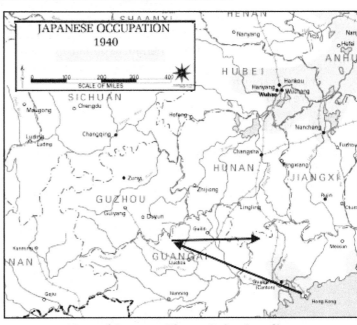

Map of Reverse Three-Point Landing

Hong Kong westbound to Kunming. After being hit by lightning, turned east to meet sunrise. Landed on a narrow, muddy road.

Chinese road crew. Each person pulled a rope attached to the heavy stone roller yoke to level the road.

Carl and Shelly Mydans wrote their article about Higgs and myself but the New York Office struck my name out since Higgs had just had a big Life Magazine write up about "Terry and the Pirates", anyway the trip was very pleasant with them and they are a grand couple.

Mac, March 5, 1941

The Hemingways are out here now and are writing articles for their respective papers and magazines. Mrs. Martha Hemingway is planning on writing an article in Colliers magazine about CNAC. She just made a round-trip to Lashio with Roy Leonard. It was on this trip that she secretly met with Cho-En-Li and literally fell in love with him. She would have dragged him off to bed had he been willing, which he was not.

Mac, March 5, 1941

Two weeks ago, I flew Dr. Lauchlin Currie, Mr. Roosevelt's special representative to China, Mr. [Nelson T.] Johnson, our ambassador and party from Chengtu to Chungking. Had a nice talk with Currie, he is a live wire and seemed to like China very much and left here with a recommendation for more help to China.

Mac, March 5, 1941

Many American military observers pass through here and one of my former Commanding Officers, Colonel Gerald Brewer, who I met and talked with last October, was killed in Egypt last month. The next important person to come is due today. He is General Clagget who was in command of Brooks Field in 1930 when I was a flying cadet. I doubt if he will remember me there but he will remember the Trapeze team..

Mac, May 13, 1941

A lot of important people have been passing through Hongkong. Capt. James Roosevelt, Hemingway and his wife, Martha Gellhorn, The Luces, Mr. Henry Luce and his very pretty wife Clare Boothe, the Novelist. The Luces went to Chungking with me and I let both of them sit up front in the cockpit so they could see the country better. They were very nice. The American Club gave a luncheon for them and they both spoke. Personally I like Mrs. Luce's speech better than his simply because she is a better public speaker. Both stated it was up to Uncle Sam to save the world for a democracy.

It is rather interesting to meet people that do so much for other people. Luce, a self-made man, now Publisher of Life and Time, and Mrs. Luce a very successful novelist. Hemingway as a writer and a regular guy and Martha Gellhorn as swell a girl or lady as you ever ran across.

Mac, May 13, 1941

IMPORTANT PEOPLE FLEW WITH MAC

LEFT Clare Boothe Luce and Madame Chiang.

MIDDLE LEFT Dr. Lauchlin Currie, advisor to President Franklin D. Roosevelt, 1939.

MIDDLE RIGHT Shelly Mydans reports from China, 1942.

Actually, our work is very interesting from the viewpoint of passengers carried on our planes, Ambassadors and high officials of every kind besides countless newspaper writers. We usually get some good information from them from time to time.

Mac, March 5, 1941

Originally published in *Life* magazine on June 30, 1941, the first few paragraphs of this article mention Mac by name and the Luces' trip to Chungking aboard Mac's plane.

The Luces, Mr. Henry Luce and his very pretty wife Clare Boothe, the Novelist...went to Chungking with me and I let both of them sit up front in the cockpit so they could see the country better. They were very nice.

It is rather interesting to meet people that do so much for other people. Luce, a self-made man, now Publisher of Life and Time, and Mrs. Luce a very successful novelist.

Mac, May 13, 1941

CHINA
TO THE MOUNTAINS

STORY by HENRY R. LUCE   PICTURES by CLARE BOOTHE LUCE

Henry R. Luce, editor of *Life*, and his wife, playwright Clare Boothe, clippered across the Pacific to China in May to have a look around that embattled country. They flew to Chungking, went through many a Japanese air raid, had their first of several meetings with the Generalissimo and Madame Chiang Kai-shek, and traveled by airplane, train and pony to the Northern Front where Chiang's troops face the Japanese across the Yellow River. They then inspected the armies of the Northern Front at many points and returned to Chungking where they studied the complex economic and political situation.

On his return to New York June 7, Editor Luce, as is his custom when he travels to the far corners of the world, wrote a report of his China trip for the private information of his editorial associates. The excerpts published herewith give *Life* readers a vivid, authentic picture of a few hours in Free China.

Mrs. Luce, an able amateur photographer, has generously supplied the pictures she took at odd moments at breakneck speed during the extraordinary exploration of China at war. - ED. at *Life* magazine

JUNE 30, 1941

At 2:30 AM we were routed out of our beds in a Hong Kong hotel and driven to an airport. By the strange light which lights all baggage rooms and places of departure, we shake hands with our pilot, an American, tough, hearty, clean-cut. He tells us that one of the other pilots on the line was the inspiration for Dude Hennick, one of the heroes of Terry and the Pirates. Our pilot and the Dude and four other Americans run the most dangerous passenger airline in the world. Their four Douglas DC-2's and two DC-3's are one of the only two connecting threads between Free China and the outside world. The other is the Burma Road, still new and inefficient. The long route to Moscow is hardly a route to the world. Today there is only one DC-3 on the line because, the day before we finally left Chungking, one of them got its right wing bombed off by the Japanese just after it had landed its passengers safely at a small airport far up inland.

At 3 AM we take off on our five-hour flight in complete darkness - no lights in the plane and no smoking allowed. Pilot McDonald zooms the ship up through the intricate hills of the harbor of

Hong Kong where the lights of an imperial city still twinkle in rows. Soon all is black and we are over Japanese-occupied territory. In 40 minutes we pass to the right of Canton, the graveyard city where 1,000,000 Chinese have resumed living but there is no life and where Japanese pursuit planes are concentrated. As the sun comes up and the clouds clear, we look down upon a land of intricate and fairylike beauty. It is the land of the terraces of rice paddies and the land of thousands and thousands of hills, each hill terraced nearly to its top with rice paddies of infinitely varied shapes, some square, some round, but mostly like the sliver shape of the new moon, shapes within shapes until all but the wooded hill or mountaintop is full. It is the landscape which might have been dreamed by a child of pure imagination. The hills in Chinese paintings which seem quite fantastic are representative of those hills.

An hour passes. The hills become higher and broader-sloped and while the myriad shapes remain, they now become a great vastness of beautiful acreage of rice. We are in Szechwan, the province which has been an empire in itself. The fields are very wet. We are glad to see this. People in Washington, in the government of the world's greatest democracy, have been praying for rain in Szechwan.

Suddenly we see a place where two great rivers turn and twist in great circles, cutting the hills and coming together and flowing on, one river through the mountains to the sea. At their juncture is an old, old city—Chungking. The plane zooms low. We looked for bombed areas but our eyes pick up only what is, not what isn't. And we land below the hills in the middle of the river bed because the water has not yet risen above that convenient runway.

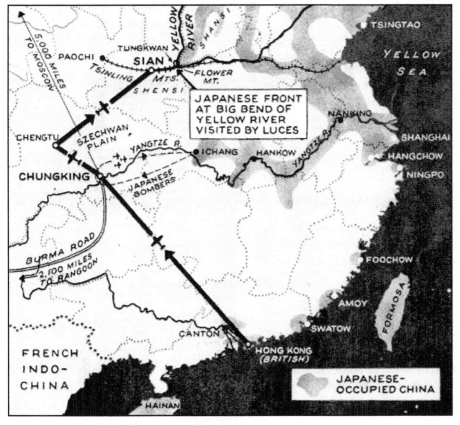

The full article in *Life* magazine is filled with sympathetic portraits of people at many levels fighting against the Japanese. While in Chungking, they endured bombing which they described and photographed.

This map from the article shows the Hong Kong to Chungking route flown by Mac and the Luces.

In the north and at the harbors, the dark shading indicates Japanese-occupied areas.

LEFT Luces' trip with Mac, Hong Kong to Chungking, 650 miles.

Hongkong
April 7, 1941.

One year ago I arrived in Hongkong more or less on my way home when all of a sudden I got this job and here I am one year today. The year has been extremely pleasant. I have enjoyed my work and have also enjoyed living in a modern environment once again. So I am well pleased.

Mac, April 7, 1941

Only one American CNAC pilot's wife will remain after tomorrow. All the others have already left. It may be the proper thing as right now the situation is very "Wishy Washy." No one seems to know anything. Yet everyone seems certain something will break very sudden. It's purely guesswork.

If things should bust wide open here we will move our base to Rangoon, Lashio or even Calcutta. We have already surveyed the route to Calcutta. For some reason I don't believe Japan wants to tangle with the U.S.. They desire diplomatic moves of evasion and would risk war with the U.S. if we became involved in the European war.

Mac, May 13, 1941

With the moon full, the Japs are raiding Chungking day and night. They have destroyed the British Embassy and wounded one of the staff. This makes it a bit difficult for us but we have a pretty good system worked out and fly mostly all night.

We are expecting to open a new line from Hongkong to Calcutta sometime around the end of this month. Actually it will be two extensions. One, an extension of the Rangoon run on up to Calcutta and the other an extension from Lashio to Calcutta. Then there is also talk in the air that we may be asked to fly alternate weeks to Manila as the Clipper goes to Singapore on odd weeks. So before long we may be a busy airline.

Mac, July 10, 1941

Hongkong
June 28, 1941.

Dear Dad,

This morning Higgs and I decided we would golf a little and so we did.

...[CNAC will have] three DC 2's and three DC 3's. About the first of the year we expect to get three more DC 3's. So we are pretty well fixed up for equipment.

I expect to start flying the DC 3's the first part of next week. They are much better planes than the DC 2's. And it is so much easier because of the automatic pilot. Just take off, set the auto pilot, and relax.

Mac, June 28, 1941

CNAC loses a DC-3 but gains a DC-2½

Hongkong
May 20th, 1941

Dear Folks,

This letter is a special. Firstly,because it will be given to Sharp, Operations Manager, who will take it to Manila. Now the rest of the letter will be devoted to why he is going to Manila.

CNAC LOOSES ANOTHER PLANE. Somewhere in China. Yesterday afternoon in a cloudless sky some thirty six Japanese bombers bombed a field far in the interior of China and destroyed several enemy planes. This would probably be the way the Jap papers would state the case. But here is the story - fresh. Yesterday morning three CNAC planes left Hongkong for Chungking. Higgs, (Roomate or Rummate) myself in two Douglas DC2's were on special flights and were to return to Hongkong last night, Which we did. Woods was flying the third ship. A DC3 which had been in service for only four months. Spank brand new. He was scheduled to go to Chengtu then back to Chungking and Lashio. About fifteen minutes after Woods tookoff the first Alarm was sounded in Chungking and this information was that 36 Japs were headed toward us. This info was also radioed to Woods who then elected to select an isolated field and go to Chengtu after the raid. The field at Chungking was suddenly turned into rapid activity. Higgs and myself got our passengers aboard and took off for parts where the Japs were not liable to pester. Then we took off shortly before dark from Kweilin and came on to Hongkong. Shortly after I took off from Kweilin my radio operator told me that he heard one of our stations reporting that the DC3 had been bombed and destroyed. Finally we got the whole story. It was bombed but the crew and passengers were safe and the plane had the right wing damaged. So that's that. We have sent a plane to the place with a crew to hide the plane in case the Japs come back today and try and finish it off. We are extremely happy that no loss to personnel and that the plane was not completely destroyed. We say never a dull moment.

Sharp is going to Manila to telephone New York for them to rush a new wing and report the incident or accident.

The DC-3 mentioned

We are extremely happy that no loss to personnel and that the plane was not completely destroyed. We say never a dull moment.
Mac, May 20, 1941

Mac's letter ends as Sharp phones for a new DC-3 wing. None was available. The famed DC-2½ salvaged by gifted mechanic Zygmund Soldinski, who replaced the DC-3's right wing with a smaller DC-2 wing, and patched shrapnel holes in the left wing and tail (rudder, elevators and ailerons) with dark fabric. The plane flew and became world-famous.

Hpngkong
July 30,1941.

Dear Folks,

The Clipper came in yesterday when I was away on a trip to Chungking and I am abput to get left out with a letter to you that will have missed this Clipper unless I can get one of the crew tp take it to LA.

The Japanese are raiding the cities of Chungking and Chengtu in a most ferocious way. For the past two or three days they have raided all day long. Yesterday there were some 100 or more Jap planes in Szechuan Province alone. And to make matters worse every place I headed for safety there was a raid there also. I finally ended up by flying about three hours changing course every time I got information from the radio. I finally decided to go to the one and only place in China where there was no alarm. Kweiyang, the capitol of Kweichow. I had been there several times before but not in the last two years so it seemed nice to get ther So peaceful and rather cool since it is 3000 feet above sea level. I stayed there for four hours and then on to Kweilin and in here last night at ten eclock.

I hope you have received the money I instructed the bnk to give you inre the house/.

There is a little more tension her, in Hongkong now but not much. Personally I think the Japs are Saps if they start any trouble withtthe USA. Of course I think they are saps all the time/.

With all the bombing of the Chinese they have accomplished absolutely nothing towards ending a victorious war for the Japs.

There is one thing that I have forgotten to mention. My vacation has been postponed until next May. So I am afraid that unles something unusua; happens I will miss another Christmas at home/.

Hurriedly,

Hongkong
Sunday Aug. 10,1941.

Dear Dad,

This time there is no question about the seriousness of the situation out here. Actually Hongkong seems to me to be one of the safest spots in the East. The situation is not unlike a typhoon that has changed it's course at the last hour and missed us here. Regardless of what happens we will be in a rather tight spot but not attacked as was first thought. Still I can be wrong because things change out here overnight.

Today the Pres. Coolidge leaves for Shanghai and then the States. She carrkes a goodly passenger list of business men and evacues from Manila, Hongkong and will get more at Shanghai. On board the Coolidge is a very good friend of mine, Carl Schaeffer, who has in his possession three pairs of bedroom slippers for Mom Lucie and Cricket. I didn't forget you and Malcolm, I just could not decide what to send that would take up so little space.

Pottschmidt, one of our pilots from Cinncinatti (well make it Cincinnati)is leaving on Tuesdays Clipper for home leave. He will return sometime in February. Leonard is next and will leave sometime in December. Then I follow. However, two more new pilots have been hired. One of them arrived here yesterday so the chances are better for me getting home Christmas but I am afraid it won't work out. I am a little sore the way things have worked out because these other two pilots were not going home at first so I put my bid in to go and then their wives went home and they now want to go. So as usual I am holding the bag. My time will come, tho.

I presume that you have received my remittance inre the purchase of the house. I think you should have asked the company from whom the house was bought to have built two more bathrooms upstairs. A bath for each room will certainly go a long way towards making a friendly household.

I saw Mr. Henry Luce&s June 30th writeup. It was well done. Told more about China than anything I have seen in a long time. Photography wasn't bad either.

I have been swimming quite a bit. Lost 7 pounds and am as brown as a full fledged life guard or something. Still could afford to loose about ten more, especially around the waist.

Give my regards to Alice Whitfield, I enjoyed her note.

Love to all,

The Japanese are raiding the cities of Chungking and Chengtu in a most ferocious way. For the past two or three days they have raided all day long. Yesterday there were some 100 or more Jap planes in Szechuan Province alone. And to make matters worse every place I headed for safety there was a raid there also. I finally ended up by flying about three hours changing course every time I got information from the radio. I finally decided to go to the one and only place in China where there was no alarm. Kweiyang, the capital of Kweichow. I had been there several times before but not in the last two years so it seemed nice to get there. So peaceful and rather cool since it is 3000 feet above sea level. I stayed there for four hours and then on to Kweilin and in here last night at ten o'clock.

There is a little more tension here in Hongkong now but not much. Personally I think the Japs are saps if they start any trouble with the USA. Of course I think they are saps all the time.

With all the bombing of the Chinese they have accomplished absolutely nothing toward ending a victorious war for the Japs.

Mac, July 30, 1941

Hongkong
September 10, 1941.

Dear Folks;-

Again I have failed to coordinate m...
Clipper schedule. I don't which is the more to...
pretty bad of late.

Several letters have reached me in...
and I am mighty happy to learn that you got th...
the house. I know you all must feel happier ab...

Mother has asked me several times...
young lady that brought the rugs over for me.
Francis Cade and she can be reached at Oberli...
thank her for me while you are

Apparently a coupl...
censored and perhaps rightly...
I sent a clipping to you abou...
amuck and bit several Chines...
the same time. Maybe excepti...
letter away or maybe you re...
answers.

I wish you wo...
fanny and marry that nice...
looks like I am having a...
or Uncle or something...

In another...
chances for getting ho...
...ike it will be somet...

We are doing a lot of flying now. I am now making two or more trips a month as far as Rangoon and there is a possibility that we will open a one day service Hongkong to Calcutta.

I have seen Colonel Chennault a couple of times and he is as busy as a bee. He wanted me to go back to work for him but I have had my share of working like a slave and living in unpleasant places. So I told him—thanks but I would rather stay where I am—this at least has a future and it doesn't have so many headaches.

Mac, September 10, 1941

Hongkong
September 26, 1941.

Dear Dad,

Had two letters from you folks and one from Malcolm this past week. As you know the Clippers only come to Hongkong twice a month and this makes our communications very slow. There is talk that Pan American will open a new service of twice a week from Manila to Hongkong. I hope they do this as it will certainly be a help to us here.

My chances for coming home Christmas have almost faded. However, I haven't given up completely. The score stands a little lopsided with the following present status. Pottschmidt is now on home leave and is due back in February. Leonard is supposed to go on leave in December and return next June. And now Sweet has taken a sudden case of homesickness for wife and children and is going home next month. (For keeps). This last blow is what hurts my chances so much but there are others just as bad. We have two pilots in the hospital. One with a recent operation for infected mastoid and the other from injuries received in a motor car accident. So now we have a definite shortage of pilots. Still things can change overnight. I hope so anyway.

The feeling here in Hongkong is still as unconcerned for Hongkong as ever. People more or less feel that the war has just completely passed Hongkong and now everyone feels that they should try and get all the women and children back here. I think this is as foolish as anything that the people have done yet. Now more than ever war clouds are evident in the Pacific and there is no telling when it will break out. Hongkong may have been passed up but there is a chance of the danger turning around and deciding to drop in and pay a visit. 'Tis possible.

Last week we had another typhoon scare. I took off on a Rangoon trip about 8 hours before it hit and didn't experience the big wind. Some damage was done but not much.

Mac, September 26, 1941

...Mrs. Chalmers and Mr. Wofford.

...e - so

Love to all,
Wm

Hongkong
October 8,1941.

Dear Dad,

Our communication worries are over at last. Effecti
October 12th Pan American will start a bi-weekly service Hor
Manila. Everyone are very happy over this new service.

Well the Chinese,as I thought and mentioned in my
letter, lost Changsha but turned right around and trapped t
Army and gave them a bang up beating. The Chinese place arg
deal of significance on this battle and claim it is the beg
of the end for the Japs.

Many prominent Americans have been visiting Hongko
their way to China. The latest is Dr. Henry Grady, Presiden
American President Lines and President Roosevelts Economic
the Far East. I attended a rather scrumptious Cocktail Part
him last night. He was my passenger from Rangoon to Kunming
became fairly well acquainted. Also there is General MacGru
military Mission that has just arrived. One of the members,
Ross Hoyt was at Selfridge Field when I was there in 1931.

Dad, what is going to be the results of inflation if it
occurs? Give me your idea. All our fellows are worried about it.

I don't remember whether or not I have mentioned this
or not but I have sent a few presents home by Mr. Carl Schaeffer.
He is already in the States and you may have them by now. Actually
I had almost forgotten about it and I am not sure what it was.

Your last letter was full of more news about home than
any that I have received in months. I enjoy hearing about the folks
back there and what they are doing.

well, I am moving from this apartment to a house. Higgs
and myself are a little restless and this place has suddenly become
very noisy. Our new place is very nice and I will send you a picture
of it soon. A nice big yard for the Duchess to play in and much more
privacy. 31- KADOORIE-AVe,

Many prominent Americans have been visiting Hongkong on their way to China. The latest is Dr. Henry Grady, President of the American President Lines and President Roosevelt's Economic Envoy to the Far East. I attended a rather scrumptious Cocktail Party for him last night. He was my passenger from Rangoon to Kunming and we became fairly well acquainted. Also there is General MacGrunder's military mission that has just arrived. One of the members, Colonel Ross Hoyt was at Selfridge Field when I was there in 1931.

Mac, October 8, 1941

Well, I am moving from this apartment to a house. Higgs and myself are a little restless and this place has suddenly become very noisy. Our new place is very nice.

Mac, October 8, 1941

Making Nuro, a traditional Chinese dish that Mac adopted as a signature dish for parties for family & friends.

FROM LEFT Unknown, Roger Reynolds, Mac, unknown, Frank Higgs.

Hongkong
November 6.1941.

Dear Folks;-

Well th[...]
in yesterday a[...]

B ecaus[...]
between the Jap[...]
one day here in[...]
States in an ef[...]

In my l[...]
Chungking and K[...]
for us to scram[...]
would not envade[...]
just sit tight a[...]

The real[...]
far now that she[...]
seems to me that[...]
will make little[...]
very, very rough[...]
reach their desti[...]
if they compromis[...]

About the only thing Japan could do instantly would be for
them to denouce their afiliations with the Axis and turn their Navy
over to the Allies in order to stop what now appears to be a first
class international chaos. But that is a dream !?

Frank and I have moved - lock, stock an d barrel. We now
are living in one of the nicest homes in Kowloon. Two story, with
a nice yard for the dogs. Yes, Frank has another now, a female Dach s
like mine but a puppy and her name is Geraldine Celeste.

I ran into a man the other night on my plane that was from
Bessemer. His name was Carter and his brother lives at Muscogee. He
will be home sometime before the 1st of January and he may call you.

Dad, have you picked out that farm near York that I am going
to buy ? Or how about your old place could that be fixed up ? If
money goes all to hell it will be better to have property so keep a
sharp lookout for a good buy and let me know.

Love to all,

Wm

Because of some very special diplomatic negotiations between the Japs and the States they are holding the Clipper up one day here in order to take Ambassador-at-Large, Kusura, to the States in an effort to smooth the troubled waters out here.

In my last trip the following feelings were noticed. At Chungking and Kunming everyone was warning that the war was on us, for us to scram out of Hongkong. — At Rangoon — people said the Japs would not invade to Siberia or South Seas. Here in Hongkong people just sit tight and carry on normally but with an ever watchful eye.

The real status of the situation is that Japan has gone so far now that she is almost compelled to take some action. And it seems to me that she is definitely behind the "Eight Ball." It will make little difference which road Japan takes, either will be very, very rough and is certainly questionable if they will ever reach their destination. If they fight they are sunk without a doubt, if they compromise they lose all they have gained.

About the only thing Japan could do instantly would be for them to denounce their affiliations with the Axis and turn their Navy over to the Allies in order to stop what appears to be a first class international chaos. But that is a dream!?

Mac, November 6, 1941

CNAC at War

Flying over the highest mountains in the world, in the worst weather, at night, in a war zone, unarmed, with Japanese Zeros hunting them

CNAC is a darned good company and they certainly do a lot of interesting work.

Mac

Likiang Mountain, landmark on the Hump route. Photo by Gifford Bull.

CNAC hangar and remains of planes after Japanese attack.

America and Britain Enter the Fight Against Japan

In Rangoon, Burma, with a CNAC DC-3, Mac prepared to pick up a load of passengers on his usual route. The other CNAC planes were parked at Kai Tak Airport, Hong Kong, after a regular night of flying.

Mac was stunned to hear that the Japanese had hit Hawaii, the Phillipines and Malaya just hours before. Six hours after the attack at Pearl Harbor began, at 8:00 AM on Monday, December 8, 1941 (one calendar day later due to International Date Line), the Japanese bombed Kai Tak Airport and began a ground attack on the British colony of Hong Kong. The Japanese were at war with the Allies.

Mac's first letter home and other accounts emphasize the heroic efforts of many. CNAC airport staff stayed on the job despite Japanese threats to behead any they caught. For three days and nights, eight American pilots and their crews flew into the war zone for a total of sixteen trips between Kai Tak Airport and airports in Namyung and Chungking, saving 275 people. Pilots Chuck Sharp, Hugh Woods, Harold Sweet, Frank Higgs, Robert Angle, P.W. Kessler, S.E. Scott and Mac evacuated CNAC personnel and families and high-ranking Chinese officials and family.

Mac's family would not be the only family waiting to hear news after the attacks, but the telegram Mac sent on December 21 must have brought a great deal of joy to his family. His mother had written to Pan Am on December 19 to find out news. Imagine that wait…

LEFT Kai Tak Airport after bombing by Japanese. Shattered airplanes in front of hangars.

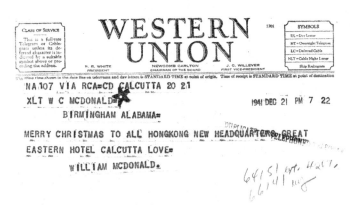

Mac and the other CNAC people had been very busy, but Mac remembered to telegram his family on December 21 from Calcutta. Judging from his mother's letter of December 19 and Harold Bixby's January response, this was the date when his family found out he was alive.

HOTEL TELEPHONE Nᵒˢ 253 254
OFFICE TELEPHONE Nᵒ 255

THE GREAT EASTERN HOTEL LD.

TELEGRAMS
"GREASTERN CALCUTTA"
CODES
A B C 4ᵀᴴ & 5ᵀᴴ EDITIONS A I AND BENTLEY'S

POST BOX 192

CALCUTTA Dec. 20 1941

Dear Dad,

All hell has broken loose. The damned
little Japs have gone completely mad. I need
not mention the rage and furor that their
dastardly attack caused. I know all of you
must feel the same as we all do here.

The War has inconvenienced many people
and I shouldn't complain but I must tell
you what I had planned.

I had not written to you for several
weeks because I had arranged home
leave and was going to try and make
Birmingham by Christmas. All reservations
had been made. I was flying day and night
the first week to get my full months flying
time in so as to get a full months pay
for December. And I had planned to send
you a cable as soon as I was

Evacuation of Hong Kong
December 8, 9 & 10

en route. I was scheduled to leave Hongkong on Dec. 11th and get a Clipper out of Manila on the 13th but look what has happened? I would, off hand, say that my plans have been just a little upset.

On Monday morning, Dec. 8th, I was in Rangoon. All of our other pilots and planes were in Hongkong. Our agent rushed into my Hotel room and told me that Japan had attacked Hawaii, Phillipines, and Malaya — I was stunned with the news and immediately realized that Hongkong must be in danger — so I took off from Rangoon at 8:00 a.m. Rangoon time and 10:00 a.m. Hongkong time, for Chungking. All the way there I began to get reports. Some good some bad, about Hongkong — and for a while I feared that my plane was the only one CNAC

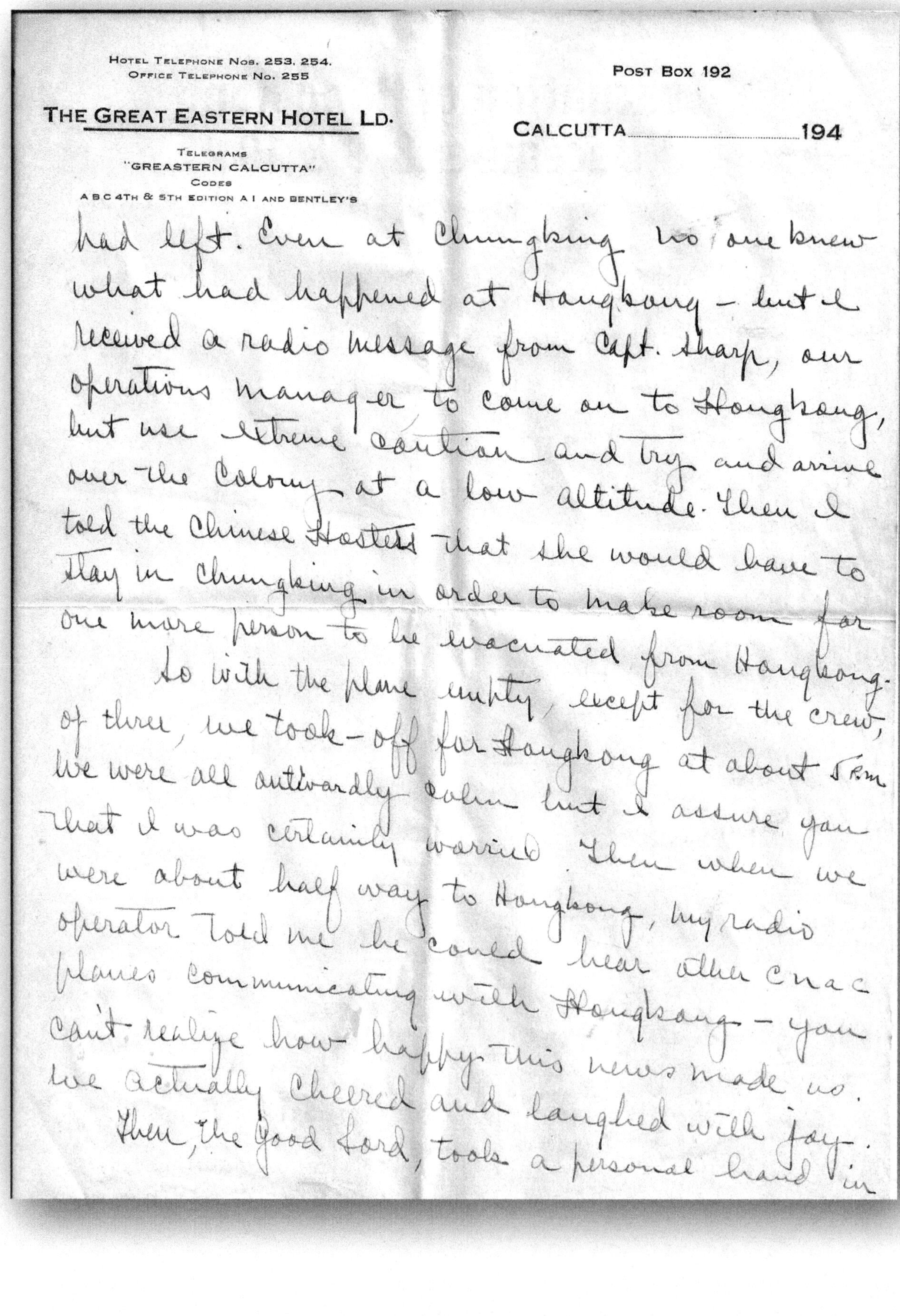

HOTEL TELEPHONE Nos. 253, 254.
OFFICE TELEPHONE No. 255

POST BOX 192

THE GREAT EASTERN HOTEL LD.

CALCUTTA_____ 194

TELEGRAMS
"GREASTERN CALCUTTA"
CODES
A B C 4TH & 5TH EDITION A I AND BENTLEY'S

had left. Even at Chungking no one knew what had happened at Hongkong — but I received a radio message from Capt. Sharp, our operations manager to come on to Hongkong, but use extreme caution and try and arrive over the Colony at a low altitude. Then I told the Chinese Hostess that she would have to stay in Chungking in order to make room for one more person to be evacuated from Hongkong.

So with the plane empty, except for the crew, of three, we took-off for Hongkong at about 5 P.m. We were all outwardly calm but I assure you that I was certainly worried. Then when we were about half way to Hongkong, my radio operator told me he could hear other CNAC planes communicating with Hongkong — you can't realize how happy this news made us. We actually cheered and laughed with joy.

Then, the Good Lord, took a personal hand in

HOTEL TELEPHONE Nos. 253, 254.
OFFICE TELEPHONE No. 255

THE GREAT EASTERN HOTEL Ld.

TELEGRAMS
"GREASTERN CALCUTTA"
CODES
A B C 4TH & 5TH EDITION A I AND BENTLEY'S

POST BOX 192

CALCUTTA_____ 194

the situation he made us ideal weather. overcast
And once again we cheered — the night, tho
illuminated by half a moon was suddenly
wonderful because it meant we could
land safely and stay on the ground for
gas and passengers without fear of a sudden
Jap attack.

We arrived over Hongkong at 5000 feet,
flying blind in the clouds, but this time the glow
of the cities lights warming the clouds, which
was so much a welcome home sign to
CNAC pilots for three years was no more. I
circled down breaking out of the clouds at 3000
feet to see Hongkong, completely blacked out, I
saw one small light across the harbor as I
made my approach to land.

I was instructed by radio to land south
of several red lights - that were in the center of

the landing area — I didn't have to be told why these lights were lit for me — bomb holes on airdromes was not new to me.

When I was some 1000 yards from the field the boundary lights flashed on, I turned on my landing lights and we were down. Almost as soon as my wheels touched the field lights were snapped off and I turned off one of my lights and taxied to a flash light signal from a ground crew. Engines cut, lights out, I jumped out of the plane to greet our gang — they were damned glad to see me and I was more than happy to see them — then I turned to see the burned skeletons of five of our planes, like tired birds with broken backs, lined up and gruesomely displayed by a soft moonglow fused thru thin places in the clouds overhead.

Three of the planes were obsolete freight planes

HOTEL TELEPHONE NOS 253 254
OFFICE TELEPHONE NO 255

POST BOX 192

THE GREAT EASTERN HOTEL LD.

TELEGRAMS
"GREASTERN CALCUTTA"
CODES
A B C 4TH & 5TH EDITIONS A I AND BENTLEY'S

CALCUTTA _____ 19

and two were DC-2's # 24 and # 26, our oldest Douglas 14 passenger planes.

These planes were parked wing-tip to wing-tip outside of the hangar and it was a very apetizing target for the Japs but little did they know that the Hangar was full of our best planes; as they machine gunned and set the old war horses on fire, no bombs were dropped on the field this first raid.

As soon as the all clear signal sounded all CNAC personnel turned out – and got the three newer planes out of the hangar and hid them 1/2 mile off the field – and luckily so – for the Japs came back in the afternoon and bombed the field – very poorly tho – even one bomb hit the hangar but failed to explode.

HOTEL TELEPHONE NOS 253 254
OFFICE TELEPHONE NO 255

POST BOX 192

THE GREAT EASTERN HOTEL LD.

TELEGRAMS
"GREASTERN CALCUTTA"
CODES
A B C 4TH & 5TH EDITIONS A I AND BENTLEY'S

CALCUTTA 19

My plane was gassed and the passengers loaded and I took off about 2 a.m. for Chungking – arriving there just at day break I had been flying about 2 4 hours – I was dead tired – but there was still work to do – so after 3 hours sleep – I again took off with the two other ships and back to Hongkong to rescue more people. This night we all took two complete loads out of Hongkong.

Again we were blessed with an overcast and our work was done without worry of Jap attacks.

We all arrived back in Chungking at 8 a.m. and we all piled in beds in quick time.

I also made an effort to get back to Hongkong on Thursday night. but the

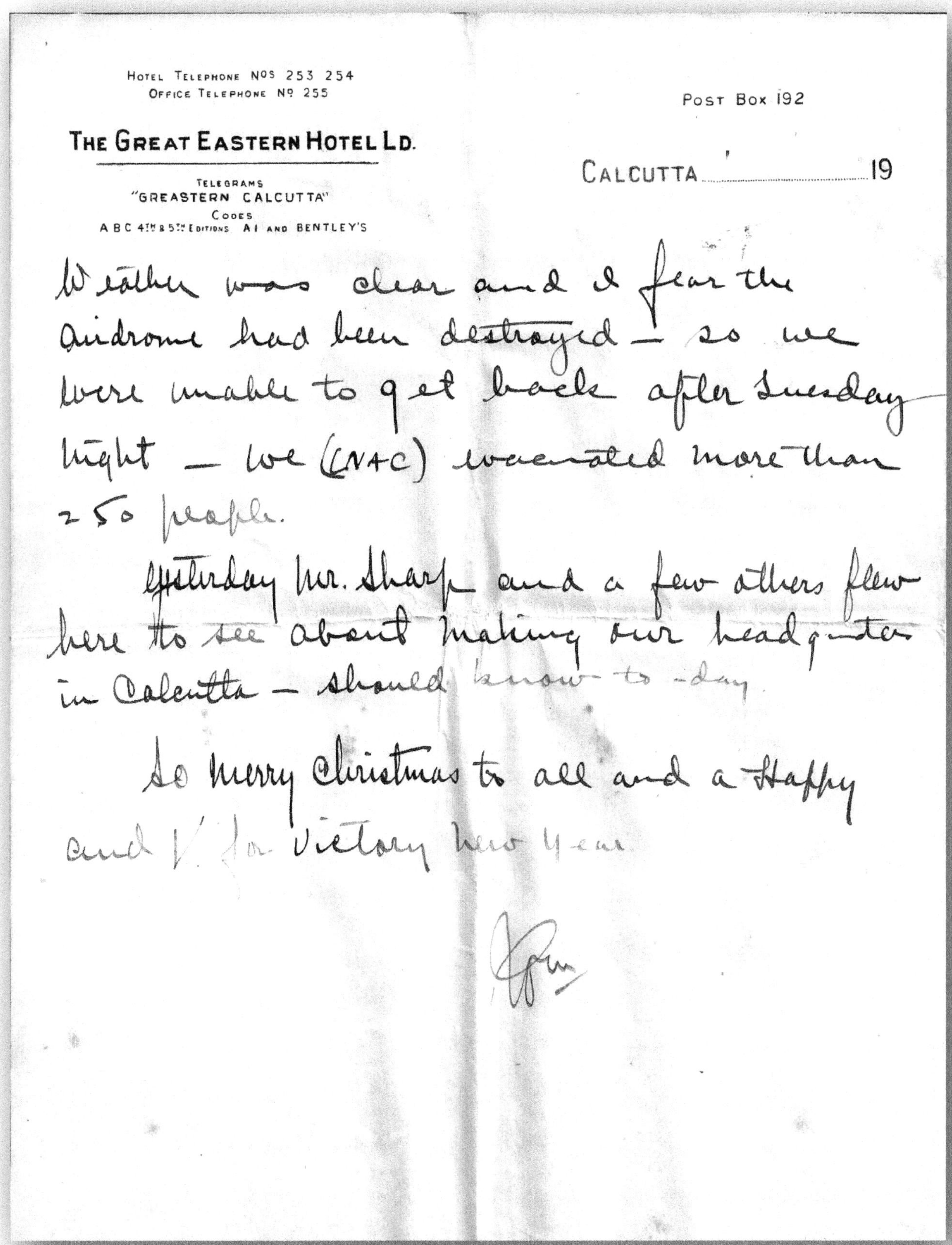

Hotel Telephone Nos 253 254
Office Telephone No 255

Post Box 192

THE GREAT EASTERN HOTEL LD.

TELEGRAMS
"GREASTERN CALCUTTA"
CODES
A B C 4TH & 5TH EDITIONS   A I AND BENTLEY'S

CALCUTTA 19

Weather was clear and I fear the
aerdrome had been destroyed — so we
were unable to get back after Tuesday
night — we (CNAC) evacuated more than
250 people.

Yesterday Mr. Sharp and a few others flew
here to see about making our headquarters
in Calcutta — should know to-day.

So merry Christmas to all and a Happy
and V for Victory New Year.

A BRIEF STOP AT TOUNGOO, BURMA
Chennault & Flying Tigers, Guns Ready

On the morning of December 8, 1941, after hearing the news about Pearl Harbor and unsure of the situation in Hong Kong, Mac started back from Rangoon, Burma, on his way to Chungking with passengers, which included Bill Pawley. He made a brief stop that he did not mention in his letters. It is unlikely that he reported it over the radio. Only long after, when it no longer endangered the war effort, would he tell more of the story.

Mac knew that Chennault was likely to know what had happened at Pearl Harbor and at Hong Kong. "For a little while," Mac said years later, "I worried that I had the only remaining CNAC plane." So Mac flew to the British base at Toungoo, Burma, where Chennault was training the new Flying Tigers, the pilots of the First American Volunteer Group (AVG). They had yet to go into combat against the Japanese.

"Here," said Mac in a speech years later, "I found guns loaded, pilots in the cockpits and engines warm. The 'Flying Tigers' were ready, as no one else in the East was and that day was the beginning of the big job they did."

These men had volunteered to fight for China, and now they were fighting for their own country as well. Chennault may have taken this opportunity to sketch out a plan for moving ground crews and support staff to Kunming. Without transports, he relied on Mac and CNAC to move AVG equipment and people.

Then Mac flew his regular route to Chungking to drop his passengers and was advised not to continue to Hong Kong. He went anyway. There, "I saw the flashes of guns and sweated a little, but kept going," Mac told a reporter.

After the evacuation of Hong Kong, moving people and supplies from Namyung to Chungking, and establishing the new base of operations in Calcutta over the Hump—three CNAC planes landed in Toungoo just after midnight on December 17 to move the Tigers' support teams to Kunming. Mac and Frank Higgs were flying two of those transports.

> "Here," said Mac in a speech years later, "I found guns loaded, pilots in the cockpits and engines warm. The 'Flying Tigers' were ready, as no one else in the East was and that day was the beginning of the big job they did."

...on 18 December, the flyable planes of the 1st and 2nd Squadrons left for Kunming... Some of us joined Chennault in a Chinese National Aviation Corporation DC-3 for the trip to China, with a stopover in Lashio, Burma.

The Japs had been making bombing runs on Kunming without opposition so they didn't bother with a fighter escort. This time we had a surprise in store for them.

The 1st Squadron which had the top cover assignment dove on the bomber formation and in a running fight, brought down four of them and reported damage to most of the others. Several of our planes were shot up, but all the pilots returned uninjured. We were a jubilant bunch, and the Japanese did not return to Kunming again during our stay in China.

Dick Rossi, *A Flying Tiger's Story*

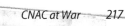

Smoke from bomb landing on runway at Kai Tak airport. Hong Kong harbor and ships in the distance.

Unhappiest Man in Alabama

William Langhorne Bond, president of CNAC at the time relates in his book, *Wings for an Embattled China*:

Mac had come into my office the last day of November, 1941. Mac said he had been in China for four years and that he would like to go home.

He felt that he needed it. I was sure he did but he had been with CNAC for less than two years. I told him we had two pilots on home leave. He was obviously disappointed, but said he was willing to wait. When Pearl Harbor and the attack on Hong Kong and the Philippines happened, Mac flew into Hong Kong from Rangoon about 10 pm.

The first thing he said to me was, "Damn! Am I glad you didn't let me go home as I requested about 10 days ago. If I were home now I would be the unhappiest man in Alabama."

U.S. Pilots Brave Guns, Rescue 275

CHUNGKING, Dec. 15.—(INS)— The stirring saga of eight American civil aviation pilots and one Chinese pilot who flew through a hail of anti-aircraft fire to rescue 275 persons, including Madame Sun Yat Sen, from besieged Hongkong had something of an anti-climax today when all nine refused to see anything unusual in their actions.

The nine pilots, all employees of the Chinese National Airways corporation, are:

Charles L. Sharp, CNAC operations manager of Fort Worth, Texas; Chief Pilot Hugh L. Woods of Winfield, Kan.; Harold A. Sweet,

Pasadena, Calif.; P. W. Kessler, Chicago; William McDonald, Birmingham, Ala.; Frank L. Biggs, Columbus, Ohio; Robert S. Angle, Calif.; S. E. Scott, Waco, Texas, and the Chinese pilot, Moon Chin.

McDonald started his rescue trips after finishing his regular commercial schedule in Chungking.

"I saw the flashes of guns and sweated a little, but kept on going," he drawled.

Starting Monday, the pilots continued their ferry service until Wednesday, when they were warned to stop by the Hongkong radio.

McDonald started his rescue trips after finishing his regular commercial schedule in Chungking.

"I saw the flashes of guns and sweated a little, but kept going," he drawled.

Mac, quoted in newspaper article, December 1941

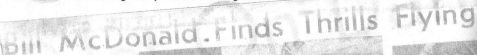

W. C. McDonald, 34, Birmingham flier, who's living an adventure book in real life as a commercial aviator in China. Remember him? He used to be one of the Army's crack pilots as a member of the "Flying Trapezers," the Air Corps' close-formation aerobatic trio who stunned spectators at the Air Carnivals here with their exploits.

PAN AMERICAN AIRWAYS SYSTEM

GENERAL OFFICES, CHRYSLER BUILDING, 135 EAST 42ND STREET, NEW YORK, N.

January 6, 1942

Mrs. W. C. McDonald
1040-43rd Street
Belview Heights
Birmingham, Alabama

Dear Mrs. McDonald:

I sincerely regret that, through misrouting, your letter of December 19 did not reach me until this morning.

I am hopeful that long before this you have received word direct from your son, informing you that he is safe, well and in good spirits. Doubtless modesty would not permit him to add that he shared with his fellow CNAC pil accomplishment of one of the most heroic tasks undertake since the outbreak of war. These men made sixteen trips into Hong Kong during the first forty-eight hours that p was under siege and evacuated over 275 Americans, impor Chinese officials and other persons. As accustomed as to the impossible jobs done by CNAC, we are neverthele ticularly proud of this latest feat.

We are informed that CNAC is operating se between China and India over a route far removed from scene of hostilities. These services are transporting ficials, materials and supplies, essential to Chinese sistance.

No doubt you will wish to correspond wit son and, in that connection, I suggest that if you po letters to him airmail, they will reach him without siderable delay. I believe it would be best, at lea the present, to address your letters to him in care National Aviation Corporation, Chungking.

Sincerely,

H. M. Bixby

HMB:MS

Helped
275 In
Hong

[Mac] shared with his fellow CNAC pilots accomplishment of one of the most heroic tasks undertaken since the outbreak of war. These men made sixteen trips into Hong Kong during the first forty-eight hours that port was under siege and evacuated over 275 Americans, important Chinese officials and other persons. As accustomed as we are to the impossible jobs done by CNAC, we are nevertheless particularly proud of this latest feat.

We are informed that CNAC is operating services between China and India over a route far removed from the scene of hostilities. These services are transporting officials, materials and supplies, essential to Chinese resistance.

H.M. Bixby, January 6, 1942

His Mathematics Wasn't Good Enough For Army—

Birmingham's Own Bill McDonald Plays Hero's Role As Civilian Pilot On Dangerous Airways Of Far East

By William Bennett

TONIGHT, if its rainy and foggy, with a ceiling near zero, a Douglas transport plane probably will lift its wings in Burma and point its nose toward Chungking, winging its way wearily through the steaming China night with a sharp lookout for the Japs.

Aboard the plane, the dim light from the instrument panel will illuminate the bronzed features of Pilot Bill McDonald, as his blue eyes coolly glance over the quivering indicators, then once more bore steadily through the blackness outside, looking for the Japs.

Tonight, too, Mrs. W. C. McDonald, his mother, will sit beside her radio in the family home at 1040 43rd-st, Bellevue Heights, listening to every scrap of war news from the Far East. She doesn't need to look at a map, for she's looked at so many maps of China and the Pacific during the last five years, she knows exactly where the mentioned spots are and can probably pronounce their names more accurately than the radio announcer.

Adventure Seemed To Seek Him Out

To the outside world, William C. McDonald is a celebrity, a member of that daredevil band of American civilian pilots who evacuated 275 people from Hong Kong by air in the middle of the Japanese attack. He was known all over the United States as one of "The Flying Trapezers," the daredevil trio of U. S. Army pilots who made aviation history in the '30's with their close-formation acrobatic flying.

But to a lot of Birmingham people, he was young Bill McDonald.

You might have known him. He went to Ensley High School, where he couldn't learn mathematics, but managed to graduate in 1929. He spent a year at Washington and Lee, then a couple of years at Howard College, but he was too restless for books. He spent a lot of time out at old Roberts Field in Ensley Highlands. Big and ruddy-faced, he was an outdoors boy all through. He seemed marked for an unusual life, for adventure seemed to seek him out.

Finally he wangled an appointment to Kelly Field, and started to go to town. He graduated a second lieutenant and went to Selfridge Field, Mich., where he was named one of 12 Army fliers to make the first high-flying tests with oxygen tanks.

Denied Commission In Army He Went To China

Two more years and Maj. Claire Chenault picked him as a wingman for the trapezes, meaning he was one of the three best fliers in the Air Corps.

Even Army life palled. He had gone to Maxwell Field, Montgomery, as a private, was made a sergeant, then Washington brass hats refused to give him a commission, despite his flying, because he couldn't pass a mathematics examination. So in 1936, he went to China and married adventure.

For two years he taught Generalissimo Chiang Kia Shek's young men how to fly, then went with the Pan-American Airways China company, called China National Aviation Corp. Since then, he half a dozen brother pilots been writing the most thri...

W. C. McDonald, 34, Birmingham flier, who's living an adventure book in real life as a commercial aviator in China. Remember him? He used to be one of the Army's crack pilots as a member of the "Flying Trapezers," the Air Corps' close-formation aerobatic trio who stunned spectators at the Air Carnivals here with their exploits.

chapters in commercial aviation's book.

Jap fliers were looking for them. So they flew their passenger runs ...what they called "protective" ...h fog a...

able in every other country in the world. They figured the Japs either wouldn't be flying, or couldn't see their passenger ships if the bombers were out on the hunt.

He Lands At Night On Blacked Out Fields

Their landing fields not only are not marked for night flying as American fields are with beacons and flood lights, but are throughly blacked out and camouflaged. Bill wrote that they found the fields with their "homing" instinct, like a pigeon, coupled with a little figuring. Today Bill McDonald, the man the Army didn't want because he couldn't pass a mathematics test, is doing practically all his flying by night and by "dead reckoning" with mathematical instruments. Even radio and radio beams must be used as sparingly as possible to keep from guiding the enemy to cities.

This every-day heroism, however, is being constantly highlighted with adventures that read like fiction.

Not so long ago, Bill McDonald left Hong Kong for (censored) with five million dollars and a bank guard in his plane. It was midnight. An hour out, he ran into a cold storm that piled ice on his wings. The icy fog was solid clear to the ground. He started to turn around and ran into an electrical storm. In four minutes his radio antenna, which acts like a lightning rod on a plane, was hit three times by lightning.

His radio set fused into a pile of ...seless metal and the cabin caught ...e. They put out the blaze and ...covered the navigating instru... [Page Two]

Adventure Seemed To Seek Him Out

To the outside world, William C. McDonald is a celebrity, a member of that daredevil band of American civilian pilots who evacuated 275 people from Hong Kong by air in the middle of the Japanese attack. He was known all over the United States as one of "The Flying Trapezers," the daredevil trio of U. S. Army pilots who made aviation history in the '30's with their close-formation acrobatic flying.

But to a lot of Birmingham people, he was young Bill McDonald.

Mac's mother, with the book she kept of his letters home

In early 1942 I was assigned to fly Madame and the Generalissimo and about a dozen high officers of China to India for conferences with Mahatma Ghandi, Nehru and other Indian officials. The Generalissimo sat in the co-pilots seat and asked many questions about the terrain and the weather. We arrived in Calcutta in the late afternoon and I was most pleased to be asked to join them for an informal dinner. It was a magnificent meal, their cooks had been part of our passenger list. News men announced that the Chiangs were in India and I was most uneasy about our return trip since the Japanese might try to intercept us and kill the Chinese leaders. We decided to fly at night and we used an RAF fight fighter escort for the first part of the trip. I was delighted to land in Kunming where General Chennault met us and took charge of my VIP passengers.

Trip to India
Note from a
speech card
Mac, unknown date

A Trip Home, With Submarine

By 1942, Mac had been away from home for six years. William Bond, Operating Manager of CNAC, hatched a plan whereby Mac could take a vacation to the States and then ferry an airplane back to CNAC.

Mac was able to spend some weeks at home, visiting with family and friends. While there he hoped to buy a car but found wartime rationing prevented it. Bond wrote to the head of the Wartime Rationing Board and the next day, Mac was able to purchase a car. When he headed back to China, he left the car for his family.

While over the Atlantic ocean, Mac was intrigued by a dark spot in the ocean. He flew closer and discovered it was a German submarine when the sub shot at his plane. He escaped damage but flew more carefully for the remainder of the ocean flight.

"Saw your son safe in Africa and he sends regards = Rodieck"

Mac's parents on the phone with Mac in New York. Photo was taken by the local newspaper as it reported on Mac's trip home from China and the evacuation of Hong Kong

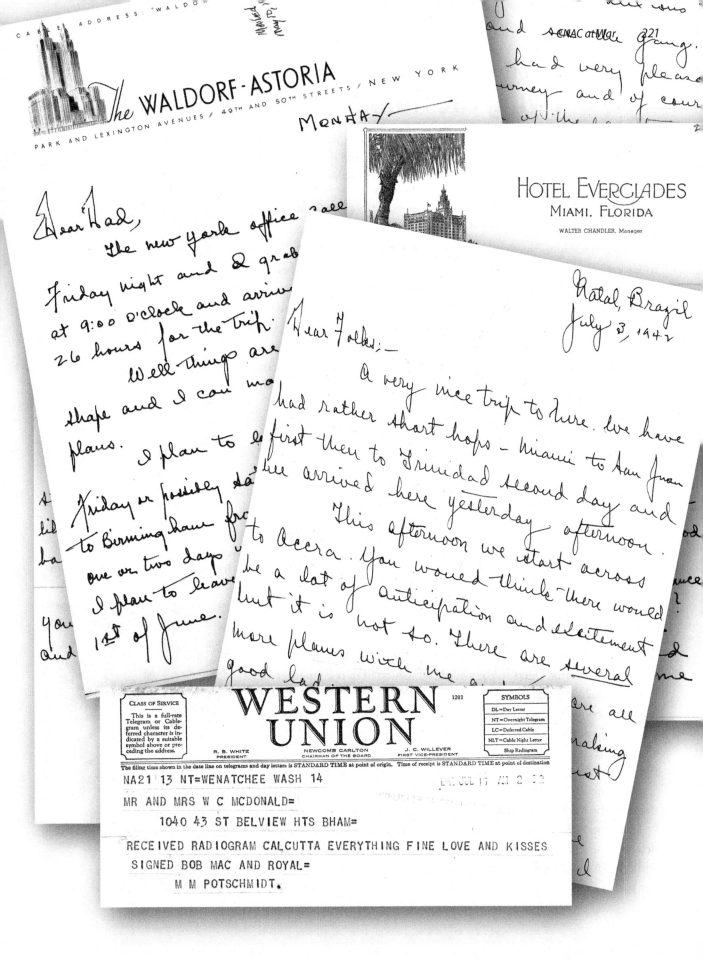

CABLE ADDRESS: "WALDORF"

The WALDORF-ASTORIA / NEW YORK
PARK AND LEXINGTON AVENUES / 49TH AND 50TH STREETS / NEW YORK

Mailed
May 9

MONDAY

Dear Had,

The new york office call...
Friday night and I grab...
at 9:00 O'clock and arriv...
26 hours for the trip.
Well things are...
shape and I can ma...
plans.
I plan to l...
Friday or possibly Sa...
to Birmingham fr...
one or two days...
I plan to leave...
1st of June.
you...
and...

HOTEL EVERGLADES
MIAMI, FLORIDA

WALTER CHANDLER, Manager

Natal, Brazil
July 3, 1942

Dear Folks:—

A very nice trip to here. We have
had rather short hops — Miami to San Juan
first then to Trinidad second day and
we arrived here yesterday afternoon.
This afternoon we start across
to Accra. You would think there would
be a lot of anticipation and excitement
but it is not so. There are several
more plans with me a...
good lad...
...are all
...nalizing

...and SCNAC at War 321
...had very pleas...
...rney and of cour...
...of the...

SUPPLY TO CHINA, FLYING TIGERS AND ARMY AIR FORCE
Flying the Hump

After the Japanese took over Hong Kong, CNAC had six usable planes and nine pilots. This small airline became, along with the Burma Road, the only supply line that China had. The United States and her allies were officially at war with Japan now, so China began to receive official help. Mac, Chennault, the Flying Tigers, Chinese Air Force instructors and CNAC were now part of an official U.S. war effort.

Mac got home to the States only because there were planes to ferry to China. The routes over the Himalayas, pioneered by CNAC before the evacuation of Hong Kong, were now the lifelines for Chinese resistance. Most supplies would have to be flown in to keep China and its fight alive, and to keep a million Japanese troops away from the Pacific.

President Roosevelt ordered General Marshall to take twenty-five DC-3's from US airlines and place them on lend-lease to CNAC. An additional seventy-five US military planes and support troops were to arrive by June 15, 1942, to start a military airlift.

CNAC's management team searched for routes over the Himalayas to move the most cargo and kill the fewest pilots. The Hong Kong maintenance shop was moved to Calcutta, India, with secondary repair shops in Kunming and Chungking. The main cargo base for CNAC was established at Dinjan, the city in India nearest to Kunming. CNAC's Chungking to Chengtu route remained open but all northern and coastal routes fell into the hands of the enemy.

ABOVE AND BELOW The planes sometimes flew at high altitudes, which required supplemental oxygen. Mac participated in testing new oxygen delivery systems during his time at Selfridge. Photos from Mac's collection.

The Japanese invaded Burma, taking Rangoon in March, 1942, and heading north. CNAC's lend-lease planes arrived in time to evacuate approximately 2,400 people and fifty tons of freight from Myitkyina, Burma, under the noses of the Japanese.

Another of CNAC's jobs was to pick up loads of 100-gallon barrels of gas from Lashio, Burma, and fly them to Kunming to keep Chennault's Flying Tigers in the air, until Lashio fell to the Japanese in April of 1942. Now everything had to come through India, and CNAC flew whatever was needed—gas, gunpowder and gold, for instance.

With the loss of Myitkyina, CNAC and the US Army Air Transport Command adopted the Dinjan-Kunming route during May and June, 1942. The Hump was dangerous, but it was China's only supply line.

On June 26, 1942, most of the 10th Air Force transports were ordered to the Middle East. This left a huge gap in flights over the Hump.

In the month of July 1942, with twenty-five planes the US Army delivered seventy-three tons of material (about three tons per plane), while CNAC with ten planes delivered 129 tons (almost thirteen tons per plane).

CNAC engine on fire. Photos from Mac's collection.

Captain Pete Goutierre took this 1943 photo of the plane minutes before Captain Jim Fox's fatal crash.

Fire and Ice: Crashes

The Himalayas offered fierce weather and high, sometimes uncharted mountains. Wings iced over or engines caught fire. Not every plane made it home. Each crash reverberated through the small organization.

As Chief Pilot for several years, Mac investigated at crash sites. He took photos and made notes. These detailed investigations were important in creating safer planes, routes, procedures and pilots.

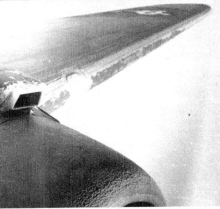

BELOW Photo of icing on the wings. Icing happens when water droplets forming the cloud are below freezing but still liquid, so they freeze on impact. Above this level is colder air, where the water has turned into snow which does not stick. Below that level the water is liquid and won't stick. CNAC pilots knew to move up or down. Moving down was risky in the mountains. Moving up required planes able to climb higher. Photo from Mac's collection.

RIGHT Tiger Leaping Gorge on the Yangtze River. CNAC pilots sometimes followed rivers to help with navigation. Photo by Pete Goutiere.

The Hump was the large spur of the Himalayan range that stretched across the north end of the Assam Valley of India, then turned south to divide Burma and China. There, peaks rose from twelve thousand to nineteen thousand feet. Further north they rose to twenty-four thousand feet.

The earliest flights over the Hump were made without the benefit of maps, in unpredictable weather. Even late in the war maps were sometimes inaccurate.

Map of Northern Hump Routes

CNAC Folding Cockpit Map

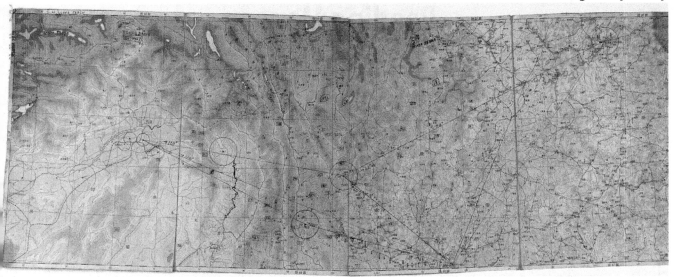

Navigation Tools: Maps

ABOVE CNAC Folding Cockpit Map. The original contour map was annotated by hand with elevations, airfields and routes.

TOP LEFT Example of what the crews saw as they flew over the mountains.

BOTTOM LEFT A terrain map showing two of the northern Hump routes.

When CNAC started flying the Hump in 1942, there were no good maps of the region, nor were there radio navigation stations along the route. Accurate elevations on maps were especially important because the early aircraft used by CNAC, like the C-53s, were not equipped with superchargers. Without these, engine power decreased at the altitudes needed to cross the mountains. Overloaded airplanes could barely clear the mountains of the route.

In addition, a camouflaged aircraft flying low over a jungle is very difficult to spot from above, whereas a high-flying airplane is easy to spot against an open sky. Therefore in good weather, to avoid Japanese fighters, pilots tended to stay as low as possible. Of course, in bad weather, flying low increased their chances of running into mountains.

Pilots wrote on their maps noting where they could find important lower passes through the higher mountains, as well as noting the higher peaks to avoid. They marked new radio beacons and routes.

Later in the operation, newer aircraft were equipped with two-stage superchargers that enabled higher operation, and the threat of Japanese fighters had also diminished. But maps continued to be critical for safety and reliability.

Reading Maps

A **RADIO RANGE** was installed near each major airport to allow landings in bad weather. Four towers broadcast signals that were arranged to form four distinct narrow beams. A pilot could follow these beams by listening to tones in his headphones that indicated which direction to go if he deviated from the beam. When flying directly over the towers, the audible signal stopped briefly, and this marked the start of a defined approach procedure. This allowed the pilot to descend safely, intersect and follow another of the beams which led to the runway.

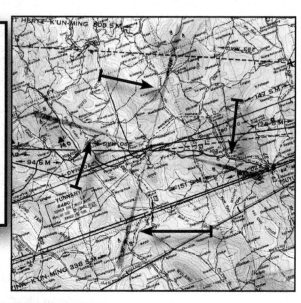

RIGHT RADIO RANGE. Map shows the four beams at Yunnanyi airport.

A **RADIO BEACON** was a small AM radio station that continuously transmitted an identifier signal, in Morse code, on a fixed frequency in all directions. A loop antenna mounted on the airplane could be tuned to this signal and rotated to find the direction from the aircraft to or from the transmitter. Passing a radio beacon provided a check of ground-speed that helped with dead reckoning. Determining directions to several radio beacons provided a good current location.

Unfortunately lightning in a thunderstorm generated radio signals that interfered with determining the direction of the radio beacon. Strong thunderstorms could render the system useless, and bad weather was just when the information was most needed. In any event, the range of radio beacons was usually around fifty to a hundred miles, depending on weather conditions and power of the transmitter.

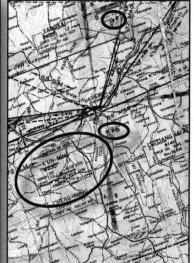

ABOVE COMPASS ROSE. This circle shows the difference between true north and magnetic north.

LEFT The smaller ovals show smaller radio beacons and their two-letter symbols, which were Morse code identifiers.

LEFT AIRPORT INFORMATION. Larger oval shows Kunming airport information. Under the name, on the left, is the station or airport elevation in feet.

Rbn means radio beacon, followed by its frequency and two-letter Morse code signal, broadcast continuously to confirm station.

LF (low frequency radio signal).

DF is direction finder, a ground-based movable antenna that could determine direction of a lost airplane's radio signal.

"Tower" and number is frequency used to call tower for landing and takeoff instructions.

Range is frequency of narrow-beam radio range for instrument landings.

DEAD RECKONING is a way to estimate your plane's current position. In bad weather or at night the routes had to be flown high enough to clear the mountains in the clouds. Winds at these altitudes could be much stronger than at the surface and estimating the effect of wind was an important part of navigation over the hump.

Pilots carefully noted the times they took off and when they passed any of the few radio beacons available early into a crossing. This information allowed them to compare their airspeed with their actual groundspeed and so estimate the strength and direction of the wind aloft. Knowing the time and direction flown since the last known location and the effective wind then allowed them to estimate their current position, a process known as "dead reckoning".

This had to be used in the middle of a crossing when over Japanese-held territory or over jungles where there were no radio stations within range. If the wind strength or direction changed, an estimated current location could differ substantially from the actual location.

For example, if an estimated headwind of 100 miles an hour diminished to 50 miles an hour, then after two hours of flying, one would be 100 miles further than estimated. This could be beyond the range of radio beacons positioned near the intended destination!

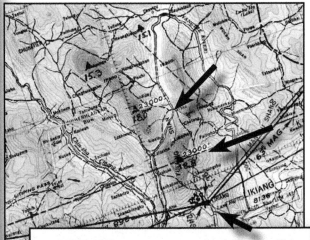

ELEVATIONS were important to get right. This section was printed showing two of three high (darkest) mountains at 23,000 feet. Actual elevations are hand-written as 15.3, 18.0 and 18.8. Likiang Mountain is the one labeled with 18.8.

The official routes fly by the radio beacon at the town of Likiang, southeast of the mountain itself.

In good weather, the shortcut following the Yangtze River northwest of Likiang Mountain cut flight time down. Pilots took that route, evidenced by photos of Likiang and the river gorge.

FLIGHT PLANS AND AIR TRAFFIC CONTROL
from Learning To Fly, or How I Got To Where I Am, by CNAC Captain Gifford Bull

Weight was important to us, and meant everything in the world if one engine quit. With a load the airplane would not fly high enough on one engine to clear the mountains. It was imperative to throw the load out and find the lowest route to an airport, or jump out. We didn't like loads that were too heavy to move, like big machinery that we couldn't possibly throw out. This was one of the reasons why CNAC pilots tried to know exactly where they were and which were the valleys that would lead to somewhere in case you lost an engine.

These thoughts were always in your mind and influenced your actions. If possible, you'd pick the lowest route, and if you could, stay under the clouds so you could see the valleys. Lots of the time you had no choice. Weather or the route forced you to go high over the high mountains.

We had flight plans that specified the route and the altitude so we wouldn't collide with other airplanes, just like Air Traffic Control in the States. I flew at any altitude I chose on whatever route seemed best under the circumstances, and I ignored the flight plan. I figured the sky was big and the airplanes were little and the chance of collision was minimal. Weather and terrain were far bigger risks. In the terminal areas, where all the airplanes were clustered around one radio beacon, I paid attention to ATC for separation from other traffic.

If the weather was bad, with lots of precipitation static that made the radios useless, I assumed the wind was strong and had swung around to come from the south. That would drift you to the north, where the mountains were higher, the radio stations fewer, and the ice was likely to be worse. With no help from the radios you had to fall back on dead reckoning navigation. I based my navigation calculations on my assumed strong south wind, which would be the "worst case scenario". If the wind really was that bad, I would get where I wanted to go. If the wind was more benign, in either direction or speed, I would end up south of where I wanted to go, but where the mountains were lower, there were more radio stations and airports, and the ice was likely to be less fierce. You had to take protective measures to save your skin.

K'un-ming, China to Chabua, India (US Army Air Forces # 133)
Revised October, 1944. Aeronautical Chart Service, U.S. Coast and Geodetic Survey, U.S. Army Air Forces

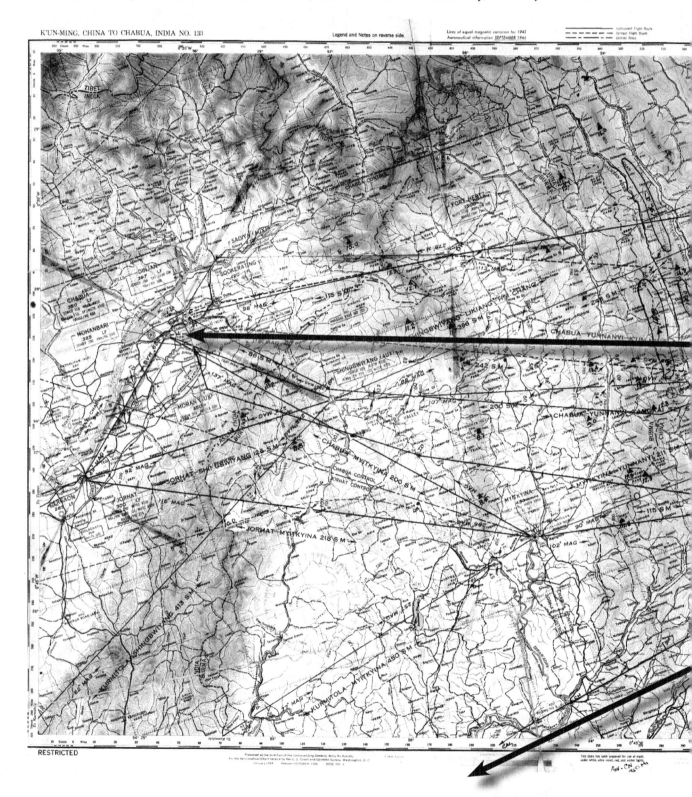

This began as an ATC map dated October 1944. Its owner wrote in specific elevations next to triangles (ex. 18.3 = 18,300 feet) and airport beacons and frequency (ex. DM 425, DM 350). Other abbreviations in use on the printed map include SM (Statute Miles, 1 SM = 5280 feet). MAG (Magnetic North = compass heading). Airports are boxed, and include information like name, elevation and broadcast frequency. Used by courtesy of Peggy Maher.

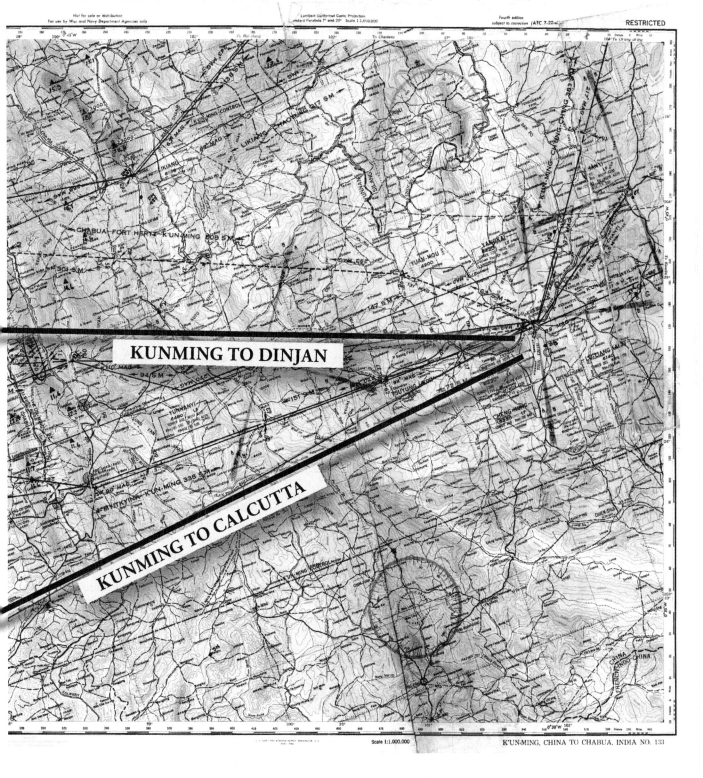

Calcutta, India,
August 27,1942.

Dear Folks,

This is my first letter since my return. I have cabled twice and sent messages thru friends. As a matter of fact a Colonel Mayer left here sometime ago with a message as to my welfare. You more than likely have it now.

Lucie's letter of July 15th reached me the other day along with one from Jenny that was mailed on the 28th – so apparently mail is beginning to get thru fairly well.

I have been pretty busy since my arrival and am enjoying the work more than ever. My vacation really did me worlds of good and it is easy to see now just how badly I needed it.

I saw General Chennault the other day and he is getting along pretty nicely – he sends his regards and was glad to learn that Lucie was so much better.

I have been living on a Tea Garden (Plantation to you folks) for the past month. It has been a little trying because of the prevalence of Malaria and general fevers. Our crowd has been fortunate – not more than one or two have been down at the same time. Luckily I haven't been a <u>victum</u>.Anyway I know how tea grows and how it is manufactured.

The situation in Russia doesn't look to hot these days. The Germans are throwing everything in the battle to win before the winter sets in and the Russians are doing everything they can to prevent them. I think it is without question one of the most gigantic struggles in all history. Should Russia collapse it will mean things will definitely take a bad turn out here. And I don't know if even Alabama will be a safe spot.

Today – right now is the real spot to open up the much talked of " Second Front ". It must come or – ??.

China is doing right well these days. Finally after five years of fighting the Chinese soldier is seeing planes over his head that are friendly. I have always said –"give the Chinese soldier air support and he will beat the Japs hands down."

I hope you Folks enjoyed your trip out to see Malcolm ? I know you must have enjoyed riding on four good tires for a change,too.

The weather is just about as hot here as [...] are just beginning to break for their finish an[...] trying of the season. Have been swimming a litt[...] other hand I have been out playing a little gol[...] work out O.K.

Drop Mr. Gover Keyton a line and tell hi[...] credited to my account.

Lov[...]

The situation in Russia doesn't look too hot these days. The Germans are throwing everything in the battle to win before the winter sets in and the Russians are doing everything they can to prevent them. I think it is without question one of the most gigantic struggles in all history. Should Russia collapse it will mean things will definitely take a bad turn out here. And I don't know if even Alabama will be a safe spot.

Mac, August 27, 1942

Aluminum Trail on the Hump

Army ATC crash site, January 17, 1945, photographed by Gifford Bull during his check ride for promotion to CNAC captain. Definitely a reality check!

Trust in CNAC

On December 24, 1941, two VIPs were to fly to a meeting in Chungking with the Generalissimo. The pilot of General Brett's plane told him in Rangoon that he was doubtful about his ability to safely make the landing in Chungking. He recommended that they take CNAC to the meeting, which they did. They made the trip into Chungking with CNAC, which also returned them to Rangoon during a Japanese air raid.

The Allies were aware of the valuable experience that CNAC had gained in China and flying the Hump routes. President Roosevelt sent Eddie Rickenbacker, then president of Eastern Airlines, to China to find out how to improve tonnage carried by the U.S. military transport and reduce its accident rate. Mac and Rickenbacker had a long conversation. Mac and others believed that much of the difference between CNAC and the U.S. military was obvious: CNAC pilots were more experienced flyers and had better training before they flew solo. CNAC also had crack ground crews which included many well-trained Chinese mechanics with years of experience.

Wartime Censorship & the End of Mac's Detailed Letters

Understandably in war, Mac's post-Hong Kong letters no longer contain detailed observations about his work and insight, information that might aid the enemy if intercepted. He talks a little about friends, his dogs, family news. Specifics about the rest of his time in China are in short supply in his letters. *Terry & the Pirates* may have contained more detailed information!

Some letters were simply lost, and whether to war or the Post Office, no one would know.

Censorship is the main topic of conversation when it comes to discussing mail from home. As a matter of fact I have tried to place myself in a censor's shoes and try and understand his job. Of course they have rules and regulations that they must go by but it is absolutely impossible to have a guide that will cover everything a person would write about. Anyway I always try and write about things that won't give out data that should the letter fall into enemy hands they would not profit by me.

Mac, October 5, 1942

Calcutta, India,
October 5, 1942.

Dear Folks,

Since July I have received one letter and one answer to my cable. I know that there are letters somewhere but unfortunately I don't seem to be able to get my hands on them. The worst part is that the American Express people have closed their offices here. So what the Post Office is doing with my mail is beyond my comprehension. However, just in case you haven't received my new instructions in re mail – please address my mail to me at this address; 3/1 Middleton Street, Fountain Courts, Apartment No. 20, Calcutta, India.

I am anxious to know how the deal ended with Drennen Motors ? Perhaps this information will be included in letters that may appear soon. The air mail service seems to be fairly good now. People are getting letters home in two weeks and replys in around three weeks. So now that we know our letters are getting thru we can write a couple of times a month.

Censorship is the main topic of conversation when it comes to discussing mail from home. As a matter of fact I have tried to place myself in a censors shoes and try and understand his job. Of course they have rules and regulations that they must go by but it is absolutely impossible to have a guide that will cover everything a person would write about. Anyway I always try and write about things that won't give out data that should the letter fall into enemy hands they would not profit by me. So you folks must consider the same thing when you write to me. In fact the censors in the States are new at the game and they are apt to censor things that are of no value wher the censors here have been at the game for several years and know what this war business is all about.

Mother, this is indeed a strange and small world. The other day, near the place where I sent you a cable, I had a rather unusal experience. I was talking to a group of young men and one of them asked me my name and when I told him he asked me if I remembered him. His face was familiar but of course I couldn't place him. He told me that you, Mother, taught him in school. His name is Endsley. He was extremely excited on seeing some one from home and he gave me a B'ham paper dated three days before I left Miami. Anyway I asked him to write you.

Also get Lucie to write my Bank and ask them if they received a deposit in my favor from Pan American Office New York for a $1000.00?

For the past month I have been having a little trouble with one of Dr. Carmichals tonsils. I am afraid that I must have it removed. I rather hate to do it out here but there is no other choice now. It could have been done so easily when I was there in the States. But I have found out that there is an expert here who can do almost the same type of work so it won't be so bad after all.

Duchess has just recovered from a summer seige of fever. She was in the hospital for two months but not all at one time. She is in pretty good shape now and sends her regards to Punk.

Tell Lucie to drop in Brombergs and see Bob and he will give her some stones that I left with him to send to the Gem Institute for study.

Write to Mr. William Van Dusen, Public Relations ? Pan American Airways Chrysler Bldg., N Y and enquire if he has received mail from me. I think it is very hard to get thru to him.

Love to all,
Wm

P.S. October 13,1942.

I have been holding the attached letter fro Chuck Sharp, our Operations Manager, to take back with him when he goes on " home Leave " which looked like he would leave on the 7th—now he is scheduled to depart tomorrow and I thought I might as well get in a few lines to add to the first letter.

I have had two letters from you during the past week. One dated the latter part of August and the other the middle of September. I was extremely glad to hear from you thru these letters as I received information in them that I have been waiting for.

I am so glad that you are enjoying the car. You must have had a nice trip when you went out to see Malcolm. I certainly enjoyed [...] while I was home – it is a very nice running machine. How is t[...] up ? They were beginning to show signs of rust in Mia[...] that the metal in the new cars was of inferior qulaity[...]

My message from Dinjan must have been considera[...] Mother must have looked all over the map looking for [...] because it isn't on the map. It is however, near Dibr[...] Duchess to more or less fill in words. She is splendi[...] tick fever during the rainy season or monsoons but sh[...]

It is too bad that the powers to be are jealous[...] he has done in China. They act as if the stakes in th[...] rather than world wide. But regardless of the handica[...] witted individuals trying to give orders in such a wa[...] get the glory – Chennault is doing a job that will o[...] unsurpassed in history. But then again no one has ev[...] was worth while without having to brush aside a lot [...]

Calcutta is now passing thru a period of weath[...] monsoons and the coming of the fine weather. In abou[...] will be wonderful. Clear and cool. Golf will definit[...] has been no air raids here but Jap observation plane[...] at an extremely high altitude. So high that they ca[...]

Lucie;- are you collecting any money from tha[...] won't pay unless you ride him. So send him a dirty [...] young life that he should establish a trai[t] of trus[...] The money don't mean anything it pure principal. An[...] even if I have to write a dun to his commanding off[...]

From all appearances it looks as if the Unite[...] hold their own and the battle from now on will be n[...] nature. I am betting that we will be back in Hongko[...] after all somebody has got to hope.

I guess that is about all for this time so "[...] meet Sharp – he is a swell gent.

Love to all,

It is too bad that the powers that be are jealous of Chennault and all that he has done in China. They act as if the stakes in this game are purely personal rather than world wide. But regardless of the handicap of having a bunch of half witted individuals trying to give orders in such a way that they personally will get the glory—Chennault is doing a job that will one day be regarded as a feat unsurpassed in history. But then again no one has ever accomplished anything that was worthwhile without having to brush aside a lot of obstacles.

…

So far there has been no air raids here but Jap observation planes come over almost daily at an extremely high altitude. So high that they cannot be seen from the ground.

…it looks as if the United Nations are beginning to hold their own and the battle from now on will be not of "strategic retreat" nature. I am betting that we will be back in Hongkong next July. A dream but after all somebody has got to hope.

Mac, October 13, 1942

CHINA NATIONAL AVIATION CORPORATION

DUM DUM AERODROME

CALCUTTA :: INDIA

TELEPHONE DUM DUM 85

November 11,1942.

Dear Dad,

I have been writing about twice a month but I suppose that my letters have gone the way of the fish or something. Your letters have not been reaching me either.

Day before yesterday a package of mail came in from PAA office N.Y. and there was one letter from you in it. I was mighty glad to hear from you and learn a little about what is going on at home. Fortunately you only had one word censored and I am afraid that mine will or has had many censored – as a matter of fact that may be the reason you haven't received any mail from me.

Well the Duchess is back in the limelight. I have found a husband for her and expect additions to my family in due course. People have asked me for a pup from the Duchess from Chungking to Karachi. She is certainly a well known dog.

Well it looks like the old packard is going to die a gallant death. What could be better than to retire right on the old homestead. Maybe someday we can sell her for scrap iron . Anyway don't worry about it.

Sorry to learn that Brother Minnie hasn't received his promotion. But time will tell and from all appearances he will get his chance.

We are experiencing somewhat cooler weather – I can't say anymore about it but it does make life a little easier when the weather doesn't cause you to perspire all day.

I see Chennault nearly every time I go out on a trip. He is in good spirits and fairly good health altho his work now is much harder – if that can be possible. He is a great man and will go down in history as one of the out- standing men on the age.

Life is becoming more and more interesting out here and I can't hardly wait until we have marched back into my former home in Hongkong.

I am sending this letter back with Frank Sinclair, who should be leaving Sunday.

Love to all,

I see Chennault nearly every time I go out on a trip. He is in good spirits and fairly good health although his work now is much harder — if that can be possible. He is a great man and will go down in history as one of the outstanding men of the age.

Life is becoming more and more interesting out here and I can't hardly wait until we have marched back into my former home in Hongkong.

Mac, November 11, 1942

Calcutta, India,
Dec. 4, 1942.

Dear Folks,

According to the date—there are only 21 shopping days until Xmas. Out here there is hardly any evidence of the coming season. Yesterday I did see some Xmas decorations in Bata's Shoe Store.

Capt. Sweet brought us a new plane and the mail from New York that Owen Johnson assembled for us. Your letter dated Nov. 8th came with this plane. This month I have had four letters from Malcolm, Lucie and yourselves. I have thoroughly enjoyed them.

I have written the Ailshies, Pete Woods, Red Aycock and Don Trenman. A Major Adair is on his way to the States with mail for you.

Eugene Graham is now stationed here. I had him out to dinner several nights ago—he is looking fit and we had a long talk.

I am enclosing a letter to the Boy Scout Troop that was so kind and thoughtful. I really appreciate their gesture. Please mail this letter to Sailor Eddens.

I am very pleased to learn of Malcolm's promotion and I know Jane must be happy, too.

The Duchess is beginning to show some signs of pregnancy—but I won't count my puppies until they are here.

Merry Xmas and Happy New Year to All—Remember me to the Rays next door and the gang at the mill.

Mac

Capt. Sweet brought us a new plane and the mail from New York…

I am enclosing a letter to the Boy Scout Troop that was so kind and thoughtful. I really appreciate their gesture…

Mac, December 4, 1942

Terry & the Pirates
Artist Milton Caniff drew adventures based on CAF/CNAC pilots

Frank Higgs as Dude Hennick and Mac as Captain Mack

Pulling many of his plots from the real adventures of pilots in China, Caniff did his best to explain the unfamiliar world where the flyers lived to the American public. Caniff remained a lifelong friend to the military man and to Mac.

His story lines were close enough to reality that Caniff was investigated as a potential spy.

The strip has been republished recently in a series of books by IDW Press.

Terry & the Pirates comics used with Permission, © 2015 Tribune Content Agency, LLC.

November 2, 1941

FLYING THROUGH THE ONLY WEATHER OFFERING PROTECTION FROM MILITARY ATTACK, THE COMMERCIAL AIRPLANE FROM CHUNGKING TO HONGKONG DRONES ALONG...

MEANWHILE: BACK IN CHUNKING...

HELLO...IS THAT THE FLIGHT SUPERINTENDENT OF THE AIRPORT?... ....THE OFFICE OF THE POLICE IS AT THIS END...

WAS ONE NAMED CHIN YANG ON THE PASSENGER LIST FOR THE FLIGHT TO HONGKONG TONIGHT?

YES! HE JUST MADE IT IN TIME!

ALAS — AN UNPLEASANTNESS HAS TAKEN PLACE!... ONE RUFFLED PERSON IS AT HAND — SAYING HE WAS SET UPON, STRUCK DOWN, AND ROBBED OF HIS PAPERS AND TICKET ON THE AIRCRAFT...YOU WILL NO DOUBT FIND THIS INTERESTING...

YOU SAY THE MAN CALLING HIMSELF CHIN YANG WHO BOARDED THE HONGKONG PLANE TONIGHT WAS AN IMPOSTER? YOU HAVE THE REAL CHIN YANG AT THE POLICE STATION — HE WAS ROBBED OF HIS TICKET AND PAPERS?

THAT IS SO! HE IDENTIFIES HIMSELF BY JEWELRY AND HIS NAME ON HIS CLOTHING!

THANKS!

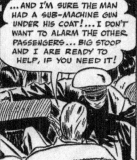

CHUNGKING CALLING MAC IN FLIGHT FOUR! COME IN, MAC, FOR PETE'S SAKE!

I'M RIGHT HERE, DUCKY... ARE THE CHUNGKING BABES LONESOME FOR ME ALREADY?

THERE'S A CHINESE ON YOUR SHIP WHO CALLS HIMSELF CHIN YANG ON THE PASSENGER MANIFEST... JUST GOT A CALL FROM THE COP HOUSE ON HIM...HE'S A PHONY!

...BETTER CHECK ON HIM BEFORE HE PULLS SOMETHING...GO AHEAD, MAC.... I SAID GO AHEAD!...

...BIG STOOP! THAT MAN WHO WENT UP TO THE PILOT'S COMPARTMENT JUST NOW... HE OPENED THE DOOR WITH A KEY... WHICH NO ORDINARY PASSENGER WOULD POSSIBLY HAVE! WHEN HE CRAWLED OVER ME I FELT A SUB-MACHINE GUN UNDER HIS COAT!...THERE'S TROUBLE COOKIN'! I'M RINGING FOR THE STEWARD!

...AND I'M SURE THE MAN HAD A SUB-MACHINE GUN UNDER HIS COAT!...I DON'T WANT TO ALARM THE OTHER PASSENGERS... BIG STOOP AND I ARE READY TO HELP, IF YOU NEED IT!

...IS LOCKED! FROM OTHER SIDE!

OKAY, HEIST GUY... YOU'VE GOT THE ACES! WHAT DO I DO?

VERY SENSIBLE CONCLUSION! PILOT WILL FOLLOW COMPASS DIRECTIONS GIVEN BY ME! SHIP WILL LAND AND SURRENDER CARGO AND PASSENGERS TO SOLDIERS! UNPLEASANT MOVE WILL PROVE MOST UNDESIRABLE!

SO THE INVADER SECRET SERVICE FINALLY SLIPPED A MAN WITH A MACHINE GUN ON BOARD THE CHUNGKING TO HONGKONG RUN...

DO NOT REACH FOR THE RADIO SWITCH!...YOU WILL LAND THIS AIRPLANE AT ONE OF OUR MILITARY AIR FIELDS...THEN YOUR TROUBLES WILL BE ENDED!

DOOR TO PILOT'S PLACE LOCKED ON OTHER SIDE!

AND THAT GUY WITH THE SUB-MACHINE GUN UNDER HIS COAT IS IN THERE, TOO! STOOP!.. GOT TO DO SOMETHING!

WAIT... I THINK MAYBE THAT PILOT IS BEATING US TO IT! ...LOOK!

...ABOVE THE DOOR TO THE PILOT'S COMPARTMENT A SIGN FLASHES ON...

NO SMOKING FASTEN YOUR SEAT BELT

禁止吸煙
繁來座帶

from 1943

HI, CAPTAIN MACK, CAN YOU USE A HOSTESS ON THIS TRIP?
OPERATIONS TOLD US YOU WERE COMING, GRETT! WE CAN ALWAYS CARRY DEAD-HEAD WHEN THE HEAD IS AS PRETTY AS YOURS!

WHAT ARE TERRY LEE AND FLIGHT LIEUTENANT BONNY DOING MACK?
THE TOWER SAID THEY'RE SIMULATING A BOMBER-ESCORT MISSION WITH US —WHICH DOESN'T MAKE ME MAD—WITH THESE IMPORTANT CHINESE OFFICIALS ON BOARD!

MEANWHILE...

YOU COME EARLY TODAY, NIGOSHI!
AND WITH REASON...THE SPY IN THE FRENCH UNIFORM DROPPED A MESSAGE INTO MY BASKET... WE MUST HASTEN TO TRANSMIT ITS CONTENTS OVER THE SHORT WAVE WIRELESS..

SO! OUR IMITATION FRENCH CAPTAIN DOES WELL AT ESPIONAGE! WE WILL TRANSMIT THIS INFORMATION AT ONCE!
WHEN I SAW THE 'CAPTAIN' LEAN AGAINST THE WALL AT THE APPOINTED PLACE I LEFT MY WORK ON THE AIR FIELD...

...AS I PASSED, THE 'CAPTAIN' DROPPED THE PELLET INTO MY BASKET, AS AGREED! THE YANKEES SUSPECT NOTHING!...
NOR DO THE STUPID YANKEES SUSPECT THE PRESENCE OF THIS TRANSMITTER!

DO THEY NOT HEAR THE STRONG IMPULSE OF THE TRANSMISSION FROM SUCH A NEARBY POINT?
OF COURSE -BUT THEY DO NOT EVEN UNDERSTAND JAPANESE-MUCH LESS OUR CODE!

THEY THINK IT IS A JAPANESE AIRCRAFT IN THE AREA!..BUT I MUST HASTEN...THE COMMANDER WILL WISH TO WELCOME A CHINA NATIONAL AVIATION TRANSPORT CARRYING IMPORTANT CHINESE FINANCE EXPERTS...

....OUR 'CAPTAIN MIDI' IS AT WORK, EXCELLENCY... HERE IS A MOST IMPORTANT COMMUNICATION FROM OUR SHORT WAVE WIRELESS NEAR THE YANKEE AIRDROME!
A CHINA NATIONAL AVIATION TRANSPORT DEPARTS FOR INDIA CARRYING CHINESE FINANCE EXPERTS!

...TWO FIGHTERS WILL ESCORT THE TRANSPORT PART WAY... ORDER THREE OF OUR AIRCRAFT TO ATTACK WHEN THE ESCORT TURNS BACK...
I HASTEN TO OBEY, EXCELLENCY!

AH, LIEUTENANT TUCKAIR, COLONEL CORKEEN... I WAS LOOKEENG FOR FLIGHT OFFICAIR LEE - I HAVE A LEETLE GOOD LUCK TOKEN FOR HEEM...
HE'S IN THE AIR, CAPTAIN MIDI...

THAT CAPTAIN MIDI SEEMS LIKE A NICE GUY... HE HAS TAKEN SUCH AN INTEREST IN TERRY...
HUH? — OH...YEAH —CAPTAIN MIDI TAKES AN INTEREST IN EVERYTHING AROUND HERE...

NEED ANY HELP CHAUFFEURING THIS THING, CAPTAIN MACK?
SIT IN, GRETT! MACK THINKS YOU'RE PRETTIER THAN I AM, ANYHOW!

HOW DOES THE BIRMINGHAM KID LIKE RUNNING OVER THE HUMP WITH AN ESCORT?
WHY, FLIGHT OFFICER LEE AND FLIGHT LIEUTENANT BONNY ARE JUST EXCESS WITH YOU ALONG, LIGHT OF MY LIFE!

-BUT I HEAH YOU'VE BEEN HIGH-EYEIN' THIS UPSTART, TERRY LEE... I'M A MEAN THING WHEN MY JEALOUSY'S AROUSED!
WHY, MACK, I NEVER KNEW YOU CARED- AREN'T YOU GOING TO TAKE ME IN YOUR ARMS?
DAWGONNIT, YOU SAY A THING LIKE THAT WHEN I'M PUSHIN' THIS TRUCK UP-GRADE WITH BOTH HANDS FULL- BUT WHEN WE LAND, YOU'LL RUN!...GO AWAY, WOMAN, YOU'RE A MENACE TO NAVIGATION!

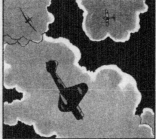

COL. CORKIN, SIR, IT'S FLIGHT OFFICER LEE... MAY I COME IN?

YOU MAY COME IN AND STAND AT EASE, LEE—AND I'LL TAKE THAT MESSAGE FROM CAPTAIN MACK YOU PICKED UP ON SHORT WAVE...

LT. FENNEY, I WANT A C-53 GASSED AND ON THE LINE WITH A FULL COMPLEMENT OF CHINESE PARATROOPS ... GIVE ME THE TOWER...

COL. CORKIN SPEAKING... CONTACT THE CIVILIAN AIRCRAFT SEARCHING FOR THE LOST TRANSPORT...

...THAT'S RIGHT... FIRST BIG BEND OF THE WALEEN RIVER...TELL 'EM NOT TO CIRCLE THE SPOT... JAPS MIGHT NOT HAVE FOUND THE PLACE..

SO...COL. CORKIN GOES BRASS HAT ON ME JUST 'CAUSE HE'S SORE!... I DID TALK TOO MUCH IN PUBLIC, BUT...

...I BRING BIG NEWS AND HE PULLS HIS RANK WHEN I COME INTO HIS OFFICE —AND I THOUGHT HE WAS SUCH A SWELL GENT... I GUESS THESE BIG SHOTS JUST LIKE TO GRIND A LITTLE GUY UNDER THEIR FEET...

WE'LL DROP PARATROOPS FROM A C-53....FLIGHT LIEUTENANT BONNY AND I WILL COVER THE JUMP— MAC DAVEY WILL TAKE TOP COVER IN A P-38 ...

COL. CORKIN IS IGNORING ME...IT WOULD BE BETTER IF HE'D BAWL ME OUT—OR BREAK ME—OR SOMETHING!

IF THE JAPS HAVEN'T SPOTTED THE WRECK OF THE CHINA NATIONAL TRANSPORT, WE DON'T WANT TO MOVE TOO MANY AIRCRAFT IN AND GIVE THE LOCATION AWAY...

I GUESS I'VE LOST MY BEST FRIEND IN THE AIR FORCES...

WE'LL TAKE OFF AT 0500 HOURS... ROGER!

HE'S NOT EVEN GONNA LET ME GO ALONG...

AS FOR YOU, LEE, SINCE YOU SAW THE COURSE CAPTAIN MACK WAS MAKING, YOU WILL RIDE SUPERCARGO IN THE C-53 TO DIRECT THE PILOT TO THE APPROXIMATE SCENE OF THE CRASH...

LEE, YOU'RE NOT READY FOR COMBAT IN A FIGHTER, ...BUT I THINK YOU CAN DIRECT THE TROOP CARRIER TO THE SCENE OF THE TRANSPORT CRASH...DO YOU?

YES, SIR, COLONEL CORKIN!

FLIGHT OFFICER LEE, I'VE FAILED IN ONE PHASE OF MY JOB HERE...DO YOU THINK I DESERVE ANOTHER CHANCE TO MAKE GOOD?

WH-WHY, WHAT'S THAT, SIR?...

I'VE TRIED TO STRESS THE IMPORTANCE OF EVERY MAN KEEPING HIS MOUTH SHUT ABOUT MILITARY MATTERS —BUT I GUESS I DIDN'T MAKE IT STICK...DO YOU THINK I COULD SUCCEED IF I TRIED AGAIN?

I CAN MANAGE IT ALONE, GRETT!

DON'T BE SILLY, MACK...YOU'RE HURT... GET BACK INTO THE WOODS

DO YOU THINK ANYONE PICKED UP OUR S.O.S., MACK?

CAN'T TELL, GRETT...OUR RECEIVIN' EQUIPMENT IS SHOT...WE'LL HAVE TO WAIT AN' SEE...

IF AN AMERICAN STATION PICKED IT UP WE MAY BE HEARING FROM THE BOYS PRETTY SOON... IF THE JAPS GOT IT...

WE'LL HEAR FROM THEM EVEN SOONER... AND HERE THEY COME, NOW!

Chennault and Joe, 1944 Christmas card

Roster of Senior Pilots
(from a mid-1943 CNAC report)

1. W.C. McDonald, Operations Asst (PAA)
2. Robert Pottschmidt, Operations Asst (PAA)
3. Frank Higgs, Chief Pilot (PAA)
4. Royal Leonard (PAA)
5. Robert Angle (PAA)
6. Paul Kessler (PAA)
7. Sydney de Kantsow (Canadian citizen)
8. Moon Chin (U.S. citizen)
9. Donald Wong (U.S. citizen)
10. George Huang (British)
11. Harold Chen (Canadian)
12. K.Y. Liang
13. M.K. Lo
14. Ed Chin
15. Hugh Chen
16. Gordon Poon
17. Robert Hedman (AVG)
18. Robert Moss (AVG)
19. Eriksen Shilling (AVG)
20. Van Shepard (AVG)
21. C.J. Rosbert (AVG)
22. Allen Wright (AVG)
23. E.W. Loane (AVG)
24. C.H. Laughlin (AVG)
25. Robert Raines (AVG)
26. Einer Mickelson (AVG)
27. Clifford Groh (AVG)
28. William Bartling (AVG)
29. Richard Rossi (AVG)
30. Carl K. Brown (AVG)
31. LJ. Hall (AVG)
32. Weldon Tutwiler
33. Richard Snell
34. Charles Sundby (R.A.F. Ferry command - Danish citizen)
35. Ace Richards (R.A.F. Ferry command)
36. R. Royer (R.A.F.)
37. Charles Sharkey (R.C.A.F.)
38. Alfred Oldenburg (R.C.A.F.)
39. Edward Leatherbury (R.C.A.F.)
40. Douglas Cunningham (R.C.A.F.)
41. Russell Johnson (R.C.A.F.)
42. Joseph Dionne (R.C.A.F.)
43. James Lane (Air Transport Auxiliary)
44. Aleck Gingiss (A.T.A.)
45. Joseph Genovese (A.T.A.)
46. Richard Newmeyer (A.T.A.)
47. Julius Petach (A.T.A.)
48. George Robertson (A.T.A. and PAA-F)
49. William Cooper (A.T.A. and PAA-F)
50. Raymond Allen (A.T.A. and PAA-F)
51. Orin Welch (PAA-F)
52. James Fox (PAA-F)
53. James Gregg (PAA-F)
54. Samuel Anglin (PAA-Africa)
55. Charles Hammell (PAA-Africa)
56. Peter Gutierre (PAA-Africa)
57. Raymond Hauptman (PAA-Africa)
58. E.C. Kirkpatrick (PAA-Africa)

Mac is Operations Assistant & Chief Pilot as CNAC Expands

By mid-1943 Mac served as Operations Assistant in Calcutta, while Robert "Potty" Pottschmidt was Operations Assistant in Dinjan. Frank Higgs was Chief Pilot at this time. Mac signed documents as Chief Pilot by the end of 1943.

Mac helped manage a rapidly expanding organization. CNAC had just a handful of pilots in December 1941. A report from Bill Bixby to W.S. Youngman of China Defense Supplies Inc. in mid-1943 listed fifty-eight Senior Pilots (list shown to the left on this page). It included fifteen pilots from the AVG as well as pilots from the British Royal Air Force (RAF), Royal Canadian Air Force (RCAF), the Air Transport Auxiliary (ATA) and various Pan American branches.

Under "Copilots" the report said, "Chinese copilots are employed from the various Chinese Government schools in accordance with immediate needs." It reported 175 radio operators and mentioned that additional personnel were available from the same schools. Of the sixteen Americans in maintenance, ten were originally from PAA-Africa. They headed a group of 350 Chinese mechanics.

The same report lists eleven C-53s (Lend Lease), eight C-47s (Lend Lease), and two DC-3s (CNAC). By June, 1943, the report expects that twenty-nine planes will be in operation after eight more C-47s are delivered.

At this time, CNAC flew the following routes:

Freight (Lend Lease planes)

Sadiya (Dinjan)–Kunming

Passengers and Airmail (2 CNAC planes, 1 Lend-Lease plane)

Calcutta–Sadiya (Dinjan)–Kunming–Chungking (3 times weekly)

Chungking–Chengtu (3 times weekly)

Chungking–Kweilin (3 times weekly)

Chengtu–Lanchow (2 times monthly if load warrants)

Mac at a desk. He continued to fly, too.

ABOVE, THREE OF CNAC'S FINEST. LEFT Juliang Lam, CNAC radio operator, promoted by Mac to deputy chief of CNAC's Xiamen office; one of five survivors when Foxy Kent's plane was shot down. MIDDLE Hugh En Chen, with CNAC since 1933, first Chinese-born Captain (1942); stayed with CNAC until 1949. RIGHT Mac, Chief Pilot.

RIGHT Mac and Robbie Roberts in front of CNAC Operations in Calcutta.

BELOW LEFT TO RIGHT Captain Frank Higgs, exective secretary Frieda Wong Chen, Captain George Huang, Mac's secretary, Lucille "Lucy" Lee, Chief Pilot Mac.

RIGHT Mac is head over heels for a girl.

BELOW Milton Caniff writes to Mac's sister about putting Mac into *Terry & the Pirates*.

Dear Miss McDonald:

   I was delighted to hear from you and to learn of your reaction to your brother's appearance in the strip as "Captain Mack".

   It was pleasant, too, to know that he was pleased with the likeness.

   "Captain Mack" appeared on the scene every day from November 15th through November 29th and again on December 5th. Fortunately, I have extra tear sheets covering those dates and I am happy to enclose them.

     Cordially,

     Milton Caniff

          March 10th, 1944

Dearest Peggy,

   Here I am again - to-night things have been called off because of a little bad weather. So I am back in the Bungalow a little early and now I am sitting by a fire listening to a radio program from London. It's nice music - soft strings and a feature piano playing Russian folk songs, and now they are playing " A Tropical Moon ". Can I help it - I wish you were here to listen to it with me.

   At 6:30 A.M. I am leaving to go back to the big city. I will be there over the week end. I will be extremely lonesome for you espeßially at the races and on the golf course Sunday and tiffin Sunday afternoon. Anyway I will be thinking of you constantly.

   I will be there only a few days as I think I will come back up here Monday. If things work out as I plan I will try and stop in to see you. Also I will try and call you long distance on Saturday afternoon after I arrive there.

   I have been visiting. I went over to see " Hooks" but got tied up on business calls and when I went over to " Hooks" place I found that he was ill in quarters. Nothing serious just a little tummy trouble. I will see him when I come back up next week.

   I have recieved several letters from Mother since I have been up here. They are all expecting me back home this month but I am afraid I will have to dissapoint them . (Excuse the spelling) I would like very much to see them but on the otherhand I would be leaving you out here and I don't think that's such a good idea. However the schedule is for me to go back on the first of May. I must see you before I go back.

   My back is about broken. I have been holding on to a jeep for about a 30 mile journey today and believe you me the roads are not unlike a washboard. I think that I will survive with the proper attention and care.

   This morning on the way out to the field we ran over a striped Krite. One of the most poisenous snakes in this part of the country. I never liked snakes and when I saw this one I was sure that I would never change my mind about them.

   I hope when I arrive at my destination tomorrow that there is a letter for me there. If there is I will be one very happy person. I wonder if you think of me as much as I think of you. I guess when I read your letter I will find out. That is if you write me ?

   By the way do you still want that Coco Cola syrup ? Does a duck like water ? O.K. Sweet I will drop off a gallon when I go up Monday.

   I still think you are mighty sweet and I miss you very much.

        Love, Mac

CNAC Captain Pete Goutiere on meeting Mac for the first time

In December of 1942 I am on a CNAC plane headed for "Dum Dum" Airport which is the main Base for CNAC in Calcutta. On entering the CNAC office I met the secretary by the name of Freida Chen. She led me into another office where I saw three or four people standing around a lonely desk! One of the fellows wanted to know who I was etc. I introduced myself, and that I had been flying as copilot for Pan American Africa; that I was interested in joining CNAC!! One of these men came forward and introduced himself as Capt. Bill McDonald. He then introduced me to Captains "Chuck" Sharp and Frank Higgs. The fourth fellow left without introduction. I later learned he was one of the mechanics. It was Captain McDonald that asked Miss Chen to get some forms for me to fill out. I sat at the desk with McDonald by my side. He would ask questions every so often; mainly in regards to flying and my flight time etc. Once completed, I handed the form to him. The next moment Bill McDonald gave a shout to his friends! "Guess what? This guy Pete…"—he couldn't pronounce my last name!!—"This pilot Pete was born in India." All three looked curiously at me and asked if I knew how to speak any of the "Hindu" language?!! I said "Yes", I can speak it fairly well." McDonald wasted little time in calling one of the CNAC servants from outside. He asked me to say something to him in "Hindu"!! I muttered away in "Hindi" and the bearer was shocked, and then laughed. McDonald wanted to know what I had said? I said that I asked the Guy to find me a pretty young Indian girl!!! Everyone had a great laugh. When all that was over, Capt. McDonald gave me instructions of where to get my CNAC Wings etc at a shop in town called "Hamilton's Jewelry Store." That he would also take me into town a little later and have me set up at the Grande Hotel. Then Captain Higgs mentioned to Captain Sharp, that he would like to give me some local training and then take me on my first flight with him in the next few days!! "Wow" Things were happening fast.

So it was that I had now joined CNAC and met the main Operations people for CNAC. All this in no time at all. I rode into Calcutta with Captain Bill McDonald. He told me a lot about the Company and Flying the "Hump." In time Bill and I would become good friends.

Some CNAC stories show up again and again. The first attack on a commercial flight, the DC 2½, Rosbert and Hammell's near-miraculous survival. The Crocodile Flight is another one told and re-told.

In part, this is because the Crocodile Flight showed each part of the rescue—a brilliant landing by the crew, an heroic effort by maintenance crew and local villages, and an almost unbelievable take-off by a fearless and skilled pilot, an Old China Hand. It showed the random nature of the danger and the importance of every person in the CNAC family.

*Pilot Glenn Carroll wrote up the original crash for publication in the CNAC Association publication **Wings Over Asia** (Volume 1), which sets the scene.*

*In his book **Saga of Flight #53**, CNAC Captain Fletcher Hanks claims that Mac's take-off from a sandbar on the Manas River was one of the great flights of WWII. He devotes an entire chapter to it, excerpted here.*

Captain James Atlee wrote a letter recounting how Mac was able to pinpoint the location of the wreck when others couldn't, then flew the plane out.

*Mac wrote his take on the story for **Wings Over Asia** as well. It is notable that he gave credit to all of the others involved, and in particular, to the unsung heroes, the mechanics.*

***Wings Over Asia** came out in five volumes. Mac helped publish several of them to keep the memories of the CNAC years alive. Many of the best CNAC stories are told in these, available as reprints from the CNAC Association and on Amazon.*

The Crocodile Flight
in Four Stories

FORCED LANDING IN THE MANAS RIVER
by Glenn H. Carroll
Reprinted with permission from *Wings Over Asia* (Volume 1)

Late in the afternoon of March 11, 1944, we left Kunming in C-47 Number 81 with co-pilot Pai and radio operator Hsu plus some six to eight tungsten bars as a token load. Except for the heavy smoke-haze that is common to India and Burma at that time of year, the weather was clear. There was a partial moon. Our ground speed from Kunming to Yunnanyi was normal and the engines were performing well. Approaching Yunnanyi, it was still light enough for visual confirmation of our direction-finder bearing.

The next check point was Yun-lung and it was there that our troubles began. We received what appeared to be a good DF bearing on Yun-lung, but by then it was too dark and hazy for visual confirmation. The elapsed time between Yunnanyi and Yun-lung indicated an alarming ground speed of 70 miles per hour instead of the usual 170 MPH. The questions that immediately entered my mind were: Did I check the time wrong? Did I get an erroneous bearing on Yun-lung? Or was there actually a 100 MPH headwind? Yun-lung is in a deep valley practically in the middle of the Hump. The strong winds prevailing in the Hump could be expected to alter direction or slacken as we proceeded Westward. I assumed that the headwind would not

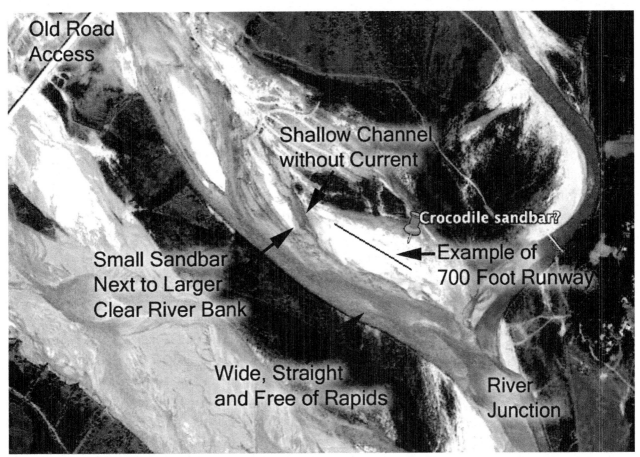

Old Road Access

Shallow Channel without Current

Crocodile sandbar?

Small Sandbar Next to Larger Clear River Bank

Example of 700 Foot Runway

Wide, Straight and Free of Rapids

River Junction

Google Earth view of a best guess on location of Carroll's plane. Image © CNES / Astrium, © 2016 Google

hold but that it would nevertheless reduce our ground speed. We would be able to check the latter when we picked up DF bearings from the Assam stations.

We proceeded beyond Yun-lung on a normal course at 18,000 feet which put us well above the smoke-haze level. As soon as there was any possibility of picking up the Assam stations, I began the search for DF bearings. As we progressed we began to get Assam signals and started calling for assistance. In all cases the DF needle swung directly toward the mountains of Tibet and an aural check yielded the same bearing. During the entire remainder of the flight we never received a reliable bearing and were unable to make contact with a ground station. Flying at night, on top of a thick smoke-haze layer, with unknown ground speed, unknown wind and no navigational aids, our only

chance was to hold to our course and hope for a break.

We continued in this manner until the gas needles indicated almost empty tanks. I decided that we should do something while we still had power available. We dropped down into the haze in an effort to locate ground lights. We were at around 10,000 feet and preparing to bail out when Pai saw moon reflections on water and shouted, "River, river below!" If the river was large enough, I decided we would be better off belly landing the aircraft in the water, where we might have access to our emergency supplies, than bailing out over solid jungle.

One low pass over the water with landing lights on revealed that two streams, which issued from the Himalayan ranges, joined below us. The water was shallow, fast and turbulent; the river bed was curved, irregular and composed of large boulders. Due to our bad fuel situation, I was afraid to make more than one low-level pass because engine failure at that altitude could be fatal. We pulled up from the inspection pass to about 500 feet, held a reciprocal course for about a minute, during which time I quietly requested assistance from higher authority, made another steep turn with the lights on, then throttled down, and landed in the water with the gear up. The curve of the river was such that we were perfectly lined up when we came out of our final turn.

The landing was smooth and the left wheel, meeting a gravel bar, gently swung us around 90 degrees to a full stop with the forward part of the aircraft well out of the water. As we flew with one generator removed, our batteries were never fully charged, but, in this instance, we had enough power for Hsu to get off two messages describing the river junction and our situation.

Pai and Hsu remained in the aircraft the remainder of the night while I donned my fleece-lined flying suit and huddled against a pile of driftwood on the gravel bar. From this vantage point, I could see anyone approaching and would have time, if necessary, to slide into the water and float away.

When daylight came, we carried our emergency supplies to the shore; laid out a large white arrow, composed of strips torn from

parachutes and cargo tie-down ropes and then started down river. As I was walking in and out of the water my Calcutta shoes soon turned to mush and had to be dicarded. I replaced them with the fleece-lined flight boots and held them snug with lashings of cargo rope.

Both banks of the river were covered with thick elephant grass some eight to ten feet high. Except where there were game trails, these formed an impenetrable barrier. We were concerned about the possibility of meeting an enraged water buffalo or some other pugnacious form of wild life who would wish to dispute possession of the trail with us. Our only weapon was a flare pistol. In addition, we had, as emergency supplies, K rations, two bush knives, a canteen, mosquito nets, and cigarettes, which I don't use.

The river was getting deeper and wider. After walking about two miles, we decided to build a raft of elephant grass stalks. The raft proved adequate for only two men, so I swam along behind, guiding the raft by means of a rope. After progressing in this way for about a mile, the raft became snagged in hip-deep water. Just as we were moving our gear ashore to proceed on foot, a large wild bull with curving horns that pointed straight up crashed through the grass to the river bank about fifty yards below us. He started toward us, pawed some sand, snorted, then, apparently thinking better of it, trotted on across the river.

He was a huge animal, definitely not a water buffalo, so big that, as he crossed the river, the water barely came above his knees. I have since learned that there is a relatively rare bull of this size and description in Asia.

For three more days, we walked along the river, in and out of the water, occasionally disturbing wild water buffalo and seeing crocodile tracks, but not encountering any crocodiles. During the cool nights, we were

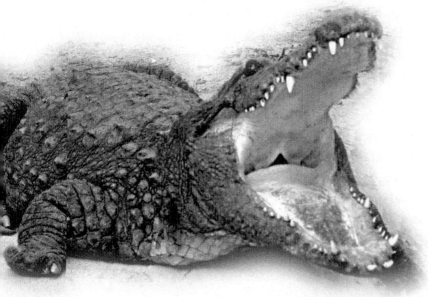

comfortable in our fleece-lined suits and were generally able to make a good fire with the plentiful driftwood.

By the third day, large water blisters formed on the soles of my feet due to walking in the constantly soaked flight boots. Pai and Hsu wore cheap rubber-soled oxfords, which held up beautifully and gave them no trouble. On the fourth day, we met a group of natives who were heading upriver and engaged one of them to guide us to the nearest town. This proved to be Sorbhog. We also learned that the two rivers emerging from the Tibetan mountain range were the Manas and the Mora Manas. This, incidentally, is the general area where the Chinese Communists invaded India several years ago.

By the last day, my blisters were so painful that I had to rest every hundred yards or so, but fortunately we came to a road and were picked up by some British officers in a station wagon. At about the same time, a CNAC plane which had been searching for us made a low pass, recognized us, and landed in the Sorbhog airfield, which had not been activated. The British gave us water, but offered our rescuers Scotch; then turned us over to a GI railroad detachment that was running the local railroad. Shortly thereafter, we were picked up by the CNAC crew and flown to Dinjan.

Pai and Hsu proved to be excellent companions for this caper. They were good-natured, ingenious and hard-working. They spoke enough English to make our evenings around the camp fire pleasant and interesting. We boiled all of our drinking water in our canteen. Each man lived on one K ration a day, normally one meal; yet we never felt particularly hungry. Except for my blistered feet and a profound thirst, we finished the adventure in excellent condition. Pai and Hsu later threw a huge Chinese dinner in Calcutta, which took care of the latter problem.

Possible path of overshoot, Manas River landing

Image © CNES / Astrium, © 2016 Google

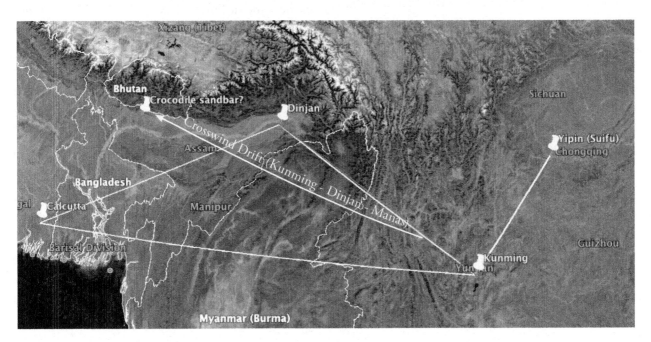

GLENN CARROLL'S C-47 FLIES AGAIN

by William C. McDonald, Jr.

Reprinted with permission from *Wings Over Asia* (Vol.1)

The men behind the scenes rarely get credit for a job well done. So I want to tell the story of how Art Prendergast, one of our leading mechanics, and his fine Chinese maintenance crew salvaged the C-47 which Glenn Carroll had abandoned.

The day after we located Captain Carroll's ditched plane in the Manas River, about a mile south of the Himalayas, Art and his crew were on their way to the site of the ditching to see whether the plane could be refitted for service or should be written off as a loss. To reach the stranded No. 81, Art and his crew had to walk to the head of the Manas River about a mile upstream from the C-47. Then they used rubber rafts to float downstream to the small island in the river where the plane had been left. On one of these trips downstream a Chinese mechanic fell out of the flimsy, bobbing raft and before he could be hauled back into the boat, was attacked and devoured by a 25-foot crocodile.

A survey showed that the left propeller and engine of Number 81 were damaged and would have to be replaced. This was impossible, however, on the small island where the plane had been abandoned. Accordingly, Art's first step was to hire local labor and elephants to drag the C-47, with its landing gear down, onto a dry overflow bed where repairs could be made.

Barely a month after Carroll had made his nighttime ditching, Art Prendergast sent word to Calcutta that all necessary repairs had been made, the engines had been tested, and the plane was ready to be flown out of the jungle.

Captain C. L. Sharp, our Operations Manager, asked me if I would do the job and I replied affirmatively. Accordingly, I was flown into Sorbhog on the Brahmaputra River and then driven in a jeep almost to the head of the Manas River. There I took a life raft on the same turbulent river route which had claimed the life of our Chinese mechanic down to where the plane was waiting.

Art was there to meet me and gave me a warm welcome. We inspected the C-47 and he told me about the repairs he had made. We then looked at the emergency take-off strip which had been prepared for the flight out. Rocks and boulders about the size of basket balls lined the dry river bed. On pacing the improvised runway, we found it was only 150 feet long. Moreover, there was a three-foot bank of sand at the end of our take-off area. I asked Art to have the bank smoothed out and tilted with a 10 degree upsweep so

Art Pendergast in the grass in front of a downed C-47, like Carroll's plane. He and his skilled crew got Carroll's plane ready to fly again in less than a month.

we could be catapulted aloft. This seemed to me absolutely necessary because the Manas River was dead ahead, a mere fifteen feet beyond the sand slope.

Art had put only 50 gallons of gas in a main tank to minimize take-off weight. A Chinese mechanic, who was very sick wanted to fly back with us so he could receive medical attention. It was difficult to refuse his request. After Art and I were in the cockpit, the other mechanics smuggled the sick mechanic aboard and shut the door. Fortunately his extra weight did not jeopardize our take-off.

We made our routine checks very carefully. Then came the time of decision. We ran the engines up, gave the O.K. signal, and opened the throttles wide. The first fifty feet of the take-off seemed to last an eternity, but at a hundred feet our tail lightened and rose a little. Just as we reached the upslope of the sand,

I pulled firmly, but not too hard, on the wheel and we catapulted into the air. I let old No. 81 settle toward the water and Art raised the landing gear. We had used 10 degrees of flap and, just before touching the water, I realized we had her under control. Slowly we began to climb and at a hundred feet we milked the flaps up and knew we were home free. C-47 Number 81 was back in the air and would soon be on the job again carrying cargo over the Hump.

Captain Carroll, co-pilot Pai and Radio Operator Hsu are to be congratulated for their fine flying teamwork in getting No. 81 down safely. Art Prendergast and his Chinese maintenance crew did an outstanding job of salvage. Moreover, Art showed a great deal of courage when he volunteered to fly as my co-pilot on a never-to-be-forgotten take-off from the banks of the crocodile infested Manas River.

FLETCHER HANKS, *SAGA OF CNAC #53*, EXCERPT FROM CHAPTER 4

FLYING A TRANSPORT OFF A 700-FOOT SANDBAR

The complete Chapter 4 includes a fascinating and detailed account of the repair work, which included more than two dozen local villagers and elephants to the rescue! It is clear just how heroic the mechanics and support crew were, and the dangers that they faced, to keep CNAC flying. It is also clear how CNAC depended on the goodwill and hard work of local people at every turn. Virtually all rescue stories, whether crew or plane, includes heroic efforts by local villagers with the cooperation of officials.

I thought about the great flights the pilots made during WWII. One that stands out was Bill McDonald's flight of CNAC #81.

Art radioed Dinjan and reported that the plane was ready to fly and the runway was completed. Woodie said Bill McDonald, the chief pilot, would arrive before noon the next day to fly it. The chief pilot knew all of the finer points of escaping from short runways and he knew no fear. He had lived dangerously in the aviation field all his life. He was one of the famous stunt pilot trio of Chennault, Williamson and McDonald, 'Three Men on the Flying Trapeze.' Many a young boy had set their sights on aviation after seeing them perform. Bill was now married and had reached the age when an aviator was old enough to know that he had cheated death several times thanks to quick decisions, but now his reaction time wasn't as quick as a younger man's. If he had declined the assignment and picked a younger CNAC pilot with quicker reactions, one who was cheating death every month, it would have been understood. An active CNAC pilot's delicate touch on the controls had to be better because he was flying 120 hours a month. To take a pilot from a desk job was questionable.

Bill walked up and down the 700-foot runway many times. He placed stones opposite the 100-foot, 350-foot and the 500-foot points on the left side of the runway so he could see them easily. He ordered the last ten feet of the runway rebuilt with a greater upsweep so he would be catapulted into the air. He ordered the ramp rebuilt with the biggest rocks they could find. He wanted to make sure the big stones would stay in place when the 17,500 pound airplane hit the incline with both engines at full power at 60 miles an hour. Bill said, "She won't fly off at 60, and when it bounces in the air the airspeed will drop to 55, but she'll be at 65 before she hits the water and she'll be flying."

The question was could the plane get up enough speed rolling over the uneven rocks? He'd have to make a judgment of that at the halfway mark, 350 feet.

The chief and Art had everyone working on the ramp, including the mechanics. Thunderheads were building up to the south, with bolts of lightning. Bill called Woodie on the radio to discuss the weather at Dinjan. Woodie said it was raining down the valley and he expected it to rain there at any minute. The wind had already shifted to the northeast, feeding the storm.

Art was sending his tools back to Dinjan in the Jeep that had brought up Bill McDonald. The three mechanics would ride back in the truck. One mechanic was very ill with malaria. Bill refused to take him in the plane because the plane had to be as light as possible.

Bill approved the ramp and, while the last workers left it, he stood at the end of the ramp on his last walk with Art and counted crocodiles. He turned to Art and reported, "I count fifteen."

Art replied, "If they are a concern to you, don't go. I don't expect to die fighting crocodiles."

Bill smiled, "Me neither. I'm ready to go. We've got to go while we have the little breeze in our face. When that thunderstorm gets nearer, the wind will change here and give us a tail wind. Then we can't go. You watch my run-up. If you see something you don't like, stop me. After I bring the engines to full power, I will let the engines cook one minute before I release the brakes. You watch the instruments and hold the throttles open with your left hand. If an engine backfires, you adjust the mixture with your right. If an engine can't hold 1600 rpm, feather it. Pull

Chief Pilot Mac

SENATE CHAMBER

MONTGOMERY

ALABAMA

J. BRUCE HENDERSON, SENATOR
22ND DISTRICT
WILCOX COUNTY
MILLER'S FERRY

June 2, 1943

Dear Mr. & Mrs. Mc Donald :

The Governor held a reception for Madame Wei and Miss Tag and Mr. Robert Tsonhywin Huang at the Governor's home yesterday evening. The legislature was invited. I went because I thought they might know William Mc Donald. Madame Wei knew him and spoke well of him. Mr. Huang was especially well acquainted with him but had not heard form him since 1938. He seemed very anxious to lean about him . He said the Chinese Govenment and the Chinese people though very highly of William Mc Donald. I an inclosing card which he gave me with theor names on it. thot Mrs. Mc Donald would be interested in this.

With every good wish , I am .

Sincerely,

The Governor held a reception… Mr. Huang was especially well acquainted with him…He said the Chinese Government and the Chinese people thought very highly of William McDonald.

Senator J. Bruce Henderson, June 2, 1943

the gear lever when the wheels leave the ramp. Watch the instruments, because once we pass the 350-foot point, there will be no aborting the take-off. I'll ask for ten degrees of flap at 500 feet, so they'll be down just before we hit the ramp. I don't want the flaps too soon because it will kill my airspeed. I will pull a light but firm grip on the wheel as we hit the ramp. I'll need 60 miles per hour at that time. You call out the airspeeds after the tail lifts off.

"Once she's in the air., I'll take off the back pressure on the wheel and she'll settle into a horizontal attitude and pick up flying speed. If I think it might hit the water, I'll ask for quarter flaps. We've got to make it to that sandbar on the other shore. I can't use much control before she flies because it will kill our speed. She'll be flying before she touches the water. One other thing; cowl flaps open on run up, closed when we start rolling, and don't open them until we are 50 feet above the water. Watch the instruments. Remember, if we don't abort after 350 feet, we'll go with what we have left even if it is only one engine, because we don't want to skid off the end of the runway into that bunch of crocs. Disregard the head temperatures. I don't mind burning up these engines to get out of here."

Art replied, "That sounds easy." He gave a nervous laugh as he flicked his cigarette into the river.

They climbed the steps to the plane, walked to the cockpit, buckled up tightly. Bill called Dinjan operations. Woodie answered and he said they had a nasty squall. Bill said he expected to be in the air within ten minutes, if the wind didn't change. He slipped a thick rubber band over the microphone button so they could hear the take-off. Woodie said he would call the M.D. in Calcutta so he and Chuck Sharp could hear it also. Bill turned down the volume on the receiver so he couldn't hear the static from the lightning.

Bill started the engines and ran them up very carefully while watching the gauges. "Art, do you see anything you don't like?"

Art replied, "The engines are ready. Go for it."

Just before Bill moved the plane into take-off position on the runway and both of them closed their side windows, the cargo door slammed shut. Bill asked, "What's that?"

Art looked back and saw the mechanics had slipped their sick comrade inside at the last moment. Art said, "We've got a sick passenger, whether we want him or not." Art waved violently to the passenger to come forward, next to the cockpit, because he wanted the tail as light as possible. Bill never broke his trance-like concentration. He turned the plane onto the very end of the runway and lined it up. He set the brakes and ran both engines to full emergency power. The plane danced there for a minute until Bill let off the brakes. When he did, the plane lurched forward. Bill announced so they could hear it on the radio, "Number 81 has started to roll," but Bill could feel every boulder it rolled over. He announced, "I have a problem. The rocks are uneven." The plane changed its direction slightly with each boulder, but Bill didn't touch the brakes to straighten its course. He needed speed immediately. He wondered if the tires were fully inflated. The plane straightened its course, as there were equal numbers of boulders on each side. At one hundred feet, the tail lifted and the plane started to gain flying speed. Bill ordered, "Ten degrees flaps."

Art applied them and announced, "Ten degrees flaps. Forty-five, fifty, fifty-five."

Everything seemed to take forever, but suddenly they hit the ramp at the end of the runway. Art called out, "Sixty," and pulled the gear lever. They were in the air.

The plane leveled out and sank to what Art thought was dangerously close to the water. The gear came up and the plane staggered a couple of times with the change of temperature in the air over the river. They were heading for the jungle on the other side of the river, but the plane was flying. Bill said in a normal voice, "We've got her now. Cowl flaps open."

Art said, "You scared the shit out of me. I thought the props were touching the water."

"Not by a half-inch," Bill replied. "But I almost asked for quarter-flaps."

The speed increased and she climbed steadily. At fifty feet Bill milked up the flaps and banked a little to miss the trees on the other shore.

Bill picked up the mike and said, "Just like it was supposed to be."

All the Burrah Sahibs picked up their mikes and congratulated Bill.

Marrying the Princess

In 1944, Billy McDonald met a young woman who changed his life. Also from Birmingham, Alabama, Peggy Spain was a volunteer with the American Red Cross in Calcutta. In high school, she and her classmates had gotten out of school to see the Men on the Flying Trapeze perform.

They were from different worlds. She was a debutante, the daughter of a wealthy family. From more modest roots, he was a dashing flyer, romantic and well-liked. He had risen to Chief Pilot in CNAC, but he had not found the girl of his dreams until he met Peggy.

Peggy wrote home in April to tell her friends about the interesting pilot showing her the sights. He swept her off her feet, and she dazzled him. By early summer they were engaged.

Chennault wrote to say that he wished he could attend to give both bride and groom away.

On August 1, 1944, they married in Calcutta. Frank Higgs was best man at the celebration, which was attended by many of CNAC's finest.

They left shortly after for a honeymoon in Kashmir. Peggy wrote home describing their time in Kashmir as "the most perfect trip anyone ever had." The notably adventurous CNAC Captain Pete Goutiere had made the introductions to the Maharajah there.

July 15/1944

...HAM NEWS ★ The South's Greatest

TO WED—Though both from Birmingham, they had never known each other until they met the past Spring in India where Miss Margaret (Peggy) Spain is stationed as an American Red Cross club hostess, and Capt. William (Billy) McDonald is chief pilot for the North China National Aviation Corporation. They will be married Aug. 1, in India.

Local Couple Meet In India For First Time, Become Engaged

They met in India, discovered they were both from Birmingham . . . well, the story will end with wedding bells Aug. 1, on the other side of the world.

The "she" of the story is Margaret (Peggy) Spain, attractive former Birmingham debutante, now in Red Cross service, and the "he" is dashing Capt. William McDonald.

While Peggy was being admired as a belle of Birmingham, serving as she did as president of the Debutante Club and being honored at numerous parties, as well as being presented by the Redstone and Spinsters Club, "Billy" McDonald was gathering fame in the Orient as a member of Chennault's celebrated Flying Tigers. They met soon after Peggy arrived in India in the early Spring to serve as a club hostess for the Red Cross. Letters home from both of them carried increasingly frequent mentions of shared occasions, for apparently Billy was enjoying showing the girl from home the Orient that has been his home for the past eight years. Then, Friday came the big news. The formal announcement of which will be made Sunday in The Birmingham News-Age-Herald society columns.

Peggy was graduated from Bir-

mingham - Southern College, previously attending Goucher College, in Baltimore, and Sophie Newcomb College, New Orleans. She is a member of the Junior League.

After attending Howard College and Washington and Lee University, Capt. McDonald entered the U. S. Army Air Corps and became a member of the famous "Flying Trapeze," which was trained by Gen. Chenault, then a major at Maxwell Field. Later, he went to Shanghai as an instructor in the developing Chinese Air Force. With him had gone the third member of the air team that pioneered in precision flying, Luke Williamson. Chenault joined them later, to head the training program, and the three enlarged a fame that was already national.

When McDonald had resigned his position with the air force, determined to return to the States, he was persuaded to become chief pilot for the North China National Aviation Corporation, in which role he has served several times as pilot for Generalissimo and Mme. Chiang Kai-Shek.

Miss Spain is the daughter of Mr. and Mrs. [...]. Mc[...] Donald's [...] W. C. Mc[...]

LEFT Shopping in Calcutta.

ABOVE Engagement announcement in *Birmingham News*.

RIGHT Peggy Spain, letter home, spring 1944.

Among the nicest parts of the whole thing is running into people from home and people who know people from home. My drawl seems to bring the question "Where are you (or you all) from" as soon as I meet any part of the American Army with the result that everyone who's ever been in Alabama pretty soon comes around to compare [...] Rodgers Dewey's brother who's a Captain i[...] few nights later I found myself seated at [...] brother in law of Getty Snow who{s so pop[...] Major Gilbert Johnston and Major Hooks Fa[...] spent hours answering their hundreds of q[...]

Among the best known and most interesting [...] is a former Birminghamian, Capt. William [...] in Bellevue Geights. Capt. McDonald work[...] generalissimo in the training of the Chin[...] When Chennault went back to the states an[...] pilot of (censored) which is doing such a[...] The exploits of Captain Mac and his gang [...] the current "Terry and the Pirates" carto[...] to me and to all other Alabamians over he[...] in his lovely home.

Among the best known and most interesting people in this part of the world is a former Birminghamian, Capt. William McDonald, Jr., whose parents live in Bellevue Heights....Mac has been most hospitable to me and to all other Alabamians over here and has entertained us royally in his lovely home.

Peggy Spain, Spring 1944

Mr. and Mrs. Frank Edward Spain

announce the marriage of their daughter

Margaret Cameron

to

William Clifford McDonald, Junior

Tuesday August first

Nineteen hundred and forty four

Calcutta, India

At Home
Fountain Court
3/1 Middleton Street
Calcutta, India

Perks of Dating a Pilot

TOP Peggy and other passengers waiting to board Mac's plane. Mac is near the plane, in a dark suit.

ABOVE Peggy reading a newspaper at left back.

LEFT Sometimes Peggy wanted to drive, and here she has Mac's CNAC Jeep and his Dachshunds too.

1944 – Wedding in Calcutta

HEADQUARTERS, FOURTEENTH AIR FORCE
Office of the Commanding General

July 24, 1944

Dear Mac:

Work is piling up here at such rapid rate that I am afraid that I will not be able to get away for a visit to Calcutta about August 1st.

I really hate this as I would like to be there to give both <u>you</u> and the bride away. After having looked after you for so many years, I could give her a lot of good tips on your care and management, but I suppose this can wait till some later opportunity.

I am sending a small gift and regret that it is not something nicer – it is about the best I can do in Kunming and hope you will find some use for it.

There is always a bare chance that I will get away after all, but if I do not, you both have my most sincere wishes for the utmost of happiness and long life.

Looking forward to seeing you both in the near future, if I don't make it for the wedding, I am,

Most sincerely yours,

ABOVE Wedding photos for Mac and Peggy.

JUST ABOVE ON LEFT Frank Higgs (best man).

LEFT Chennault and Peggy bond over Dachshunds.

I would like to be there to give both you and the bride away. After having looked after you for so many years, I could give her a lot of good tips on your care and management…

Chennault, July 24, 1944

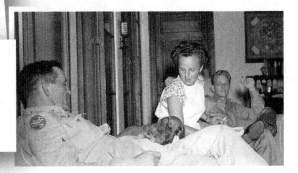

Newlyweds in Kashmir

They enjoyed the scenery, the water, golf, tiger hunts and formal dinners.

> We've just come back from the most perfect trip anyone ever had.
>
> Peggy (Spain) McDonald

Honeymoon in Cooch Behar

NEWS ★ The South's Greatest Newspaper

Birmingham

BY MARGUERITE JOHNSTON

How can Birmingham fail to gain the global concept when one-time residents are skittering casually all over the world?

From Peggy Spain McDonald in India to her parents, Mr. and Mrs. Frank Spain, comes a letter describing a recent trip she made with her husband, Capt. Billy McDonald. The letter is interestingly illustrated by this week's Life magazine picture coverage of a similar hunt.

"We've just come back from the most perfect trip anyone ever had. We flew to a native state where we landed on the maharajah's private aerodrome. There we were met by six cars and a station wagon which transported us and luggage to the palace.

"I had expected this to be either shabby and dirty or much too ornate, but it's one of the most beautifully done homes I've ever seen. There must be about 40 guest apartments and I do mean apartments in the palace, plus the living quarters of the maharajah's three sisters and the dowager maharani.

MRS. McDONALD

"Mac and I occupied the Chinese suite—a bedroom in the palest green and gold lacquer work, a lovely red and jade sitting room and a green and gold dressing room. Every touch is perfect, indirect lighting over dressing table mirrors, the best plumbing in India, tremendous pale green bath towels, the softest linen sheets I've ever slept on.

* * *

THERE ARE SEVERAL STATE DINING ROOMS, and we used the middle-sized one, since there were about 15 of us and usually some local guests. The table was stretched to seat 40 at one time, and a damask cloth, all in one piece was used on it.

"In the rear of the building is a miniature of the building furnished in detail which was built for the maharajah's sisters as a doll house.

"We woke up about 9 every morning to witness the changing of the guard which is done with all the fanfare of Buckingham Palace and a much better brass band.

"About 11 we piled into cars and drove 25 miles to a camp on the edge of the jungle where we climbed on the backs of elephants. These elephants were equipped with soft mattresses which made for very comfortable riding until we got into howdahs, little straw and steel structures carried by elephants containing two seats, gun rests, ammunition bags, etc. They'd even put in tangerines and bottles of water so that we'd not be hungry or thirsty.

"The guests were lined up on one side of a clearing in the high jungle grass. The maharajah and native mahouts on about 20 other elephants would go about half a mile away, form a solid line and beat the grass toward us. On three successive days, on the second beat, out came a tiger.

* * *

"THE TIGERS WERE ABOUT NINE FEET LONG, and averaged 350 to 400 pounds. When the kill

CAPT. McDONALD

had been made and everyone had snapped pictures furiously for a few minutes, we'd get back on the comfortable mattresses and ride to camp.

"By this time the palace card had arrived and servants spread a beautiful lunch on the lawn. In the afternoons we'd board elephants again and beat the jungle in a line, to kill whatever appeared. Got a dozen beautiful peacock, several wild boars and a leopard.

"About sundown, we'd return to the camp where there were tea and cakes or Scotch and sodas for those who wanted them. Then we'd be driven back to the palace, where we dressed for dinner, and I do mean dressed. Dinner was about 11 p.m., and afterwards the men would play billiards and the gals poker—if you could keep awake.

"There were about eight couples of us . . . The maharajah was the most perfect host, and everything

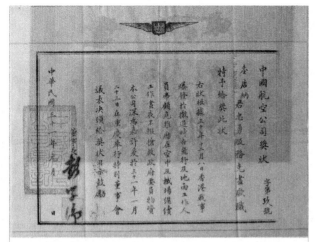

CNAC citation

Date: Jan., 1942

Ref.No: 9

Per his loyal and brave dedication to his responsibilites, W.C.McDonald is hereby awarded this citation. It is based on the facts that, on 19411208 when war was erupted in HK, all CNAC aircrews and ground staff overcame various difficulties to continue to work in the air and on the ground day and night to evacuate important government officers and supplies.

Signed: Peng Sho-pei (CNAC President)

Ministry of Communications Citation

Date: April 24th, 1945

Serial No. Aviation 6189

Per his magnificent effort and brilliant achievement in air transportation, W.C.McDonald is hereby awarded the MOC Citation.

Signed: Yu Fei Peng
         (Minister of Communications)

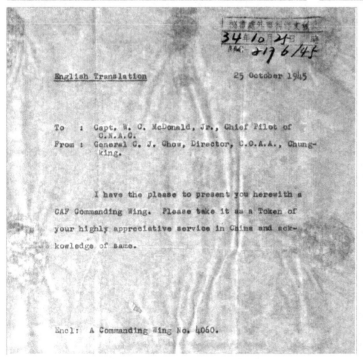

CHINESE CITATIONS

UPPER LEFT Evacuation of Hong Kong.

UPPER RIGHT For flying the Hump.

LEFT Outstanding service with CNAC.

BELOW Replica of Mac's CAF Commanding Wing.

19451025 国民政府航空委员会主任周至柔将军
在重庆向中国航空公司总飞行师麦唐纳先生
(W.C.McDonald)颁发中国空军指挥官功勋胸章
(编号4060),对其在中国所作出的受到高度赞赏
的服务表彰并感谢

Accomplishments and Sacrifices

A collection of papers attributed to Althea Lister, Pan-American historian, tells the story of CNAC's wartime accomplishments and sacrifices through statistics. These are impressive, given the airline's small size and financial challenges. While the ATC eventually brought more tonnage across the Hump due to sheer numbers, CNAC did more with fewer resources at less cost in human life.

Yet twenty-three flight crews were lost in forty-seven major accidents. China was a perilous country for any who flew its skies.

According to the Lister papers, CNAC planes crossed the Hump more than 80,000 times between April 1942, when it first established routes between China and India, and September 1945, the end of the war.

In 1944 alone CNAC pilots flew more than 9,000 round trips over the Himalayas, logging in excesss of 10 million miles.

Japan had hoped to cut off China from the world, from supplies and from foreign markets, effectively ending its ability to resist Japan's will. The handful of American civilians in aviation in China—those who worked for the Chinese Air Force, CNAC, the AVG or aviation companies—helped China to hold out against the stronger force until the U.S. entered the war. Even after, they played an important role in supplying China with essentials.

Ferrying over 50,000 tons of goods into war-ravaged China, CNAC helped thwart the Japanese efforts to strangle China. It supported Chennault's Flying Tigers, its U.S. military successor, the 14th Air Force, and the Chinese Air Force. CNAC also carried almost 25,000 tons of goods to foreign markets, much of it critical to the wartime efforts of Allied governments and manufacturing.

Mac received three different awards from the Chinese government in recognition of various accomplishments. The United States has now recognized Americans who worked for CNAC as veterans, and has retroactively awarded them various medals.

But when Japan surrendered to the Allies in September, 1945, CNAC faced the transition from wartime to civilian work. This entailed moving operations from Calcutta back to Shanghai and transitioning from the dangerous Hump flights to more routine Chinese and international routes for freight and passengers.

CNAC would face other issues as well. According to William Leary in his book *The Dragon's Wings*, a number of disastrous accidents in 1946 and 1947 related in part to poor infrastructure caused pilots to demand "minimum requirements" for safe operations such as night lighting, equipment for instrument landings, weather reporting, qualified air traffic personnel and more radios. Morale among personnel deteriorated, and CNAC faced difficulty with payroll, infrastructure and China's escalating civil war.

In the years following the war, Mac suffered a number of particularly painful losses. In 1945, just after the war ended, his best friend Frank Higgs lost his life in a horrific crash. In December of 1946, Mac was on the radio with the pilots of two airplanes, attempting to talk them through landing with zero visibility. Both planes crashed, with great loss of life.

FATAL CRASH OF FRANK HIGGS

During a flight in late October 1945, Mac's best friend Frank Higgs was flying a load of banking officials and gold from Shanghai to Canton. He was using an unreliable ATC map. He did not arrive at his destination.

The Shanghai area had no search and rescue so Mac retraced Higgs' route and found the wreckage after three weeks. The crew—Higgs, his co-pilot and radio operator—and all ten passengers had been killed. The gold was gone. The plane had crashed into a Chinese village, destroying it, killing seven and injuring others.

Accident investigation guessed that Higgs flew at 1500 feet over a mountain and was sucked into the face by an unexpected down draft. China was dangerous even for an experienced pilot like Higgs.

This was a great personal loss for Mac, and it shows in the letter he wrote to Higgs' long-time friend, cartoonist Milton Caniff. Caniff drew one final cartoon for Frank Higgs and laid Dude Hennick, his character in *Terry & the Pirates*, to rest.

Calcutta, India
November 7, 1945

Dear Milt,

This is a very difficult letter to write. Regardless of how I start it or how I say it — it is wrong. Frank has left us. He was killed in a crash on October 20th about 200 miles southwest of Shanghai. He was on a regular flight from Shanghai to Canton. There were ten passengers on board and a crew consisting of Frank, his Chinese co-pilot and Chinese radio operator. We do not have any idea of what caused the accident. The ship crashed into a Chinese village at about 3000 feet in some mountains. It was a terrific crash and the ship caught fire and all on board perished. Also the entire village was wiped out. Seven villagers were killed and a number were injured.

There was no radio contact indicating any trouble and it was unreported for almost a week before we found the ship. All the bodies will be brought back to Shanghai and Diana, Frank's wife, has instructed that Frank's body be cremated and buried in Shanghai.

This is the most awful thing that has happened to us in our history. It is a terrific blow. Frank was my best friend and I am bewildered and stunned. Diana is staying with Peg and me and we are trying to console and comfort her in every way that we can. It is difficult because we, too, feel terrible about the whole thing.

Milt, I know that you would want to hear from me about Frank and you will have to excuse the peculiar tone of this letter as I am not in any mood to talk or write much about it.

I am sorry that my letter conveys such sad news,

Mac

The Shanghai Evening Post

62 Killed As 3 Airliners Crash Here

12 Killed, Three Injured In This Crash

2 CNAC, 1 CATC Planes Lost In Fatal Tries To Land In Heavy Fog

Pilots Fail In Attempts To Make Blind-Landing

CATC Airliner Hits Farmhouse In Landing

Doctors Battle For Lives Of Crash Victims

Assembly Approves Constitution

The 1946 Christmas Crashes

On December 25, 1946, Mac was Chief Pilot. The following is from a letter that Lincoln Reyholds sent to his wife, describing the scene at Lunghwa during an unusually heavy fog that created zero visibility:

Woody phoned Tweedy, then he and I rushed out to Lunghwa. "Mac" McDonald, Chief Pilot, and three of his assistants were already there. Mac was in the tower and one of the three planes, an unconverted DC-3 was low overhead circling the field. Mac was attempting to contact him by radiophone but was having great difficulty as the plane's radio equipment was not operating properly. Positive communication had been established by CW (dot-and-dash). The plane was running low on gas as it had been released from Hankow for Nanking but had been unable to get into Nanking in three or four tries, before coming on to Shanghai. It had made several attempts to land at Kiangwan by GCA (ground control approach—radar) but was unsuccessful because of radiophone trouble. The GCA unit could receive the plane all right, but the plane could not get messages from the ground in turn. The pilot, Captain Greenwood, then came over to Lunghwa knowing that he had no alternative by that time. The nearest clear weather alternate field was Tsingtao, but he had insufficient gas to get there by this time. Apparently he decided against that course earlier because Tsingtao does not have any field lights for night operation. There was hope too that an occasional break in weather might occur, according to CNAC and Kiangwan forecasts. In summary up to this point, Greenwood had

to attempt to get in at Shanghai, and Lunghwa was a better choice than Kiangwan.

For something like forty-five minutes the plane flew around in the fog overhead. He made several attempts to "feel" his way down to a sign of the lights….Finally Greenwood told Mac on the radio that he was so low on gas that he was coming in.…Suddenly there was a dull red cone in the fog.

[CNAC Captain Rolf Preus] flew back and forth over the field several times, coming down as low as he dared.… The pilot climbed up to the altitude called for in standard approach procedure. Mac was talking to him all the time. He was calm and confident. We on the ground felt reassured.…I was back up on the hangar roof…listening for Mac. As the pilot made his turn into the final leg, Mac asked him not to reply to Mac's transmission. Mac instructed him calmly to come on down the final leg at 110 miles an hour, and at 150 feet altitude as he passed over the inner marker—a radio beacon near the approach end of the runway.…I distinctly heard him coming in… there was a sudden dull thud-like sound and then again that silence.

The death toll for those crashes, plus an ATC crash the same day, was 71, with 16 survivors. CNAC reorganized and within a few months, Mac had stepped down as Chief Pilot.

On August 1, 1947, he and his family left China.

Christmas Crashes report

After a disaster like the 1946 Christmas crashes, with such loss of life, CNAC had to take stock of its operations and procedures.

Here, a report that we believe was written by Mac, as Chief Pilot, shows the difficult and complex situation in which CNAC operated.

Not surprisingly, after the tragic events CNAC underwent an almost complete turnover in its management.

SHORTLY AFTER MY RETURN FROM TOKYO AND THE CRASH OF CAPTAIN LONGBOTHAMS PLANE HAD BEEN CONFIRMED AND IT WAS DEFINITELY ESTABLISHED THAT THE CAUSE OF.THIS CRASH WAS 100 % PILOTS ERROR. IT WAS DECIDED THAT IMMEDIATE ACTION SHOULD BE TAKEN IN ORDER TO PREVENT FURTHER ACCIDENTS OF THIS NATURE AND OF ANY OTHER NATURE.

IN A TALK WITH YOU WE POOLED OUR EXPERIENCES AND DIAGNOSED THE UNDERLYING CAUSE OF LONGBOTHAMS MISTAKE TO BE THE SAME OF SO MANY OTHER PILOTS. IT IXXXXIXWAS IMPATIENCE AND OVER EAGERNESS THAT TRUMPED GOOD JUDGEMENT. A CAMPAIGN WAS STARTED. AT THREE PILOTS MEETINGS THIS SUBJECT WAS DISCUSSED AT GREAT LENGTH. AT THE PILOTS MEETING ON SATURDAY BEFORE CHRISTMAS I AGAIN BROUGHT THIS SUBJECT UP AND TALKED XXXXXXXXT WITH THE PILOTS IN A MOST SERIOUS MANNER TO AGAIN BEWARE OF LETTING THINGS OUTSIDE OF DUTY INFLUENCE THEIR JUDGEMENT TO THE POINT THAT THEY MIGHT STICK THEIR"NECKS OUT". CAPTAIN GREENWOOD AND CAPT. PRUES WERE PRESENT AT THESE MEETINGS.

TO FURTHER THIS CAMPAIGN YOU ENLIGHTENED ALL DEPARTME HEADS AT THE WEEKLY STAFF MEETING. IN SPITE OF OUR EFFORTS THESE TWO ACCIDENTS HAPPENED.

IN EARLY OCTOBER I TOOK COMPLETE INVENTORY OF THE PILOT SITUATION AND MADE PLANS TO PREPARE THEM FOR THE WINTER SEASON.

ON OCTOBER 22nd I ISSUED A NOTICE TO ALL PILOTS THAT ONE PLANE WOULD BE AVAILABLE EVERY DAY FOR A SPECIAL INSTRUMENT FLIGHT DRILL WHICH INCLUDED PRACTICE OF THE LUNGHWA LETDOWN WITH A BLIND APPROACH TO THE RUNWAY USING THE INNER MARKER BEACON THAT HAD BEEN INSTALLED AT MY REQUEST. MORE THAN 65 PILOTS OUT OF 69 AVAILABLE IN SHANGHAI MADE THESE SPECIAL FLIGHTS. ANOTHER IMPORTANT PHASE OF THE DRILL WAS TO PROCEED TO KIANGWAN AND MAKE A PRACTICE GCA APPROACH AT THAT FIELD. 42 PILOTS ATTEMPTED TO COMPLY WITH THESE INSTRUCTIONS BUT DUE TO THE FACT THAT THE GCA WAS INOPERATIVE AT LEAST 25 % OF THE TIME FROM OCTOBER 22 nd UNTIL DECEMBER 12th ONLY A SMALL PERCENTAGE OF OUR PILOTS WERE ABLE TO PRACTICE A GCA LETDOWN. MY RECORDS SHOW THAT CAPT. PRUES WAS ONE OF THE PILOTS THAT DID PRACTICE A GCA LETDOWN. ALSO ANOTHER FACTOR WHICH CANNOT BE OVERLOOKED IS THE FACT THAT THE SHA TOWER AT KIANGWAN HAS HAD MUCH DIFFICULTY OF LATE KEEPING THEIR TOWER IN FIRST CLASS OPERATING CONDITIC DUE TO FAULTY POWER SUPPLY. THIS PREVENTED PILOTS OUT ON PRACTICE FLIGHTS FROM BEING ABLE TO OBTAIN PERMISSION TO USE THE GCA. XXXX

I WAS INFORMED ON ONE OF MY MANY VISITS TO KIANGWAN THAT THE GCA WAS OUT BECAUSE THE CHINESE GUARDS HAT GONE ON A RAMPAGE OF SOME KIND AND
                                                    AND SHOT UP THE

Some of the issues CNAC faced

Pilots taking chances

Preparation for winter season impeded

GCA at Kiangwan not working due to faulty power supply and rumored gunplay

Link trainers "inoperative due to lack of power"

CNAC operating "at full steam"

Thousands of requests for air transport from many governmental organizations

Entire capital moved from Chungking to Nanking

Operating conditions not improving

Improvements previously requested

Weather observations from airport

Long wave beacons installed in line with runways

Alternate fields equipped for night landings

How crashes might have been avoided

Tsingtao was unequipped for night landings. Weather was good there and planes had sufficient fuel, so they probably would have landed safely, had Tsingtao had night landing equpment.

EC. 23 of 1476

GCA GENERATORS. THUS CAUSING THE GCA A TO BE OUT AGAIN. THE DATES OF THESE TROUBLES CAN BE CONFORIMED FROM THE US NAVY.

THE VALUE OF LINK TRAINING HAS ALWAYS BEEN RECOGNIZED BY CNAC OPERATIONS AND EVERY EFFORT HAS BEEN MADE BY OUR MR. BABLES TO PUT THE LINK TRAINERS IN OPERATION. HE TRIED INSTALLATION IN THE AMERICAN SCHOOL AND FOUND OUT THAT THE POWER THERE WAS INADEQUATE AND THEN MOVED THE TRAINERS BACK TO LUNGHWA WHERE HE WAS INFORMED THA POWER COULD BE MADE AVAILABLE. TO THIS DATE OUR LINK TRAINERS ARE STILL INOPERATIVE DUE TO LACK OF POWER.

A STUDY OF OPERATIONAL CONDITIONS HAS BEEN IN DAILY PROGRESS SINCE OUR MAIN BASE MOVED FROM CALCUTTA TO SHANGHAI. CNAC HAS BEEN OPERATING AT FULL STEAM IN COMPLIANCE WITH THE THOUSANDS OF REQUESTS FOR AIR TRANSPORTATION FROM PRACTICALLY EVERY GOVERNMENTAL ORGANIZATION IN CHINA. THE ENTIRE CAPITAL WAS MOVED FROM CHUNGKING TO NANKING. THE WAR HAS BEEN OVER FOR MORE THAN A YEAR AND OUR OPERATING CONDITIONS HAVE BEEN LITTLE IMPROVED IN FACT THHEY HAVE STEADILY GOTTEN WORSE WITH THE ALMOST DAILY PROBLEMS THAT WE ENCOUNTER FROM MILITARY SOURCES.

SINCE OCTOBER I HAVE BEEN TRYING MY LEVEL BEST TO IMPROVE CONDTIONS BY REQUESTING THAT WEATHER OBSERVAT IONS BE MADE FROM THE AIRPORT. THAT LONG WAVE BEACONS BE INSTALLED IN LINE WITH RUNWAYS. THAT INNER AND OUTER MARKER BEACONS BE INSTALLED AS POOR VISIBILTY LANDING AIDS. THAT ALTERNATE FILDS BE EQUIPPED WITH NIGT LANDING FACILITIES. AND THIS LAST POINT IS THE MOST IMPORTANT OF ALL AT THIS TIME. I REQUESTED COL. HSIA OF COMMUNICATIONS TO INSTALL NIGHT LANDING LIGHTS AT TSINGTAO BUT HIS REPLY WAS SO LUDICROUS THAT I STARTED TAKING ACTION MYSELF AND FOUND RUNWAY LIGHTS LOCATED IN THE OPERATION STOREROOM AT PEKING WEST FIELD. I INFORMED YOU AND THE ACTION HAD NOT BEEN COMPLETED TO GET THE LIGHTS FROM PEKING TO TSINGTAO. I DO KNOW THAT CLO. HSIA MADE A TRIP TO PEKING SOME TIME AGO AND APPARENTLY FAILED TO SEE THIS EQUIPMENT AND HAVE IT MADE AVAILABLE TO OUR OPERATIONS.

ON THE NIGHT OF DECEMBER THE 25th TSINGTAO WEATHER IT WAS EXTREMELY GOOD AND CAPT. LOANE WANTED TO SEND ALL PLANES TO TSINGTAO BUT THERE WERE NO NIGHT LAND* ING FACILITIES.

I WOULD LIKE TO POINT OUT THAT ALL THREE OF OUR PLANES HAD SUFFICIENT GASOLINE ON BOARD TO GO TO TSINGTAO FROM THEIR DESTINATIONS. PLANE 140 HAD 420 GALLONS OF GASOLINE ON BOARD WHEN IT LEFT HANKOW AND TSINGTAO WAS 295 MILES NORTHEAST. LESS THAN TWO HOURS FLYING. PLANES 115 and 147 HAD AMPLE GAS TO GO TO TSINGTAO AFTER THEY ARRIVED OVER SHA. THERE WERE NO LIGHTS. THE TIME ELEMENT WAS A FACTOR. IT WAS TOO late to install lights and the planes crashed.

The McDonalds arrive in San Francisco by way of Wake Island, August 2, 1947

C. L. Chennault

1000 Cole Avenue, Monroe, La.

SUITE 601, 915 15TH STREET, N. W., WASHINGTON 5, D. C.

March 13, 1957

TELEPHONE ME 8-5797
———
CABLE ADDRESS
"CLAULT"

Mr. W. C. McDonald
c/o Roberts & Sons
530 So. 19th Street
Birmingham 3, Alabama

Dear Mc:

Your letter dated March 8th was greatly appreciated. I must admit to being rather remiss with my correspondence but I have had so much to do and so many letters to write that I lose track of some which I receive.

I know you have heard the news of Luke's death last night at 11 o'clock. Mary had called us early in the evening and told us that his situation was very serious indeed. It has been a very severe shock to me as I never expected him to die so early. We are trying to plan attending the funeral services but due to the fact that Delta does not have any early morning planes flying East from Monroe, I am afraid we will not be able to make it. I suppose you and Peggy will go over and I hope you will represent me if I do fail to make the trip.

With regard to your visit to Monroe, we will be glad to have you and your whole family at any time that you can come over. We have a guest house available that will accommodate all of your family and it would be a real pleasure to have you with us. Why not plan returning to Birmingham via Monroe when you leave New Orleans after your convention there March 27, 28 and 29. You could come up here by Southern and go on to Birmingham by Delta later.

I was sorry to learn of the death of your father and I know that you must miss him a great deal. You may recall that my father died in 1942 while I was fighting the Japs from Kunming. It was always a matter of deep regret to me that I did not get to see him again after the end of the war.

With very best wishes, I am

Most sincerely,

C. L. Chennault

em

P.S. I have called off my Friday engagements here and am going to Atlanta tomorrow Thursday night. We will attend the funeral service at 10:00 Friday and go on to New York Friday night — C.

I know you have heard the news of Luke's death last night…It has been a very severe shock to me as I never expected him to die so early.

…we will be glad to have you and your whole family at any time that you can come over.

I was sorry to learn of the death of your father and I know that you must miss him a great deal. You may recall that my father died in 1942 while I was fighting the Japs from Kunming. It was always a matter of deep regret to me that I did not get to see him again after the end of the war.

Chennault, March 13, 1957

After China

Although Mac and Peggy loved China, after the birth of their first child, daughter Cameron, the young parents decided to take a Pan-American job closer to home. Son William C. McDonald III was born in Miami, where the family lived for about 18 months. Then they moved to Brazil where Mac flew for another three years. The family was happy and Mac enjoyed the less stressful work.

However, Peggy contracted polio there. On the advice of doctors, Mac moved his family back to the States so that she could be near her parents. He stopped flying and worked in business to stay near his family. Within a few years, the family moved back to Birmingham, Alabama, where they would remain for the rest of their lives.

However, he continued to correspond and to maintain friendships with many, including Madame Chiang Kai-shek, William Bond and Bill Pawley, as well as his fellow pilots.

He remained particularly close to his mentor and friend, Claire Chennault, and looked on him as the main inspiration of his life. Without Chennault's influence, it is possible that Mac might have been just another one of the many unemployed young men in the Depression, or working at any job he could find. Instead, Chennault helped him develop skill and confidence as a flyer, and he found fame with the Men on the Flying Trapeze.

In China's fight against the Japanese, he found a cause he felt passionately about, one for which he quietly risked his life over and over. Even after Mac moved out of Chennault's shadow and joined CNAC, he and Chennault continued to work together and maintain their friendship and working camaraderie.

(continued on page 275)

Lt. Gen. Claire Lee Chennault
September 6, 1893 – July 27, 1958

- Hometown: Commerce, Texas; Waterproof, Louisiana
- Time in China: 1937-45
- Foremost expert and author of textbook on pursuit planes and tactics
- Supervised Mac on his final check ride at Brooks Field in San Antonio, Texas, in 1931
- Hired Mac for the "Men on the Flying Trapeze" in 1932
- Convinced Mac and several others to accept offers from China to serve as advisors to the Chinese Air Force (CAF)
- Formed the American Volunteer Group (AVG), famously referred to as the "Flying Tigers" by the press
- Served as the Major General of the 14th Air Force in China
- Retired just three days before the surrender of the Japanese
- Maintained his friendship with Mac to the end of his life

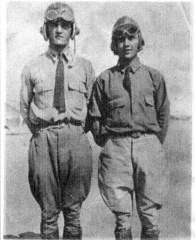

POSTAGE AND FEES PAID
Department of the Army

THE "GREAT" FLYING TIGER—MG CLAIRE L. CHENNAULT (1890-1958)—first took to the air as a passenger. In this 1918 picture, the then young lieutenant (left) is standing with LT Fred L. Edele (now a retired major), prior to catching a flight from Kelly Field to Corpus Christi, Texas. In 1937, after almost 20 years of service with the U.S. Army Air Corps, GEN Chennault retired due to physical disabilities and became an advisor on aeronautical affairs to the Chinese Nationalist Government. Chennault was an innovator of fighter aviation tactics, and in 1941, organized and trained the famous "FLYING TIGERS," who fought for the Chinese in defense of the Burma Road. In April 1942, he returned to active duty with the U.S. Army Air Forces, commanding units in China which were organized in 1943 as the 14th Air Force. He was promoted to the grade of Major General in 1943 and retired in 1945.

★ ★ ★

This pamphlet provides information and guidance for
RETIRED ARMY PERSONNEL

By Order of the Secretary of the Army:

W. C. WESTMORELAND
General, United States Army,
Chief of Staff

Official:
KENNETH G. WICKHAM
Major General, United States Army
The Adjutant General

1968

LEFT Photo of Mac and Chennault by Skip Adair. Used with permission by Stephanie Vickery Adair.

CIVIL AIR TRANSPORT
交 通 部 民 用 航 空 局 直 轄 空 運 隊

Taipei, Taiwan
30 January 1952

Mr. William MacDonald
212 Georgia Avenue
Savannah, Georgia

Dear Billy:

I was awfully pleased to receive your letter dated January 20th as
I had lost track of you. In fact, we addressed a Christmas card to
you at your old address in Rio. It is good to know that Peggy will
suffer severe ill effects from the attack of polio. Her good fortu
is probably the result of <u>clean living</u>! I am glad to know that you
have settled down to a "shore job" for you have gotten to the age w
banging an old transport around isn't as much fun as it used to be.
I hope that your Lincoln-Mercury agency will prove to be profitable
and keep you interested in life.

I have heard that there is good fishing and also good hunting around
Savannah and I am sure you will pick up a boat and maybe a bird dog
before you live there long. When you are ready to go fishing, let me
know and I will come over and string the fish for you.

I hear that Hansell has returned to active duty although I do not know
what he is doing. When you see Luke again give him my very best regards.
We still have a good many of the old hands around. Tom Gentry is our
flight surgeon. Willie Heston just left here to return to duty at Maxwell Field. Eddie Rector has come out for duty with M.A.A.G. Joe
Rosbert and Eric Shilling are still with us. I have been promoted
upstairs to Chairman of the Board and Willauer is our President at the
present time. I will pass on your message to Madame Chiang when I see
her next. I know she will be glad to hear from you. I am enclosing
some snapshots which will bring you up to date regarding the family.

We are planning on making a trip back to the States some time in the
spring. We will spend most of our time in California, Washington and
Louisiana, but will try to get in touch with you at least. I would
like very much to see Cameron and little Billy. Give them my love.

With very best wishes for your success as a businessman and love to all
from all of us, I am

Most sincerely yours,

C. L. C.

Encl. - snapshots (3)

I have heard that there is good fishing and also good hunting around Savannah and I am sure you will pick up a boat and maybe a bird dog before you live there long. When you are ready to go fishing, let me know and I will come over and string the fish for you.

Claire Chennault
January 30, 1952

I would very much like to see Cameron and little Billly. Give them my love.

IN CHINA THEY CALLED HIM 飛虎

3 January 1958

Mr. W. C. McDonald, Jr.
c/o Roberts & Son
530 South Street
Birmingham, Alabama

Dear Mac:

I appreciated your letter dated December 26th very much indeed.

I know exactly how you feel because I felt the same way when I heard that Luke was desperately ill. You know, of course, that I have enjoyed life very much. I have lived through a number of experiences which I am sure no other man has enjoyed. Nevertheless, I am not willing nor content to lay down and give up at this time.

We are returning to 1000 Cole Avenue, Monroe, Louisiana January 11th and I will enter Walter Reed Hospital January 21st to continue cancer treatments. I have felt fairly well during the month I have spent here and hope to continue to improve in the future.

With love to all members of the family, I am,

Most sincerely,

C. L. Chennault

C/lac

Claire Lee Chennault

202 SHERATON BUILDING • 711 14TH STREET, NORTHWEST

WASHINGTON 5, D. C.

CABLE ADDRESS "CLAULT"
PHONE METROPOLITAN 8-3797

April 18, 1958

Mr. W. C. McDonald, Jr.
Roberts & Son
530 So. 19th Street
Birmingham 3, Ala.

Dear "Mac":

I received your letter dated 11 April upon returning from another visit to Ochsner Hospital in New Orleans. It was nice hearing from you but I wish you would drop over to see me some time.

My schedule is very elastic due to the fact that I have to go to the hospital for both treatment and examination at unexpected times. However, we will be at home most of the time now until May 1. If you could phone me a day or two ahead, I can tell you whether we will be at home or not.

With very best wishes to all members of the family from Anna as well as myself, I am

Most sincerely,

C. L. Chennault

cm

ABOVE Chennault the farmer. Mac took this picture just a few days before Chennault's death in 1958.

After leaving China, Mac flew for Pan Am in Brazil for another three years.

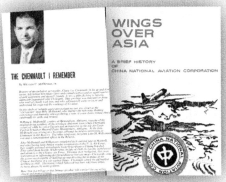

Writing & helping others tell stories

Golf

CNAC / AVG

Alabama Aviation Hall of Fame.
LEFT TO RIGHT Former Ambassador Billy Cabaniss, Billy McDonald III, Mac.

Back in the United States, they stayed in contact. As Chennault fought his final illness in 1958, Mac and Peggy visited his home in Louisiana just a few days before he passed away. After Chennault's death, his wife Anna asked that Mac come and help plan the funeral at Arlington. At the service, in a room full of dignitaries, Mac was honored when Madame Chiang Kai-shek asked to walk into the service leaning on Mac's arm, both having lost a dear friend. Not surprisingly, when Mac began a book about his adventures, he dedicated it to Claire Chennault.

Mac was always interested in those who'd shared the intense experiences in China. He worked to help keep alive the memories of that time, helping found the CNAC Association and serving as its long-time president. He helped organize its reunions, including joint reunions with the AVG alumni association with its overlapping membership.

Through his publishing company, he helped bring out several volumes of *Wings Over Asia*, each a sparkling collection of first-person stories from CNAC personnel and its friends.

Mac wrote frequently for newspapers and magazines, and spoke to community groups about his experiences. He penned "The Chennault I Remember" for *Air Power Historian.* To the frustration of many, he kept his agreement never to speak of their combat activities. He generously opened his home and files—the letters he'd written home and other documents he'd collected—for people from Martha Byrd to Sebie Smith to consult as they wrote books about China's aviation and CNAC.

Mac continued to play golf, passing a love for the game along. His son Billy and grandson Will both played the game well enough to earn scholarships to college.

He received honors ranging from awards from the Boy Scouts to election as one of the first five inductees into the newly-formed Alabama Aviation Hall of Fame.

The annual CNAC reunions seemed to be the highlight of his year; there he was always in the heart of things, telling stories or listening, surrounded by people who understood what he remembered, their respect for him obvious to all.

Late in his life, after a debilitating stroke had taken away his ability to speak, his surviving friends continued to visit. They sat with him and told stories about China, reliving the adventures and sorrows of

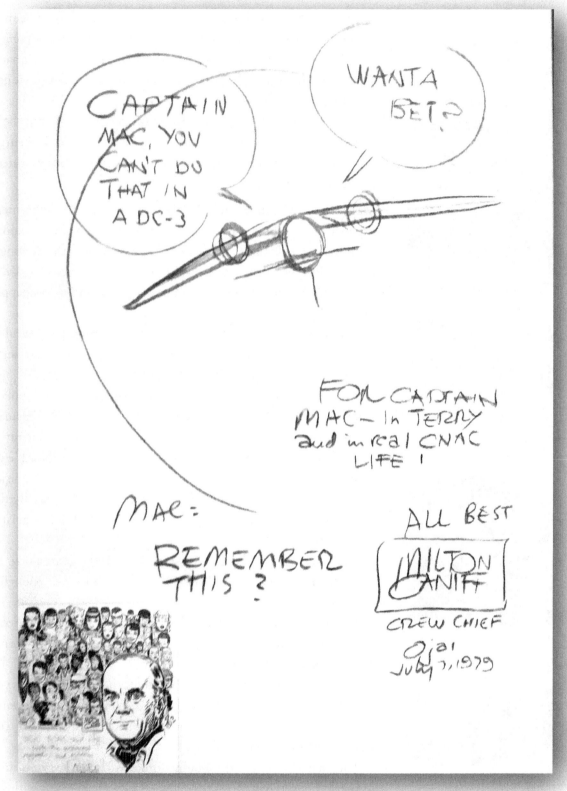

Milton Caniff developed comic strip *Terry & the Pirates* and based the character of Dude Hennick on his college friend, Frank Higgs. The character Captain Mack was based on Mac. He drew this for Mac at a CNAC reunion in 1979. He regretted not including the CNAC logo.

their youth. He played with his grandchildren in a house inspired by China.

On June 11, 1984, seven years after his stroke, Mac passed away quietly. His funeral was attended by friends from across the country, and was delayed a day to allow a Chinese representative to attend, remembering the contribution he had made to its people. Planes from Mac's first unit, the 106th Observation Squadron now flying as part of 117th Reconnaisance Wing of the Alabama National Guard, flew overhead. The Phantom IIs modified for reconnaisance, flew in a set of four, then broke into the Missing Man formation to honor their fallen comrade, a single plane peeling off from the group and flying higher.

In 1998, Mac was honored with a permanent exhibit at the Air Force Enlisted Heritage Hall, Gunter Annex, Maxwell Air Force Base. In China, the contributions of the American flyers are honored in museums throughout the country, and Mac's image hangs in those exhibits, often with Chennault.

William C. McDonald Jr. of Fairfield, Alabama, chose a difficult but rewarding journey. He faced a great many challenges along the way, and overcame them. Putting himself in harm's way over and over, he continued to do his part to fight against a strong enemy which threatened great harm. Eventually, the fight nearly won, he married the girl of his dreams. After victory, he returned home to raise his children and live a quiet life.

But he never stopped telling the stories, and encouraging others to tell their stories.

Alabama remembers where it all started

Photo Album
Friends & Family

Photo Strip with Higgs and Mac.

Patch of the CNAC Chung symbol

Mac was on the design team. Chennault suggested that CNAC put a bold symbol on its planes to make sure they weren't mistakenly identified as an enemy plane, by anyone.

CAF & CNAC

Film Star. Colonel Ming, famous actor Jin Yan known as the "Valentino of Shanghai," Mac.

PREVIOUS PAGE In the 1970s, the McDonalds built their dream home, which was inspired by their time in China, on top of Red Mountain overlooking Birmingham.

1944 Wedding in Calcutta, Mac and Peggy

CNAC wives at the apartment bar

Picking Lima beans, Dec. 25, 1951.

Fun & Friends

BELOW Peggy in Shanghai and with new hat.

ABOVE Chennault the farmer harvesting lima beans in 1951.

BELOW LEFT Mac having a beer in Kunming.

BELOW RIGHT Peggy playing golf near Sugar Loaf Mountain with friends in Rio, Brazil.

TOP Mac, Peggy, Herbert Ryding (who introduced the happy couple), and unknown.

LEFT Mac with three Pan Am pilots.

ABOVE House in Miami.

CNAC reunion

Peggy and Mac just below here.

LEFT Doc Farrar, Bill Pawley, Robbie Roberts and Mac.

BELOW With Jimmy Richenbacher, WWI Ace and President of Eastern Air Lines.

OPPOSITE Mac with Anna Chennault.

RIGHT 1966 reunion. Mac (left).

BELOW Mac using a ham radio on the way to a reunion in China.

Reunions

1956 CNAC reunion, Mac and Peggy at front right.

<small>ABOVE</small> CNAC reunion.

AVG Reunion.

Mac's Kids

TOP LEFT Jamie Watson (left) and Cameron McDonald in Shanghai.

TOP RIGHT Peggy with Billy and Cameron, and her sister Frances Hodges with her children Ellen and Chap.

BOTTOM LEFT Billy in Rio, Brazil.

BOTTOM RIGHT Billy and Cameron with Mac's parents.

MIDDLE Dutchess (dog) in Shanghai.

TOP Cameron, Sandy the Dachshund and Billy.

LEFT Peggy with children.

BOTTOM Billy and Cam posing with portraits.

RIGHT Wedding of Cameron McDonald and Scott Vowell. Billy gave Cameron away. Cameron, Billy, Peggy.

BELOW Wedding of Billy McDonald and Nancy Adams. Peggy, Billy, Nancy, Mac.

Mac's Kids Get Married

Mac's Grandkids

Billy and Nancy had three children. Mac got to meet each of them.

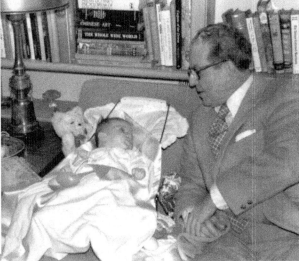

RIGHT Mac and grandson Will.

BELOW Billy, granddaughter Lucy and Mac.

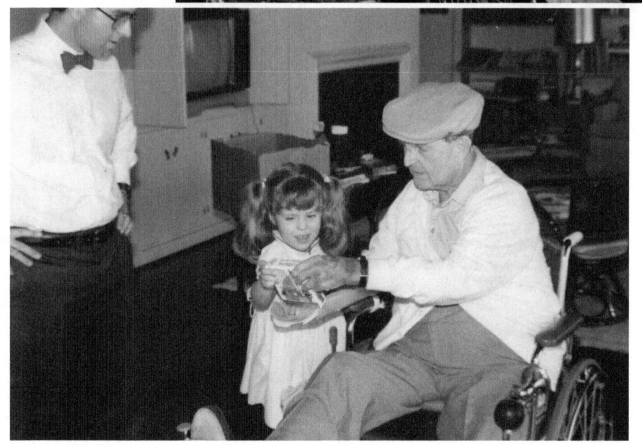

Cameron and Scott had one child, John Scott. Cameron also had quite a large family of Dachshunds.

MAC'S GREAT-GRANDKIDS

CLOCKWISE FROM RIGHT Andy (Lucy & Wade's son) cheering. Baby Frances and Elizabeth (Will & Mary's daughters). Elizabeth looking at a picture of Trapezers. Elizabeth, overlooking Birmingham. Andy in aviator hat.

TOP Brother Malcolm, sister Lucie and Mac. **JUST ABOVE** Mac and Peggy with Dachshunds.

Wade and Lucy's wedding

Mac's Grandkids
Get Married

Will and Mary's wedding

LEFT TO RIGHT Nancy, Billy, Cameron, Scott

LEFT Annual Christmas picture of Billy's family.

BELOW The family dogs, Lola (left), Bandit, Sandi and Abby.

BOTTOM Billy's family, 2016 spring

Monumental Sculpture At Museums

TOP Maggie, Nancy, Billy and Ed Boyd at NAAM. The sculpture portrays an ancient myth about an archer who shoots nine suns out of the sky, leaving just the tenth. The Chinese meaning for Japan is "sun."

BOTTOM NAVM sculpture.

The museum buildings and grounds were stunning.

2016 TRIP TO CHINA

Angie Chen, with the help of her friend Ge Shuya in Kunming, arranged the trip of a lifetime for our family.

In May of 2016, we began a three-week trip to China.

The Chinese people were warm and gracious to us at every stop. We were deeply moved to see photos of Mac and words about his work in museums throughout China, and to see how the Chinese people still remembered the people who'd been with them during their struggle so many years ago.

Dr. Ed Boyd, son-in-law of Flying Tiger J.J. Harrington, and Billy made presentations at each museum stop and we were honored with beautiful receptions and banquets.

Angie Chen, representing the CNAC Association in China, presented at CPRMM and introduced Billy and Ed. We made so many new connections and friends, and we expect that we will continue to share our research on this time period.

In Nanjing, we toured Nanjing Anti-Japanese Aviation Memorial (NAAM), Nanjing Aviators Association (NAA) and Nanjing Anti-Japanese Victory Museum (NAVM). Officials from the Hangchow Jianqiao CAS Museum visited with us.

In Beijing, we saw China Civil Aviation Museum (CCAM), Chinese People's Anti-Japanese War Museum (CPAM) near Marco Polo Bridge, and Chinese People's Revolutionary Military Museum (CPRMM). In addition, we had a gathering with a CNAC, CAMCO and Chinese Air Force (CAF) second generation group.

In Kunming, we visited Kunming Museum (KMM), and Yunnan Army Academy Museum (YAAM). We also met with the leadership of the Kunming Aviation Association (KAA) and got a special tour of places Mac had worked in Kunming. We also shared memories with a CAF and AVG second generation group in Kunming.

As an unexpected bonus, Nancy arranged a trip to Shanghai and stayed at the Jing An Hotel, previously Haig Court, where the McDonalds had a lovely apartment after the war. Nancy was welcomed there graciously, and presented the hotel with a CNAC pin, pictures and several introductory pages from the book, and a copy of a letter from Mac saying it took two and a half minutes

Remembering Mac

LEFT Maggie and Billy, with photo of Mac, in CPAM.

RIGHT YAAM exhibit showing a CNAC flight over the Hump.

BOTTOM Billy spots Mac in another picture at the KMM. In the photo, Mac is pall bearer at Chennault's funeral.

It was always exciting to find photos or mention of Mac. Ed saw a huge picture of his father-in-law.

to get from Haig Court to the hospital where daughter Cameron McDonald was born.

The Chinese media seemed very interested, and we met with many reporters and photographers. It was fun to see ourselves in Chinese newspapers and websites.

In August 1937 after the Marco Polo Bridge incident, Mac and the other Americans were ordered out of China by the U.S. Consul General.

Mac wrote home saying that he would not leave the Chinese people at the moment they needed him the most. He refused to leave and stayed another seven years.

Mac never forgot the Chinese people. Our trip was a chance to thank the Chinese people for not forgetting him.

The McDonald Family

Nanjing Aviation Association (NAA)

May 24, 2016
Nanjing, China

RIGHT NAAM deputy curator Luo ChaoJun, CPPCC vice director Pang ZhaoYin, NAA vice president Xu JiaHong, Ed, Billy, Nancy, Maggie, Angie, NAAM curator Zhang PengDou.

Nanjing Anti-Japanese Aviation Memorial Hall (NAAM)

May 24, 2016
Nanjing, China

Deputy Director Pang ZhaoYin
Curator Zhang PengDou
Deputy Curator Luo ChaoJun

UPPER RIGHT We were surprised by the press coverage of our visit. We ended up in major newspapers, on TV and radio, and of course across the internet. The Chinese people seemed very interested in finding out more about our shared history.

RIGHT Angie, Billy, Curator Zhang, Ed, Dr. Liu

Nanjing Anti-Japanese Victory Memorial Hall (NAVM)

Memorial Hall of the Victims in Nanjing Massacre by Japanese Invaders

May 25, 2016
Nanjing, China

Curator Zhang JianJun
Deputy Director Dr. Liu YanMing

RIGHT TOP View of monument and reflecting pool.

RIGHT Dr. Liu gave Billy and Ed a tour of the Memorial Hall.

Hangchow Jianqiao CAS Museum
formerly the Chinese Air Force Central Aviation School (CAS)

May 26, 2016
Jianqiao (Hangchow), China

Director Wu Yuan

LEFT TO RIGHT We met with Director Wu in Nanjing. Director Wu, Billy, Ed, Angie

Mac's first assignment was at the CAS in Hangchow. The school is now a private museum.

China Civil Aviation Museum (CCAM)

May 30, 2016
Beijing, China

Director Wang XiaoHui
Deputy Director Mao XunZhang

RIGHT The building looks like an airplane jet engine cut in half and turned upside down. The sign in front welcomes us. BELOW CCAM staff. Director Wang is center, between Billy and Ed.

威廉·C·麦克唐纳三世先生和杰斯本·J·哈林顿家族向民航博物馆捐赠藏品仪式
Ceremony of Mr. William C. McDonald III & Jasper J. Harrington Family Donating Collections to Civil Aviation Museum

China's People's Republic Military Museum (CPRMM)

May 30 & 31, 2016
Beijing, China

Curator Major General Dong ChangJun

Artifact Collection department
Director Sr. Colonel Yang HaiFeng
Deputy Director Sr. Colonel Cheng DingFei
Director Colonel An LiJuan

UPPER RIGHT Presentation made by Curator Dong.

LOWER RIGHT (LEFT TO RIGHT) Angie, Ed, Col. An, Maggie, Billy, Nancy, Col. Cheng.

Second Generation CNAC and CAMCO Group
May 30, 2016, Beijing, China

BELOW Second Generation CNAC and CAMCO group with McDonald group and CPRMM Curator Dong.

Chinese People's Anti-Japanese War Museum (CPAM)

near the Marco Polo Bridge

"Museum of the War of Chinese People's Resistance Against Japanese Aggression"

May 31, 2016
Beijing, China

Deputy Curator Luo CunKang

<small>RIGHT</small> Curator Luo (next to Billy) and staff with McDonald group.

Yunnan Army Academy Museum (YNAAM)

formerly a military academy

June 4, 2016
Kunming, China

<small>UPPER RIGHT</small> Angie Chen showing Billy an exhibit about rice drops that CNAC made for Chinese expedition force escaping from Japanese troops.

<small>LOWER RIGHT</small> Angie, historian Ge Shuya, Billy, YNAAM senior staff member Zeng YuRong

Kunming Museum (KMM)

June 3, 2016
Kunming, China

Curator Tian Jian
Deputy Curator Li XiaoFan
Assistant Li Guanzhang

<small>UPPER</small> Billy points out Mac's picture, the Men on the Flying Trapeze.

<small>MIDDLE, LEFT TO RIGHT</small> Angie, unknown, Deputy Curator Li XiaoFan, KMM curator Tian Jian, Billy.

<small>BOTTOM</small> Presentation on the book to about one hundred patrons.

Kunming Aviation Association (KAA)

June 6, 2016
Kunming, China

RIGHT KAA member Ms. Liu Rong with Billy.

BELOW, LEFT TO RIGHT Members of the KAA. Liu QiWen (upcoming president), Wang ZhengXing (incumbent president), Billy, Angie, Ge Shuya, Wang ChengZhong (vice president)

The group would like to establish closer ties with CNAC Association. Billy will carry that request to CNAC's reunion and convention in September 2016.

Yunnan Flying Tiger Research Association (YNFTRA)

June 6, 2016
Kunming, China

RIGHT Billy and YNFTRA vice president Zhu JunKun at the Flying Tiger Theme Restaurant. A P-40 plane flies overhead as decor.

Kunming Second Generation Group
CAF/AVG

June 6, 2016
Kunming, China

RIGHT In front of a tea house run by Ms. Huang JiMing (2nd from left) , whose grandfather Huang TingYao was Chennault's interpreter from 1944–1945.
LEFT TO RIGHT Ge Shuga, Huang JiMing, Mao XiangLin, Billy, Prof. Liu ZengLi, Angie, Chen XiuFeng, Dr. Yin Lun.

Jing An Hotel
previously Haig Court

May 25, 2016
Shanghai, China

General manager Li Gang

TOP General manager Li Gang, Nancy and Maggie at Jing An Hotel following the presentation. The tree sculpture inscription reads, "William C. McDonald Jr.'s Place of Cherished Memories, 1945-1947."

BOTTOM Maggie in front of hotel

JEFF SESSIONS
ALABAMA

COMMITTEES
ARMED SERVICES
JUDICIARY
ENVIRONMENT AND PUBLIC WORKS
BUDGET

United States Senate
WASHINGTON, DC 20510-0104

June 29, 2016

Honorable Deborah Lee James
Secretary of the Air Force
1670 Air Force Pentagon
Washington D.C. 20330-1670

Dear Madam Secretary,

In accordance with section 1130 of Title 10, United States Code, I request that you review the application for, and approve where appropriate, relevant campaign medals, the Air Medal and the Distinguished Flying Cross for Mr. William C. McDonald, Jr., who flew for the China National Aviation Corporation in support of Allied military operations in the China theater during World War II.

The McDonald family has requested the assistance of Colonel Jeffrey L. Newton, Director of Staff for the Alabama Air National Guard to compile the required justification and materials needed for the review. He can be reached at Jeffrey.l.newton10.mil@mail.mil; (334) 271-7266, or (205) 981-7706.

Thank you for your assistance in this matter.

Very truly yours,

Jeff Sessions
United States Senator

Always an Alabama boy at heart, Mac got his start flying with the Alabama Air National Guard (AANG). In 1984, the 106th flew the Missing Man formation to mark Mac's passing.

During his lifetime, Mac and the other CNAC pilots and crews were not officially acknowledged by the U.S. government as participants in WWII. Now Col. Jeffrey L. Newton, Director of Staff of Alabama ANG, is working with the McDonald family to have Mac's contributions recognized.

CPSIA information can be obtained
at www.ICGtesting.com
Printed in the USA
LVOW03*0042270916

506320LV00010B/17/P